J. Jeannette Lovern, Ph.D.

# Practical Assessment for 21st-Century Classrooms
## A Primer for First-Year Teachers

Cover Art: Courtesy of J. Jeannette Lovern.

Copyright © 2011 by Pearson Education, Inc.
Upper Saddle River, New Jersey 07458

All rights reserved. No part of this book may be reproduced, in any form or by any means, without permission in writing from the publisher.

This special edition published in cooperation with Pearson Learning Solutions.

All trademarks, service marks, registered trademarks, and registered service marks are the property of their respective owners and are used herein for identification purposes only.

Pearson Learning Solutions, 501 Boylston Street, Suite 900,
Boston, MA 02116
A Pearson Education Company
www.pearsoned.com

Printed in the United States of America

1 2 3 4 5 6 7 8 9 10 V0CR 16 15 14 13 12 11

000200010270789707

CT

ISBN 10: 1-256-36101-1
ISBN 13: 978-1-256-36101-5

## Table of Contents

**CHAPTER 1**         1
*Why Do We Have to Bother With All This Test Stuff Anyway?*
**Introduction to Assessment**
    Purpose of Assessment
    Validity and Reliability
    What We Assess
    Formative vs. Summative
    Norm-referencing vs. Criterion-referencing
    The Theoretical Base

**CHAPTER 2**         17
*ME? Grade four Grammer and Speling?*
**Professionalism in Assessment**
    The Neighborhood Professional
    The Teacher's Three Languages
    Teacher Dispositions
    Providing Feedback
    Grading for Grammar/Spelling

**CHAPTER 3**         39
*But I Don't Like Her...*
**The Role of Collaboration**
    Collaboration Among Teachers
    Cooperative Learning
    Grading Group Work

**CHAPTER 4**         57
*You Mean I Gotta Teach That?*
**Curriculum Standards and Assessment**
    Standards
    New Common Core Standards
    Creating a Unit
    Writing Objectives

**CHAPTER 5**         73
*Am I Getting Close to What You Want or What?*
**Formative Assessment**
    Historical Perspective
    The Stiggins' Model
    Types of Formative Assessments
    Types of Formative Self-Assessment Tools
    Formative Peer-Review Tools
    Grading Formative Assessments

## CHAPTER 6 — 99
### *Is This Gonna Be On The Test?*
**Summative Assessment**
- Description of Summative Assessment
- Types
- Usage
- Face Validity
- Use of Technology

## CHAPTER 7 — 113
### *Stems, Distractors, and Other Confusing Words*
**Creating Selected-Response Items**
- General Guidelines
- Multiple Choice Items
- Binary Choice Items
- Matching

## CHAPTER 8 — 145
### *I Wrote on the Front and the Back So Surely I'll Get Some Points*
**Creating Constructed-Response Items**
- FITB Items (Without a Word Bank)
- Listing Items
- Short Answer Items
- Essay Items
- Writing Clear Directions
- Creating A Key
- Grading Selected-Response Items

## CHAPTER 9 — 161
### *You Mean This Test Could End Up on the Principal's Desk or the 6 O'clock News?*
**Creating a Professional Test**
- Test Blueprint
- Formatting the Test for Good Face Validity
- Organizing and Ordering Items

## CHAPTER 10 — 179
### *You Mean I Should Let The Students Know How I'm Going to Grade This?*
**Rubrics and Scoring Guides**
- Holistic vs. Analytic Rubrics
- Generic vs. Specific Rubrics
- Grading Essay Items with Rubrics
- Grading Performance Assessments with Rubrics
- Peer Grading with Rubrics
- Using Technology to Generate Rubrics

**CHAPTER 11**     **195**
*You Mean It's Not Always About Tests?*
**Performance Assessments**
    Definition of a Performance
    Role of Ambiguity in Creativity
    Performance Assessment Rubrics
    The Importance of Modeling
    The Importance of Engagement

**CHAPTER 12**     **209**
*Do We Have to Look At This Stuff A Second Time—I Already Graded It Once*
**Portfolio Assessments**
    Portfolio Types
    Portfolio Development
    Scoring of Portfolios

**CHAPTER 13**     **221**
*Did I Pass?*
**Assigning Grades**
    Grading
    Determining Weights for Grades
    Report Cards
    Progress Reports and Portals

**CHAPTER 14**     **235**
*Are All Those Squigglies Supposed to Mean Something?*
**Interpreting Standardized Test Score Reports**
    General Information About Standardized Tests
    Percentiles
    Stanines
    Grade Equivalents

**CHAPTER 15**     **245**
*If Only Billy Would Apply Himself. . .*
**Communicating with Stakeholders**
    Defining Stakeholders
    Communicating with Students
    Talking with Parents

**REFERENCES**     **259**

# Author's Note

With a myriad of books available on assessment, the question might arise as to why another one is needed. However, I do believe that this book offers something new. It takes my first-hand experiences in:
- A) Doing assessment for K-12 students
- B) Grading teacher candidates' first attempts at writing assessments and analyzing outcomes (and thereby seeing many misconceptions of pre-service teachers as well as mistakes that are made by such novices)
- C) Interviewing and observing numerous novice and veteran teachers through the years about assessment
- D) Observing how teaching and learning has changed from the 20$^{th}$ Century to the 21$^{st}$, and
- E) My passion for assessment and research done on it.

Those experiences are brought together to provide a book on assessment that is totally <u>practical</u>. Many assessment textbooks seem to spend a lot of time on theory, which is of course important, and less time on the nuts and bolts related to assessment. Since the primary audience for this book will be teacher candidates in teacher education programs learning about assessment (often for the first time) as well as first-year classroom teachers, some basic theoretical concepts within the field of assessment are touched upon briefly. However, the rest of the book is strictly practical!

 At various points throughout the reading, you will find a sidebar entitled "FROM THE PRINCIPAL'S DESK". These have been written by Dr. Richard Day, a veteran principal who served as a principal for 25 years, and is now the moderator of a widely-read blog entitled *Kentucky School News and Commentary*. In addition, he is now a college professor who prepares future teachers and principals. Again, I asked him to write these sidebars from the *practical* side of assessment.

A further note: For ease of reading for the reader, gender pronouns are used throughout the book in a relatively alternating manner. When a student, teacher, or other person is referred to as *he* or as *she*, it can be assumed that that person could also be of the other gender.

**ACKNOWLEDGEMENTS**

Special thanks to my generous colleague, Dr. Richard Day, for his contribution to the book and the generosity of his time to discuss issues and concepts related to assessment.

Special thanks to my former graduate assistant and friend, Rebecca Sears, for her help with the pictures, graphics, and editing.

Special thanks to my current research assistant, Lindsey DeVries, for the research she did of various topics and for her work with the references.

And special thanks to Dr. Krista Althauser, a special colleague of mine, whose smile and sweet spirit inspires me every day!

# CHAPTER 1

# Why Do We Have to Bother With All This Test Stuff Anyway?
## Introduction to Assessment

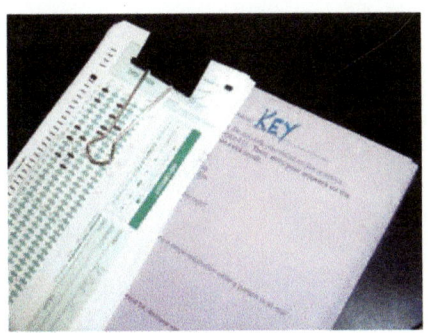

### KEY CONCEPTS:
Purpose of Assessment
Validity and Reliability
What We Assess
Formative vs. Summative
Norm-referencing vs. Criterion-referencing
The Theoretical Base

> *Three things give the student the possibility*
> *of surpassing his teacher: ask a lot of questions,*
> *remember the answers, teach.*
> --Jan Amos Coménius

The word *assess* came to the English language via the Latin word *assidere*, which meant *to sit by*. This became the Old French work *assesser*, which maintained the original meaning but added the extra meaning of *to levy tax*. With the nuance of these two meanings, we come to our modern-day meaning that involves *sitting by* and observing someone (or that someone's product) and *levying* a grade.

So, why do we do assess? Let's leave the classroom for a bit and consider assessment in another arena. When a patient goes to a doctor, the doctor will ask the patient for the reason for the office visit. The doctor will then proceed to conduct initial assessments (blood pressure, weight, heart rate, etc.) The purpose of the initial assessments is to determine a diagnosis and a plan of action for treating the ailment. How many patients would go back to a doctor who simply concluded, "Yes, you sure are sick. These tests prove it. Thanks for coming in." Obviously, the plan of

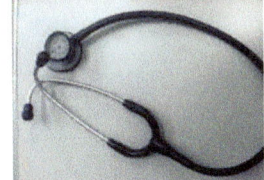

action is the most important part. A teacher assesses for the same reason: to determine what action should be taken. As we look further into the reasons for assessing, some groundwork needs to be established. Let's consider some key assessment terms that a new teacher will encounter.

## VALIDITY AND RELIABILITY

**Validity.** The *validity* of anything is based on the term *valid* meaning how well-founded or well-grounded something is. In the field of assessment, validity refers to a measure of the truthfulness of a measuring instrument (Jackson, 2009). It indicates whether the instrument (the assessment) measures what it claims to measure. Thus, we would consider that an assessment is only valid if what it purports to test *is* actually what it *does* test. An example of a nearly universal two-part assessment that is considered both valid and invalid is the driver's exam administered by most states across the United States. The first part of the exam, the written portion, is often considered invalid by many drivers in the U.S. because they feel that being able to pass that test by memorizing what is often considered mostly useless information from a rule book has nothing to do with real driving. On the other hand, the actual road test, where one has to drive with an experienced driver

who is acting as the examiner sitting in the passenger seat is considered valid. In order to determine if someone can drive a car, the best way is to have him/her drive a car!
In the classroom, an assessment is valid if it actually tests for what it purports to test. For instance, if the teacher wants a student to be able to identify adjectives in sentences, then a test where students circle the adjectives in sentences is valid. However, if a teacher actually wants students to be able to use adjectives in their writing, that test would not be valid.

*Reliability.* The reliability of anything is based on consistency or stability of a measuring instrument (Jackson, 2009). A scale used in science would be an example of reliability. It needs to measure the weight of an item the same each time a student uses it before conducting an experiment. If not, it is a useless measuring instrument.

In assessment, we consider a test to be reliable if, when administered in similar circumstances, it produces similar results. For instance, if a teacher believes she has taught her second-hour algebra class the same as her fifth-hour algebra class, and there are similar skill levels in each, she would expect the outcomes to be the same on the unit test.

To ensure reliability when grading student projects, such as a diorama depicting Native American life, a teacher would develop a rubric to score the projects in order to arrive at similar scores. The reliability would be the *reproducibility of the assessment results* for similar diorama projects.

## WHAT WE ASSESS

Since teachers have first had students, they have assessed a variety of things to determine if the students have learned. Stiggins and his colleagues (2005) have determined that what is assessed can be classified into the five areas of *knowledge, reasoning, skills, products, and dispositions*.

*Knowledge.* The use of selected-response items (multiple choice, true/false, matching) is the common method by which a knowledge base is assessed. Stiggins (2008) indicates that this type of assessment is best used when one's instruction is focusing on foundational knowledge. "From the beginning of your students' learning, both you and they will want to know what knowledge or reasoning targets are to be mastered." Further, "we want students at all times to know where they're headed, where they are now, and how to close the gap between the two" (p. 98). Selected-response items (multiple choice, binary choice, and matching) allow us to determine, and provide to students, that information in an efficient way. Since most selected-response items are written, you need to be careful that you use this type of assessment only if the students' reading skills are sufficient to give you an accurate assessment. In the case of primary students, you may actually have a series of pictures from which the students choose the correct answer to your verbal prompts.

***Reasoning***. Mental processes are represented with reasoning targets. A primary aim of schools today is to help students develop the skill of applying knowledge in context. The application of knowledge heightens the level of thinking such as when students are asked to predict, summarize, infer/deduce, compare/contrast, synthesize, classify, evaluate or analyze. Extended written response questions are a good choice for assessing reasoning. These are well written quality questions requiring students to analyze, compare, contrast, synthesize, draw inferences, and evaluate knowledge gained through study. An example would be having students analyze a bar graph showing the current trend of tennis shoes sales to predict and explain a future increase or decrease in sales. For some reasoning patterns, selected response questions can be used (e.g., choose the statement that best describes the character traits of the lawyer in the book).

Let's consider the assessement of cognitive processes, or reasoning, in the area of art. Color theory would be something that we present to students in this arena. As students learn that the mixture of red and blue creates the color purple, and later, learn that purple is the complementary color to yellow (the primary color not used to create the secondary color), they are developing reasoning skills. These theoretical concepts can be assessed on student demonstrations, assessed by the teacher walking around the room as the students combine the colors, through an interview between the teacher and the student, via homework/classwork assignments, and on paper-and-pencil tests.

***Skills.*** In addition to knowledge and reasoning, we also assess skills. Often these are assessed simply by asking students short answer type items (e.g., measure the degrees of an angle) that help you determine if the student can perform the action. In most classrooms, skills can be assessed in simple classroom activities initially and on culminating projects in which a group of skills may be assessed. Additionally, skills may be assessed on short-answer quizzes, unit tests, and exams.

A common type of skill we assess involves assessment of a student *performance*. These commonly take the form of a speech, a dramatic reading, a musical rendition, or a presentation.

***Products.*** As we have moved to more authentic assessments in the 21$^{st}$ Century, products that the students create have become commonplace. Often, teachers have students create first attempts where they demonstrate to a teacher that they can accomplish the task put before them. This is often followed up by an intermediate assessment in which the students perform the task as a part of an actual product. Finally, this task may be part of a culminating project in which students demonstrate several skills.

The way all of these work together is shown in the example below:

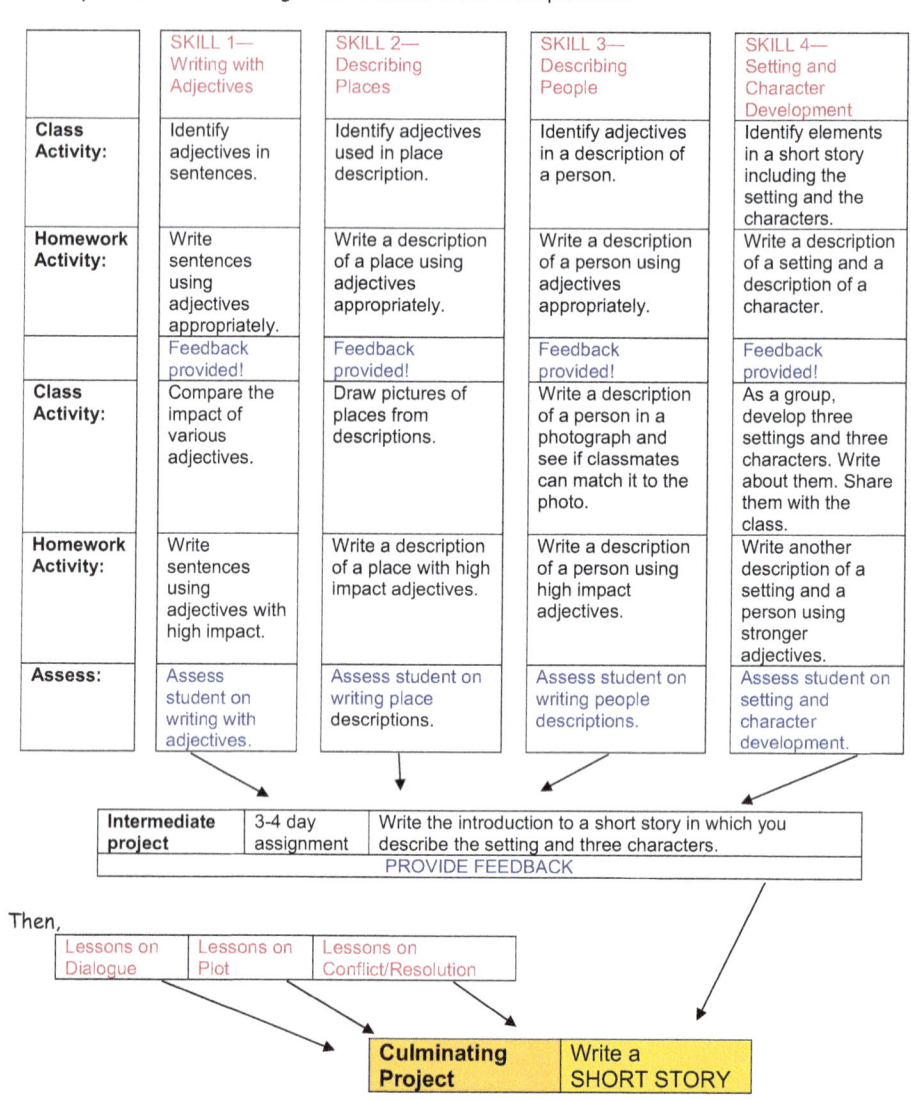

|  | SKILL 1—Writing with Adjectives | SKILL 2—Describing Places | SKILL 3—Describing People | SKILL 4—Setting and Character Development |
|---|---|---|---|---|
| Class Activity: | Identify adjectives in sentences. | Identify adjectives used in place description. | Identify adjectives in a description of a person. | Identify elements in a short story including the setting and the characters. |
| Homework Activity: | Write sentences using adjectives appropriately. | Write a description of a place using adjectives appropriately. | Write a description of a person using adjectives appropriately. | Write a description of a setting and a description of a character. |
|  | Feedback provided! | Feedback provided! | Feedback provided! | Feedback provided! |
| Class Activity: | Compare the impact of various adjectives. | Draw pictures of places from descriptions. | Write a description of a person in a photograph and see if classmates can match it to the photo. | As a group, develop three settings and three characters. Write about them. Share them with the class. |
| Homework Activity: | Write sentences using adjectives with high impact. | Write a description of a place with high impact adjectives. | Write a description of a person using high impact adjectives. | Write another description of a setting and a person using stronger adjectives. |
| Assess: | Assess student on writing with adjectives. | Assess student on writing place descriptions. | Assess student on writing people descriptions. | Assess student on setting and character development. |

| Intermediate project | 3-4 day assignment | Write the introduction to a short story in which you describe the setting and three characters. |
|---|---|---|
|  |  | PROVIDE FEEDBACK |

Then,

| Lessons on Dialogue | Lessons on Plot | Lessons on Conflict/Resolution |
|---|---|---|

| **Culminating Project** | Write a SHORT STORY |
|---|---|

Thus, when we consider the products we are assessing, it helps us understand why we are teaching the concepts that we are, and how they fit into the total picture of educating the student. Ultimately if a teacher is assessing a product, he is technically assessing if the student has a knowledge base, the reasoning it takes to understand and manipulate that knowledge, as well as the skills to use that knowledge base. Our assessments, just like the test results that a doctor puts together to make a diagnosis, fit together to give us a picture of the student's learning.

*Dispositions.* Finally, we assess dispositions. These involve behavior, attitudes, and social actions. The dispositions of students are assessed based on how they act in a group setting, while working independently, in their interactions with other individual students, and in their interactions with the teacher.

An important aspect of dispositions involves the concept called *habits of mind*. Developed by Dr. Arthur Costa, Professor Emeritus of California State University, the habits of mind include 16 thinking dispositions that enable a student to develop critical thinking and creativity skills. These sixteen habits of mind found on the *Habits of Mind* website (http://www.habits-of-mind.net) include:

| HABITS OF MIND ||
|---|---|
| 1) persisting | 9) metacognition |
| 2) thinking and communicating with clarity and precision | 10) taking responsible risks |
| | 11) striving for accuracy |
| 3) managing impulsivity | 12) finding humor |
| 4) gathering data through all senses | 13) questioning and posing problems |
| 5) listening with understanding and empathy | |
| | 14) thinking interdependently |
| 6) creating, imagining, innovating | 15) applying past knowledge to new situations |
| 7) thinking flexibly | |
| 8) responding with wonderment and awe | 16) remaining open to continuous learning |

Obviously, the habits of mind are a part of any social interaction that we assess. These are assessed by evaluating students' participation and leadership in collaborative projects, assessing students' participation in peer reviews and their submissions after those reviews, and observing how the students interact with the teacher during class, during individual conferences, and after receiving written feedback.

## FORMS OF ASSESSMENT

The purpose for which we do assessment dictates the form of the assessments that we do. There are sets of broad categories that help us further understand why we assess as we do.

*Pre-Tests vs. Post-Tests.* One of the first kinds of tests you may administer to your students is a pre-test. A pre-test is often given to students during the first few days of class (or the first day of a new unit), and the teacher makes it clear to the students that, while she wants them to answer as many of the items as they can correctly, the ones they don't know will not be held against them. The purpose of the pre-test is to provide the teacher with information in general terms about the prior knowledge the students have. Typically, a teacher will look at the test items across the tests (rather than looking at a particular student's test) to see which items need more emphasis in her classroom and which can simply be reviewed on the way to more complex items.

A post-test is given after the material has been learned. Sometimes teachers use the unit test as the post-test. However, other times, the teacher will actually use the exact pre-test as the post-test and have the students take it as a review for the unit test. By taking the post-test, they can then see what areas they still need to study before taking the unit test.

Many teachers like to use the pre-test/post-test model in their classrooms for the purpose of determining what is called the *value added*. By comparing the measures of central tendency (mean, median, mode) of the pre-tests with those of the post-test, a teacher can determine that her instruction did *add value*.

**FROM THE PRINCIPAL'S DESK**

The teaching and learning process is extremely complex. The best teachers, in my experience, have been those who have had a *second sense* about what it is their students already know, and use this information to give that hard-to-teach child just the right amounts of challenge and support. A good deal of that knowledge is derived from watching students in class, listening to their answers, observing their independent work, and other informal means. But they also rely on tests.

Perhaps, at some time in the future, it will be possible for us to place a high tech helmet on the head of every student. My imaginary helmet would be able to extract, harmlessly, from each student's brain an accounting of the knowledge they already possess. Perhaps it could also be tailored to suggest to teachers those next bits of knowledge the student needs in order to advance. But unfortunately, no such technology exists.

So, for now, in order to understand what students know, we give them tests. That is to say we ask them to respond to a set of questions which represent a small sample of the information we have been teaching. And we hope the results represent, with some accuracy, what our students know and are able to do.

*Formative vs. Summative Assessment.* When assessing students, our assessment will be either formative or summative. Formative involves checking students' abilities as they learn the material, while summative checks to what extent students have achieved. Formative assessment is a planned process to elicit evidence of current student learning and their learning progress. The information gained guides teachers on what and how to adjust what they are currently doing. Summative assessment comes at the end of a planned unit, process or learning episode. Simply put: formative is an assessment *for* learning and summative is an assessment *of* learning. Formative assessment is used for the purpose of monitoring student progress. The teacher is checking to see if the students are learning the things she wants them to learn, and if they are developing the skills, attitudes, etc. she wants them to develop. In other words, the teacher is checking if the students are on the right track. Formative assessment provides feedback to both students and teachers. This feedback serves several purposes. "Feedback to students provides reinforcement of successful learning and identifies the specific learning errors and misconceptions that need correction. Feedback to the teacher provides information for modifying instruction and for prescribing group and individual work" (Linn & Gronlund, 2000, p. 41). Through formative assessment, an art teacher has the opportunity to see what the student is doing right (for instance, holding the paintbrush correctly to create a certain brushstroke), and to encourage him/her to continue to develop the skill. Likewise, if a student is going astray (not holding the paintbrush correctly so it does not create the desired brushstroke), the teacher has the opportunity to re-direct that student before he continues to practice the skill using the wrong technique.

Summative assessment, which is done after the unit of learning has been completed, is used to determine to what extent the students have learned the things you wanted them to learn or gained the skills you wanted them to obtain. Examples of this include unit or semester tests, final projects, and cumulative portfolios.

*Criterion-referencing vs. Norm-referencing.* Another aspect of assessment involves criterion-referencing vs. norm-referencing. The first involves checking a student's work against established standards, while the other compares a student's work with that of his/her peers.

While Green & Johnson (2010) cite criterion-referenced grading as being "determined by comparing a student's performance to an absolute standard" (p. 306), in some areas, the standards are less absolute. Still, there are some aspects of foundational knowledge and particular skill techniques that do have pre-determined absolutes. For example, stating the three primary colors as red, yellow, and blue is a criterion by which an art teacher would assess a student's answer. However, in terms of skills, creating a certain brushstroke is a criterion by which the art teacher could assess a student's ability. While you know what you're looking for, and you definitely would be able to determine if a student provided an incorrect example, there may be a variety of correct responses based on the individuality of students. In terms of other criterion-referencing grading, you might ask the student to create a product in which you identify aspects they need to include. Then, you might use a rubric to grade the product according to those established criteria.

Norm-referencing often concerns either interpretation of standardized testing or grading on a curve in the classroom, or in some instances, it involves students submitting work for contests (e.g., poster contests, essay contests, science fairs). In the first two instances, students are divided into groups and receive a ranking based on how they do in comparison to their peers. However, in the final one, the teacher (or the agency sponsoring the contest) arbitrarily determine the number of students who will be awarded a certain level of distinction (for instance, first place, second place, third place, etc.) in each category.

## THE THEORETICAL BASE

**The Testing Effect.** In a meta-analysis of research done on the correlation between testing and memory, Roediger & Karpicke (2006) determined that "A powerful way of improving one's memory for material is to be tested on that material" (p. 181). They found that testing enhanced later retention of the material more than additional study at a later date. This is called the *testing effect*. In their meta-analysis, they looked first at laboratory studies conducted by psychologists, but later at studies that took place in actual educational settings. In the various studies they examined, they found that students who had been tested over material frequently had higher retention rates not only during the learning experience, but at later intervals. They concluded:

> If teachers determine what critical knowledge and skills they want their students to know after leaving the class, these points can be emphasized in class and tested repeatedly at spaced intervals to ensure that students acquire this knowledge. Frequent testing not only has a direct effect on learning, but also should encourage students to study more, to be continuously engaged in the material, to experience less test anxiety, and probably even to score better on standardized tests. (p. 206)

Throughout their meta-analysis, they determined that frequent testing (including formative assessments) boosted educational achievement at all levels of education.

**Bloom's Taxonomy in the Cognitive Domain.** For more than half a century, Bloom's Taxonomy in the Cognitive Domain has been the gold standard in terms of classification of learning objectives. Bloom & Krathwohl (1956) determined that there were six levels at which students engage with material they are learning.

They established a system of hierarchy of educational objectives which attempts to divide cognitive objectives into categories ranging from the simplest behavior to the most complex. They formulated these six levels into a taxonomy, which is defined as a classification system in which each level purports to be a pre-requisite of the level above it. During the 1990's, a former student of Bloom's convened a group to reformat the classification system. He wanted to assure that each level had to be accomplished before moving to the next higher level. They changed the terminology, and reformulated the taxonomy into five levels. However, this "updated" version of Bloom's Taxonomy has never been as fully accepted as Bloom's original. Therefore, we will use the original in our work here. The six levels of that original taxonomy are knowledge, comprehension, application, analysis, synthesis, and evaluation. These are explained in detail on the table. Note that the taxonomy is listed from the bottom up for clarity.

| BLOOM'S TAXONOMY IN THE COGNITIVE DOMAIN |
|---|
| ***Evaluation*** is using definite criteria to judge the value of the information for a given purpose. Students may determine the criteria they use or the teacher may give it to them. The criteria may be internal (organization) or external (relevance to the purpose). At this level, evaluation is the highest in the cognitive domain because students make a conscious value judgment and use elements of all the other categories to achieve the learning outcome. |
| ***Synthesis*** involves assembling several different parts of knowledge into a new whole. It involves collecting information, and then, creating a new insight. At this level, emphasis is on the formulation of new patterns or structure and creative behaviors. Students often confuse application with synthesis, but it is easy to distinguish them if you remember that the product created by a synthesis is based on a variety of sources. Often, when a product is created at the application level, it is simply a new product based on having learned a single concept, or a set of highly related concepts. True synthesis involves not only more than one concept, but a variety of concepts being brought together to form a new whole. |
| ***Analysis*** answers why and requires students to break down knowledge into component parts and organize it for clearer understanding of the relation of those parts to one another, to the concept as a whole, or between one concept and another. At this level, students are required to demonstrate an understanding of both the content and structural form of the material representing a higher intellectual level than that of comprehension and application. |
| ***Application*** involves using the learned, and understood, material in new and concrete situations. Students are expected to take what they have learned and apply it in a different situation. At this level, the teacher has students applying methods, laws, and or theories to practical situations requiring a higher level of understanding than those simply required to demonstrate comprehension. |
| ***Comprehension*** is defined as the ability to grasp understanding. Students are asked to translate material, grasp meaning and to interpret material by summarizing or explaining. At this level, the teacher takes it one step beyond simple remembering of facts and material, to a basic understanding. |
| ***Knowledge*** measures recall of information gained through instruction or observation. In other words, it involves mostly facts, and we primarily are asking students to be able to recall those facts, recognize information we've presented, or identify information formats that have been presented to them. |

The three upper levels of the Bloom's Taxonomy in the Cognitive Domain (analysis, synthesis, and evaluation) are further classified as *higher-order thinking skills* (HOTS). When teachers are creating units, lessons, and ultimately, assessments, they of course have to establish information (knowledge and comprehension) and make sure students can use it (application), but they are encouraged to make sure that HOTS are also represented. When we discuss standards, and deconstructing the standards into targets, we will examine the levels more thoroughly and determine how objectives, and items that assess those objectives, can be written at the various levels.

**Depths of Knowledge.** In recent years, mathematics educator Dr. Norman Webb, at the University of Wisconsin Center for Educational Research, developed the concept of *Depths of Knowledge* (DOKs). His DOKs were created to determine the degree of depth, or in other words, the cognitive complexity required of standards and demonstrated on assessments. Further, they were to be used to determine how *deeply* the students would interact with the content and how *deeply* the students will be expected to understand and demonstrate their understanding of the concepts.

While some people believe that Webb's DOKs are just another classification of Bloom's Taxonomy in the Cognitive Domain because they deal with the same cognitive skills, many states have adopted them because of their belief that they are simpler, they do truly build on one another (which is a complaint against Bloom's), and because there seems to be a clearer distinction between the levels.

    Webb's DOK model has four levels:
        1) Recall
        2) Basic Reasoning
        3) Strategic Thinking
        4) Extended Thinking

They are explained on the next page, and for clarity once again, are listed from the bottom up.

| **DEPTHS OF KNOWLEDGE** |
|---|
| At **Level 4, *Extended Thinking***, students must investigate the concepts, and do some work that involves application of the concepts and demonstrates significant understanding of them. Higher-order thinking skills are also involved as they relate ideas within the content or with other content. To truly reach this level, new knowledge has to be created. |
| At **Level 3, *Strategic Thinking***, students must use planning and logic to interact with the material. Their responses are more complex, and they need to support their thoughts and justify their answers. Sometimes, more than one possible answer is sought out or discovered. |
| At **Level 2, *Basic Reasoning***, students must comprehend what is taking place and be able to paraphrase the concepts. They must use the concepts to make decisions about how to approach the problem or answer the question. They may use two or more steps at this level in responding or solving a problem. |
| At **Level 1, *Recall***, students simply recall facts, information, or even a procedure, or they use simple skills. Only a very shallow understanding of the concepts is required. Simple regurgitation of material is expected as is having students do work that requires only one step (e.g., stating the state capitals, finding the nouns in a sentence, giving the definition of a word, using automaticity to respond to simple multiplication facts). |

You will often find lists of verbs for each level. However, DOKs are determined by more than the verb. For instance, a student could be asked:

A) to *list* the four chambers of the heart (DOK 1—Recall)

B) to *list* the reasons that led to the cause of the War of 1812 (DOK 2—Basic Reasoning)

C) to *list* the background events and characteristics of the main character that caused him to join the gang (DOK 3—Strategic Thinking)

D) to *list* how the examples used by the debaters either strengthened or weakened their arguments (DOK 3—Extended Thinking)

What comes after the verb is what determines the level (Webb, 2002).

Another important myth to avoid is that if the activity that students are doing involves an extended length of time, it is automatically at *Level 4—Extended Thinking*. If students are spending a long period of time simply identifying the parts of speech of words in a lengthy passage, it may simply be *Level 1—Recall*. If they are doing the same activity, but with a passage in which the identification of the parts of speech were not so clear, and analysis must take place (including possibly diagramming out the sentences), it would move to *Level 3—Strategic Thinking*. Still, it would not be at *Level 4—Extended Thinking* unless students were to go further with the process (possibly to creating a passage with similar usage of the parts of speech and then determining if the structure worked better or worse in their passage). In order to reach *Level 4*, basically new knowledge needs to be created.

## THE PURPOSE OF ASSESSMENT

Now that we have discussed what we assess, some basic terminology, and the theoretical base, let's return to the original question with which we began this chapter. Why do we assess? We assess **to make educational decisions**. Examples of educational decisions that are made include: placement, promotion, the decision to move on to the next unit or to re-teach or provide more opportunities for practice, etc. If as a teacher, you are simply assessing something for the purpose of putting a grade on the top of it, that is similar to a doctor stating his diagnosis, but not providing the patient with a health care plan to get better.

## BASIC CONCEPTS IN CHAPTER 1

A) We assess for the purpose of making educational decisions.

B) Validity means that the assessment assesses what it purports to assess.

C) Reliability means that if an assessment is given in similar situations, it will produce similar outcomes.

D) We assess students in the areas of:
    knowledge (content),
    reasoning (ability to think),
    skills (ability to do something),
    products (output), and
    dispositions (attitude and actions toward the work).

E) Formative assessment is assessment <u>for</u> learning; summative assessment is assessment <u>of</u> learning.

F) Criterion-referencing provides information about how a student's work compares to established criteria (the right answers or the expected work); norm-referencing provides information about how the student's score on the assessment compares with the scores of the other students who took the same assessment.

G) Bloom's Taxonomy in the Cognitive Domain involves:
    knowledge (the facts),
    comprehension (understanding),
    application (using the information in a new or testing situation),
    analysis (breaking into parts),
    synthesis (creating a new product from a variety of sources), and
    evaluation (judging the value).

H) The Depths of Knowledge (DOKs) are:
    DOK 1 (recall),
    DOK 2 (basic reasoning),
    DOK 3 (strategic thinking), and
    DOK 4 (extended thinking).

NOTES:

# CHAPTER 2

# *ME? Grade four Grammer and Speling?*
## The Importance of Being Professional

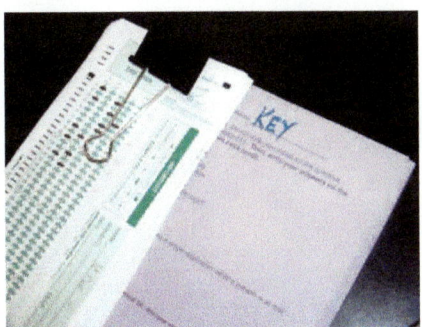

**KEY CONCEPTS:**
The Neighborhood Professional
The Teacher's Three Languages
Teacher Dispositions
Providing Feedback
Grading for Grammar/Spelling

> *In a completely rational society, the best of us would be teachers and the rest of us would have to settle for something less.*
>
> --Lee Iacocca

When I was growing up, if a less-than-clear document arrived, the grownups would get together to try to figure out what it meant. For instance, I remember once that my grandmother had received a letter about her Social Security benefits that she didn't fully understand. At Sunday dinner, it was passed around and the grownups discussed what they thought it meant. Then, it was decided that they should go and ask Mrs. Harwood. Mrs. Harwood was a retired teacher. Although her job had nothing to do with Social Security or any other part of the government, she was considered the "expert" in the neighborhood.

As a teacher, you will find that you too will be considered the expert. Part of that is related to the fact that teachers must have college degrees. Therefore, that makes you an educated part of the populace. But, it goes further than that. Teachers are considered experts by their neighbors because teachers don't stop learning once they have been awarded that college degree. Teachers are life-long learners.

Interestingly, I once had a colleague with a Ph.D. in Inclusive Early Childhood. Once we were at a restaurant and a friend of mine who worked at a daycare center came up to our table. I introduced my friend as our new professor in Early Childhood. The following conversation took place:

> "Oh, you're just the expert I need advice from," the daycare worker said. "We've been having difficulty with a child who bites. We've tried everything."
>
> "I don't know that I'd say I'm an *expert*," my colleague responded haltingly.
>
> "Well, if you're not an expert in this, *who would be*?" the daycare worker asked.

The daycare worker had a point. And, warranted or not, as a teacher, you will be considered the neighborhood "expert". And, whether you're desirous of it or not, you will also be a role model. Thus, in this chapter we will discuss those aspects of being a teacher that you will be "assessed" on by the school principal, the students, and their parents.

## THE TEACHER'S THREE LANGUAGES

As a teacher, you will be expected to speak three languages. No, this does not mean that you have to be tri-lingual (as in speaking English, French, and Spanish). The three languages that you will speak have to do with the audience. As a teacher, you will speak one language when talking to the students, a different language when talking with your fellow educators, and a third language when talking with parents. And, what all of those languages will have in common is that you will be expected to speak standard English in each case.

### The Language of Talking with Students

I think most teachers accept that they will be role models for their students while they are in the classroom. However, teachers are role models outside of the classroom as well. This means that teachers need to be careful about the speech they use no matter where they are in the school. Using standard English when responding to a student on the playground is as important as it is in the classroom. Babies obtain their native language by simply being immersed in it. The older members of their family speak to one another using language, and they automatically pick it up. That is the reason that a baby who grows up in a home where some of the people are speaking one language and some of the people are speaking another language will be bilingual. Likewise, the children you teach will come to your classroom speaking the language of their home culture. However, they will be spending seven (or more) hours a day in the school culture. And, they will pick up the language that is used there as well.

I spent several years teaching in the Caribbean. On some of the islands in the Caribbean, the Creole language that was spoken in most of the homes was also spoken in the schools. In fact, it was a point of pride that the children were being taught in their mother tongue. And, it was a beautiful language, with many colorful descriptive expressions that were so full of nuanced meanings. However, once college readiness exams (such as the SAT, ACT, etc.) became commonplace as part of the admission requirements for colleges (in the Caribbean as well as in other parts of the world where Caribbean students went to college), the attitudes changed. Children who were being educated in schools using a Creole language simply didn't do as well on those tests as the children who were being educated in schools using standard English. It wasn't that the Creole was inferior. It was that it simply wasn't the language of the test.

Let's consider the following scenario:

> **LEARNING JAPANESE**
>
> You and a group of your fellow teachers have been chosen to participate in a program. The twenty-five of you will have the opportunity to go to a college for a 12-week intensive summer course in botany. You will not be paid to attend, but, at the end of the 12 weeks, anyone who passes the comprehensive exam will win a cash prize of $10,000. And, the teacher with the highest score would receive a prize of $50,000. However, the test is in Japanese. So, while you will be having botany classes in the morning, you will have Japanese classes in the afternoon. In addition, there are three housing options available to you free of charge:
> - A) You can live in the dorm with your fellow teachers (who are all studying botany and Japanese with you).
> - B) You can live in a posh hotel, but no two teachers will be in the same hotel.
> - C) You can live with a Japanese family that uses Japanese in their daily conversation with one another.
>
> Which option would you choose?

As much as I think it would be great to spend the summer in a posh hotel, or having the luxury of being with my fellow teachers in the evenings studying together in the dorm, I would choose the opportunity for immersion in the Japanese language. With the possibility of $50,000 on the line, I would definitely want to become not only an expert in botany, but I would want to become fluent in Japanese as well.

Remember this story when you consider the language you use around your students. Immerse them in the language of the test!

In addition, when talking with students, especially in the area of assessment, be very specific about the content. Telling a student that her writing on the assignment was "poor" is not informative. Instead, point out that the second sentence lacked parallelism or the third paragraph needed more support for the topic sentence. (We will talk more about providing feedback to students in future chapters.)

### *The Language of Speaking with Other Educators*

Every profession has its "jargon". Among other educators, you will hear professionals using the language of the profession. Thus, you will need to learn the language of the profession. Throughout your teacher education training, you are exposed to the language. In addition to needing to know educational terms (like *validity, reliability, grade equivalents, Bloom's levels*, etc.) in order to pass your certifying exams to become a teacher, you will need to maintain those terms when working as an educational professional.

### The Language of Speaking with Parents

As we discuss the language to use when talking with parents, let's start with a quick story:

> A member of my family who was a medical doctor was once telling a group of us that my grandmother had had a myocardial infarction.
>
> When we asked what that was, he said, "A heart attack."
>
> I asked him why he didn't just tell us that in the first place. "They pay me big bucks to talk like that!"

I always think about that experience when considering talking with parents. While we wanted to believe that the medical professionals have the training to know the big words, ultimately, we wanted them to speak a language to us that helped us understand so we could help my grandmother recover. We needed the balance. It's that balance that you will use when speaking with parents. You obviously will use more adult language, in contrast to the language you speak with your students. But, you don't use the "jargon" of the professional educator that will make the parent feel put off. If you are the type of teacher who uses too many "big words" when talking with parents, the parents may put up a wall. Remember, no one likes to feel inferior.

When I have trouble with my car, I take it to an auto mechanic. When the auto mechanic starts using language I don't understand, he may start to see my eyes glaze over. Basically, I'm not interested in the inner workings of the engine. I want to know two things: how much is it going to cost and how long is it going to take?

You will have some parents who are like I was when our family member told us about my grandma. I wanted to know what the big words meant so I could help her. You will have other parents who are like I am with auto mechanics. They will simply want to know the bottom line. Watch for that "glazed look" and immediately get to the bottom line (e.g., *Billy has an 82% in my class, which is just above the class average.*)

Ultimately, remember the goal when talking with parents. You and the parents are on the same team. You both want the child to become educated. Having the parents on your side will make your job easier. Having a parent who encourages his/her child to do the homework you send home or to study for an upcoming test will assist you in educating that child. Therefore, make sure that when you talk with parents, you keep that fact in mind.

## THE DISPOSITION OF A TEACHER

The term *disposition* is not a term we hear often in the 21$^{st}$ Century. However, occasionally, you will hear someone say, "He has such a nice disposition" or "She's really nice-looking, but she has such a nasty disposition!" In those contexts, the person's attitude, personality, or behavior is being discussed. As teachers, you are expected to have a certain disposition. And, this disposition will affect how you assess your students as well as how you are assessed.

The National Council for Accreditation of Teacher Education (NCATE) has established six standards by which they assess teacher education programs and thereby award national accreditation to them. The first of those standards states:

> Candidates preparing to work in schools as teachers or other professionals know and demonstrate the content knowledge, pedagogical content knowledge and skills, pedagogical and professional knowledge and skills, and professional dispositions necessary to help all students learn. (NCATE, 2010)

The professional dispositions to which they are referring are set by the various teacher education programs that are seeking accreditation. At the large Southern university where I am a faculty member, which is accredited by NCATE, the following ten dispositions have been established:

1. Professionalism
2. Positive attitude
3. Prepared to teach and learn
4. Effective oral communication
5. Effective written communication
6. Self-directed learner
7. Emotional intelligence
8. Appreciates and values diversity
9. Reflection
10. Collaboration

Let's consider each of them individually.

*Professionalism.* I once asked a group of middle school students what a professional was. One girl answered, "A man who wears a shirt and tie when he goes to work." Obviously a professional involves more than that, but it certainly does remind us that a person's job is reflected in the way he dresses. As a new teacher, that should be a starting point for you. Teachers need to dress appropriately and conservatively. The school where you teach will probably provide a dress code for you. While it is not the most important part of your job, it is important that you follow it. How you dress will create the first impression you make on students each day, and being dressed professionally will set the tone in the classroom.

Another very important part of professionalism involves attendance and punctuality. As a teacher, you will be expected to be at work *every* day, and *on time!* If you are unable to go to work, you will need to inform the school as soon as you know so they can get a substitute teacher for your classroom. You will need to be in your classroom before your students arrive, and you should be prepared and ready to start class when the students arrive.

Also, professionalism involves speaking appropriately with the administration, colleagues, students, and parents. I was once observing a student teacher who said to the students, "You treat me with respect and I'll treat you with respect." After the class was over, I talked with her privately. I told her not to say that to the students again. She was the professional, so whether the students treated her with respect or not, she was expected to treat them with respect. If a student upsets you, remind yourself that you must be professional. You are getting paid to be a professional. So, while you may want to respond to a student with a sassy remark, you should not. Instead, remain the professional that you are, speak with the child semi-privately if possible (e.g., quietly at your desk) and return the conversation to the work that is being done in the classroom.

*Positive attitude.* We all have problems in our lives. However, you're being paid to be a teacher. Think again about how you would feel if you went to see a doctor, and instead of her concentrating on diagnosing the problem you came to see her about, she spent the first ten minutes telling you all about her problems and how depressed she was about the raise in her rent, the problem she was having with her neighbor, etc. You'd definitely wonder about her competence as a doctor.

As a teacher, you too need to consider that the students are there to learn. So, no matter what's going on in your life, you need to *check it at the door* when you enter the classroom. If you have just gone through a breakup in a relationship, and it's overwhelming you, think about how you'd feel if a doctor spent half your appointment talking about his recent breakup. You would feel like a boundary was being crossed. You're the patient; he's the doctor.

Likewise, you're the teacher and you have students. There are boundaries. Occasionally, if something horrific has happened (such as your favorite aunt has been diagnosed with cancer), you can share briefly with the students that you are feeling sad and state the reason why. However, then you simply move on with the school day. Students have the right to feel safe in a classroom, and one of the ways you provide them with that feeling of safety is by assuring them that the adult in charge of the classroom (you, the teacher) is going to lead a day of learning.

*Prepared to teach and learn.* It is usually obvious to students when the teacher is not prepared to teach. I particularly remember one teacher who was always reading the paper when the students walked into the classroom. Once the bell rang, he'd look up and then apparently decide at that point what was going to happen in the classroom that day. Sometimes, the students would be told to read. Other times, they'd be told to answer questions at the end of the chapter. Still other times, they'd discuss a topic. Did learning take place? It may have. But, without true preparation, I'm guessing it was far less than what could have taken place had the teacher been deliberate about what would be taught, how it would be taught, and how it fit in the big picture of the students' learning of that particular subject matter.

---

**LEARNING FROM MY STUDENTS!**

I love it when a student questions something I've just presented. I like them to check the things I've said. And, usually, what they find will validate what I said. If it contradicts it, then we discuss it. And, I learn!

I also learn from my students through their creativity. They show me new ways of looking at things. Even when they question an item I've written on a test, as I listen to their explanations of what they were thinking, I learn. I learn to write better test items. I learn how the various word choices I made could lead a student to a different answer than the one I intended.

I also really learn from my students when they give presentations, create products, etc. Sometimes, I have to look up some of the information they have provided in the products to verify that it is correct. But, it's a lot easier to do that in a 21$^{st}$-Century classroom with the Internet at our fingertips. If the information they have provided is correct, then I've had two chances to encounter it. And, repetition of exposure leads to retention of the information. So, I learn. If their information is inaccurate, I can clear up their misconceptions. The old adage that the best way to learn something is to teach it often proves true. So, again, I learn!

---

Another aspect, and one that is often overlooked, is that a teacher needs to be prepared to learn. Twenty-first Century teachers must be prepared to learn along with, and sometimes from, their students. The excellent outcome of your students being tech-savvy is that they have a ready resource at their fingertips. And, to a certain extent, it may make some of your students skeptical about what you say. That is critical thinking.

Encourage them to check what you teach. That will mean they are dealing deeply with the information. If they find other information that conflicts with what you have taught, together you can evaluate the new information. Sometimes, you may change your mind. Other times, you will help them see that the information they found is not reliable.

**FROM THE PRINCIPAL'S DESK**

As teachers, we communicate for a living. In fact, the ability to communicate clearly with children and adults is one of the first things I look for when hiring a teacher. The best teachers are those who can take a complex set of ideas and tell a simple story. This is just as true in a parent-teacher conference as it is in the classroom.

*Effective oral communication.* In addition to the usage of standard English previously mentioned and the consideration of the audience (students, fellow educators, parents), it is important that teachers be effective in the way they communicate. Teachers need to be clear when they express themselves. They also need to be specific, especially in the area of assessment. Telling the parents that their child is "doing poorly in math" is not informative (and it can insult some parents). Instead, indicate: *Thomas has a 58% on the math homework, but that includes zeros for two assignments he did not turn in. On the homework he did turn in, he obtained a 79%.* That would be more informative.

*Effective written communication.* Again, in addition to the importance of using standard English and the consideration of the audience, the teacher should choose her words carefully when providing comments on a paper, when writing a note to send home to parents, or when creating a report for the principal. Just as with his oral communication, the teacher should be clear in what he means and specific in what he writes.

*Self-directed learner.* A teacher needs to be able to go and get the information she needs. Obviously, in 21$^{st}$-Century classrooms, the most convenient source will be the Internet. Of course, it is not the only possible source. And, for things like the school policy, it may or may not work (depending on how the school distributes it). There is an old adage that states ignorance of the law is no excuse. When you encounter something you don't know, whether it is in the classroom, in a faculty meeting, or in a parent conference, it is your responsibility to learn it. If a student asks you a question you can't answer, either direct him on where to find the answer or tell him you will find out and get back to him (whichever is appropriate based on the information he's seeking). If a parent asks you for information you don't have, direct her to where that information could be found or tell her you'll find out and get back to her (again, whichever is appropriate).

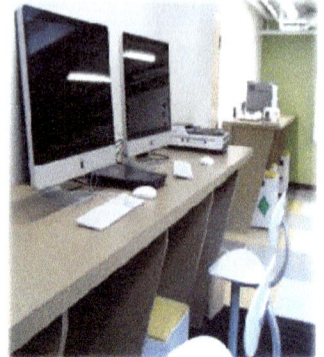

*Emotional intelligence.* Daniel Goleman coined the term "emotional intelligence" in his 1995 book of the same name (Bantam Books) in which he determined that a person's knowledge of emotions and skills in dealing with them are as important as his cognitive knowledge and skills. He shortened the term to "EQ" to contrast with "IQ".

EQ includes four parts. They are:

    A) awareness of one's own emotions
    B) management of those emotions
    C) awareness of other's emotions
    D) maintenance of appropriate relationships

EQ is very important for teachers. The concept is explained in this quote from the author and stress-reduction expert who created the HeartMath System used in many hospitals:

> With just a little education and practice on how to manage your emotions, you can move into a new experience of life so rewarding that you will be motivated to keep on managing your emotional nature in order to sustain it. The payoff is delicious in terms of improved quality of life.
> --Doc Childre

As the quote states, EQ can be developed. You can learn to be aware of your own emotions and to manage them. You can become more cognizant of the emotions of others and you can develop appropriate methods by which to relate to the people around you. And, as the quote states, the more you develop this, the better your quality of life.

*Appreciates and values diversity.* It has been politically correct throughout the 21$^{st}$ Century in the United States to tolerate persons different from ourselves. But, teachers need to go further. The word *tolerate* implies there is something wrong with the item (or person) being tolerated. People tolerate a headache. People tolerate a traffic jam. As a teacher, you should not consider that you need to *tolerate* students who are different from you. Instead, you need to *appreciate* and *value* the diversity of the students in your class. A student of a different ethnicity, who speaks a different language or has an exceptionality, or is from a different socio-economic group will be a valuable addition to your class. He will learn from you and the other students, and the other students and you will learn from him.

*Reflection.* The way to get better at doing anything is to practice, practice, practice. However, if you're practicing a wrong technique, you will only get better at doing something in the wrong way. Thus, the best way to become an excellent teacher is to reflect on your teaching regularly. There are many ways to reflect. One way is to keep a journal in which you write each day about what worked, what didn't, and what could be improved upon.

However, some days, you may simply be too busy to do a formal reflection. Still, you don't want to miss the opportunity to become a better teacher. Thus, on your lesson plan, you can jot down some quick notes (e.g., worked well but the groups needed to be larger; this activity only took 20 minutes; put more items for discussion on sheet; students did not have the necessary background for this). That way, the next time you are planning to teach that unit, you can refer to the old lesson plans and be reminded of things you need to change.

In addition to regular reflection (even daily if possible), there are other times that a teacher needs to reflect. At the end of a unit, after doing the unit assessment, the teacher should reflect on how much the students achieved, what he did to assist in that achievement, and what he needs to change to improve the outcomes for the upcoming unit (as well as for future times when that unit is taught again). At the end of a marking period, again a teacher should reflect. In looking at the grades the students achieved, the teacher can once again consider each student and think about that student's individual achievement.

In 21st-Century classrooms, the teacher may be entering the grades on an electronic report card which the parents can access via a portal provided by the school district. However, while the format may have changed, a report card still serves the same purpose. The parents want to know the percentages or letter grades, and basically, how the student is doing. In advance of filling out the report card, including the comments section, the teacher should reflect on each of her students so that she can provide an accurate informative assessment for the parents.

*Collaboration.* Very few things in life are created as an enterprise of solitude. In fact, the importance of collaboration cannot be overemphasized. Very few things in life are done without some collaboration. If you go to the grocery store, you need the collaboration of the people who have put the groceries in the store so that you can buy them. The grocery store is run through the collaboration of all its workers, and the owner of the grocery store knows that he cannot provide YOU with food unless there is a lot of collaboration.

This particular disposition is so important that I have devoted an entire chapter to it.

*PROVIDING FEEDBACK*

Teachers often complain about all the papers they have to grade. But, it will be a part of your job so it is important to learn to enjoy it.

> **LEARNING TO ENJOY GRADING!**
>
> When I was in first grade, my last name was Abbott. At that time, students sat in alphabetical order and the teacher's desk was always in the corner. Thus, for all of my elementary years, I sat next to the teacher's desk. Because I had an older sister who often came home and taught me what she had learned in school, by the time I entered first grade, I could read, write, and do third-grade math. Thus, I often finished my work earlier than many of my peers. To keep me busy, my first-grade teacher would often hand me papers to grade. It was really just doing matching between the key and the answers the students had put in the blanks, so it was easy enough for a little six-year-old to accomplish. (Note: That would not be allowed today because teachers are not permitted to allow students to see the other students' grades. However, at the time, our graded papers were often put on display for everyone to see, and teachers often called out grades as they passed out the papers.)
>
> The experience of grading papers for my first-grade teacher made me feel special, and like I was doing something important. As I moved through the grades, and still sitting next to the teachers' desks, I would actually ask them if they had any papers they wanted me to grade. Not surprisingly, I grew up to be a teacher (and ultimately a professor in teacher education). And, to this day, I love grading papers.
>
> *I tell you this story for two purposes:*
> *A) The experiences you provide your students in your classroom can have far-reaching consequences. Thus, remember, it is a great power (and responsibility) you have as you interact with your students.*
> *B) Grading papers will be a regular part of your job as a teacher, and it can be an enjoyable one.*

One way to make grading enjoyable involves recognizing the role EXPECTATION plays in the process. If the students' responses meet your expectations, it will let you know that the students are indeed gaining the knowledge and skills that you expected. When you receive a set of papers like that, it is often a joy to grade them as it reinforces for you that you are doing your job correctly.

However, when there are papers that do not meet your expectations, you may find yourself becoming irritated. It's usually that experience that makes teachers not enjoy grading. When you encounter papers like that, you *can* however even enjoy grading those. Once again, return to the disposition of emotional intelligence (discussed earlier). First, become aware of your emotions (you're feeling irritated because you worked really hard to create an exciting set of lessons related to that information). Next, look at what you were expecting. Then, become a detective! Many people like watching television shows involving clues that lead to solving a crime or mystery. Think of your grading that way. Seek to figure out where a student has gone wrong, what misconceptions he has, or what you need to do to increase his understanding. View it as doing an investigation (just like the forensics people do on those crime dramas). Once you have it figured out, plan your next action. Will you need to re-teach? Will you simply need to provide extensive feedback to the few students whose papers did not meet your expectations? Will you need to give another opportunity to the students for them to improve their grades? At the end of the grading of each set of papers, reflect. I think you'll probably find that a lot of learning did take place, even on papers that didn't fully meet your expectations. And, those sets of papers give you an opportunity to become a better teacher!

When giving feedback to students, it is important to be informative, but to not *do all the work for the student*. Again, you have to find a balance. In being informative, be specific. Instead of stating "Good writing!", indicate "You provided excellent support for your thesis statement." or "This paper was organized effectively." If the feedback needs to point out errors, it is all the more important that you be specific. Rather than state "poor writing", indicate "This sentence goes off topic" or "Your third point contradicts the first two."

Do keep in mind that you want the learning to continue for the students once they get the paper back. Thus, sometimes, you will point out an error, but not provide the answer *per se*. For math papers, sometimes it is best to indicate that an answer is incorrect without providing the correct answer. Having the students figure out what the answer should have been will extend the learning. For language arts, rather than correcting the grammar and spelling errors throughout the paper, some teachers use the CUPS model for grading.

| THE CUPS MODEL |
|---|
| C = Capitalization |
| U = Usage (word usage) |
| P = Punctuation |
| S = Spelling |

When the teacher finds an error, he simply writes the letter in the margin. The students are then instructed to find the error on that line. Because we don't want the learning to end once the papers have been turned in, the teacher is directing the students toward the error without actually correcting it for them.

Another part of grading involves allowing, even encouraging, students to <u>negotiate</u> their grades. When you are grading, you will be viewing the students' responses through the filter of your knowledge and experience as well as your expectations when you wrote the items or the prompts. However, students will have answered through their own filters based on their knowledge and experience and the way they interpreted the items or the prompts. By allowing the students to offer clarifications to you about what they were thinking that made them answer the way they did, you will learn much more about what they truly know (or don't know). Sometimes, when a student clarifies for me what he was thinking, even if his answer was incorrect, I may restore the points because his clarification showed me that he truly knew the information but simply interpreted my question in a different way.

There is an added advantage to having your students negotiate their grades. If you ask students to talk about their favorite teachers, and conversely, their least favorite teachers, a common theme emerges. That is whether the teacher was considered FAIR or not. By encouraging students to negotiate their points after the grading has occurred, and being open-minded to seeing their way of thinking, the students' perceptions of your fairness will increase.

## *GRADING FOR GRAMMAR AND SPELLING*

Several years ago, with the test scores particularly low in the areas of reading comprehension and writing concepts on the standardized tests for a local school district, the administrators postulated that it was because some of the teachers in the schools spoke with a non-standard dialect. When they had encouraged the teachers to speak using standard English, the language arts teachers indicated to the administrators that it was the teachers in what they termed the "non-academic" subjects that allowed students to use non-standard English even in their writing. Thus, at one of the regularly scheduled day-long teachers' meetings, I was called in to convince those "non-academic" teachers (their term, not mine) the importance of enforcing appropriate usage of standard English as well as the need for them to require good grammar and spelling on their assignments.

With what I considered to be a daunting task, I went to talk with several teachers in the school district in advance. With the input from them, I created my workshop.

I began the workshop by writing the paragraph in the box below on the chalkboard, and then asked what they thought of it.

> when she was first asked to speak at this conference,
>
> the professor were not happy  She didnt want to go
>
> their at all. Her had other things she want to do.

"The first word in the sentence needs to be capitalized," one of the teachers called out confidently.

"There's no period at the end of the first sentence," another stated.

"You used the wrong *there*," yet another said. "It's t-h-e-r-e."

Within less than a minute, they had all found the very obvious mistakes and the corrected board looked like this:

```
W
~~w~~hen she was first asked to speak at this conference,
                was                    didn't
the professor ~~were~~ not happy  She didnt want to go
there          She                      wanted
~~their~~ at all.  ~~Her~~ had other things she ~~want~~ to do.
```

I then asked them if they grade for grammar and spelling on the written assignments in their classes.

"It's not my job," said one young man. "I don't expect the English teacher to teach the safety rules for my shop, so why should I do her job?"

"I don't feel like I'm a good enough writer to criticize anyone else's writing," another said.

The teachers had been somewhat defensive coming into the workshop anyway, and with those comments, the momentum built quickly. They were all virtually in agreement that they either wouldn't, or couldn't, grade for grammar and spelling. I let them vent for a bit before I asked them how it was that they could so readily correct the paragraph I had written on the board.

"Your mistakes were so obvious," one defended. "Everyone could see those."

At that point, I passed out a handout I had created with the very simple rules that *everyone knew*. An updated version of that handout is found on the next page.

## Basic Writing Guidelines

**1. Punctuation**
   End a sentence with a period, question mark, or exclamation point.
   Use a comma to separate ideas.

**2. Capitalization**
| | |
|---|---|
| Proper nouns (or adjectives) | *Spain*; *Spanish* book |
| Beginning of a sentence | *The* candidate was from Alaska. |
| The pronoun I | David and *I* went to the library. |
| Entire word capitalized for emphasis | State the *MOST IMPORTANT* reason. |

**3. Subject/verb agreement**
   Number     Singular: *Billy jumps.*     Plural: *The boys jump.*

**4. Pronoun/antecedent agreement**
| | |
|---|---|
| Number | He (singular) . . . student (singular) |
| | They (plural) . . . students (plural) |
| Non-human | The dog (non-human) . . . its (non-human) |

**5. Parallelism**
| | |
|---|---|
| In series | *wearing* a dress, *cooking* a fig, and *looking* pretty |
| | (NOT *wearing* a dress, *cooked* a fig, and *look* pretty) |
| Tense | Maria *danced* a waltz before she *threw* the bouquet. |

**6. Modifier usage**
| | |
|---|---|
| Comparatives/superlatives | *more* or *–er* for two items |
| | *most* or *–est* for more than two |
| Possessives | Singular: friend's book   Plural: students' desks |
| | Ends in s: Mr. Davis' chalk |
| -ly form for adverbs | She passed *easily*. NOT: She passed *easy*. |

**7. Homophone usage** (common ones listed)
| | | |
|---|---|---|
| their, there, they're | it's, its | accept, except |
| board, bored | to, too, two | allowed, aloud |
| here, hear | affect, effect | whether, weather |

I encouraged them to simply grade for those simple rules. They begrudgingly said they would (because, after all, they were being blamed, at least in part, for the low test scores).

The story didn't end there though. A few months later, I had another opportunity to meet with many of this group of teachers again. I asked if they had incorporated grading using the simple rules we had discussed. A few had, and of those, every one of them had the same story. The quality of the work that was handed in had gone up. Not just the writing quality, but the *content* quality! "I think they are just paying more attention to what they write now knowing that I'm going to take a point or two off for simple mistakes," one shared.

Later, a friend of mine, who is a science professor, was complaining to me about the fact that the lab notebooks she had to grade were so hard to read. I suggested she start grading for the basic grammar and spelling rules.

"But, I'm teaching science, not English," she said.

I told her the story of my "non-academic" teachers and I gave her my simple rules document. A few months later, she reported the same thing that the teachers had told me. The write-ups in the lab notebooks made more sense and were better thought out. "And, only because I made the assignment worth 27 points instead of 25, with those two extra points for basic grammar and spelling," she stated.

So, my belief, whether you're a teacher or a professor, and whether you're teaching a "solid", a "special", or even a shop class, enforcing basic grammar and spelling on written assignments is a good idea. Whether you teach P.E. and only have an occasional written assignment (e.g., students write out the rules for volleyball) or science where you have students regularly record their results and draw conclusions in a lab notebook, I highly suggest that you grade for basic grammar and spelling as it will improve the quality of the overall work.

> **That which is INSPECTED is RESPECTED.**
> **--Anonymous**

## WAYS TO GRADE FOR GRAMMAR/SPELLING

There are four typical ways that teachers handle grammar and spelling errors on graded work. They are:
- A) A point (or ½ a point) is taken off for each mistake throughout the paper and simply deducted from the total points possible.
- B) The entire paper is graded for content and then holistic points for grammar/spelling are deducted.
- C) Grammar/spelling errors are pointed out on the paper, but points aren't deducted.
- D) Grammar/spelling errors are ignored.

Elementary teachers in a self-contained classroom (who have the same students for several subjects) have yet another option:
- E) Grammar/spelling errors are noted on the paper, and the points (or a notation) are recorded in the writing portion of the gradebook.

***Taking off points for each error.*** In some contexts, this may make sense. For instance, in the context of a writing or grammar class, where the emphasis is on grammar and spelling, it might be appropriate. However, in other contexts, it can be too punitive. For instance, on a 25-point opinion paper, if a student had ten mistakes, he might receive only 15 points (representing 60%) for the paper even if it was well thought out, followed the correct format, included the appropriate background, etc. Thus, if this method is used, it's often best to cap the total number of points that can be deducted. A good rule of thumb for most assignments is to have grammar/spelling represent approximately 10% or less.

***Grading the paper holistically in terms of grammar/spelling.*** Often, teachers simply figure out the points for the assignment and then add one or two points for grammar/spelling to the total points possible. Note the social studies example in the box.

| | | |
|---|---|---|
| Location of battle | Rolla, Missouri | 2 |
| Description of the geography | Small southern town; hilly terrain | 2 |
| Two reasons for deserting his post | Scared; homesick; wife expecting baby; mad at the Captain; questioning the cause | 4 |
| Effect it had on the battle | Soldiers were blindsided; many soldiers were killed in their tents | 8 |
| Effect on the war | Provided momentum to the other side | 5 |
| Grammar/Spelling | 0-2 mistakes: 2<br>3-5 mistakes: 1<br>6+ mistakes: 0 | 2 |
| **TOTAL** | | 23 |

As you can see, the content is worth 21 points and the grammar/spelling is worth 2 points. A good rule of thumb is to figure the content points and then add grammar/spelling that represents no more than approximately ten percent.

## BASIC CONCEPTS IN CHAPTER 2

A) As a teacher, you will be considered a neighborhood professional, and a role model.

B) Teachers must learn to speak appropriately to their students, to fellow educators, and to parents.

C) There are dispositions that are expected of teachers including:
    Being professional
    Having a positive attitude
    Being prepared to teach and to learn
    Using effective oral communication
    Using effective written communication
    Being a self-directed learner
    Displaying emotional intelligence
    Doing reflection
    Collaborating effectively

D) Grading is a regular part of a teacher's job, and can be enjoyable if a teacher views it as determining what the students have achieved (or still need to achieve).

E) There are basic grammar and spelling rules, and grading for grammar and spelling will improve the overall quality of the students' work.

NOTES:

# CHAPTER 3

## *But I Don't Like Her...*
### The Role of Collaboration

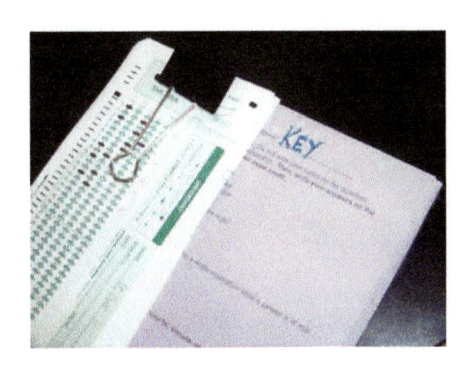

**KEY CONCEPTS:**
Collaboration Among Teachers
Cooperative Learning
Grading Group Work

*Individually, we are one drop.*
*Together, we are an ocean.*
--Ryunosuke Satoro

The word *collaborate* evolved from the seventeenth-century Latin *co-* meaning *us or two* added to *labor* meaning *to work*. Likewise, a synonym, *cooperate* evolved from the same *co-* and the word *operate* meaning *to be productive or efficacious*. Operate was a more encompassing term because it meant that one was not just working, but being very productive and as effective as possible. During the Industrial Revolution, *operate* was applied to machinery and meant that the parts were functioning well together (as in a well-oiled machine that's running smoothly). Thus, we can conclude that collaboration and cooperation have been a part of the human experience for a very long time.

Petrulis (n.d.) states that few tools in a teacher's toolkit are "as potentially powerful as small groups. Employing small groups and group projects creates possibilities for interaction and learning that could not be accomplished easily in other ways" (paragraph 24). Still, in my experience as a professor, teacher candidates often give me pushback when I require collaboration. I often get requests from students asking if they can do the work alone because either:

A) I always do all the work anyway and just put other students' names on it and I don't think that's fair.
B) I simply can't find the time to meet.
C) I don't feel I learn as much when I do group work.
D) I tried to work with HER but she simply is impossible (so I'm submitting MY work rather than her inferior work).

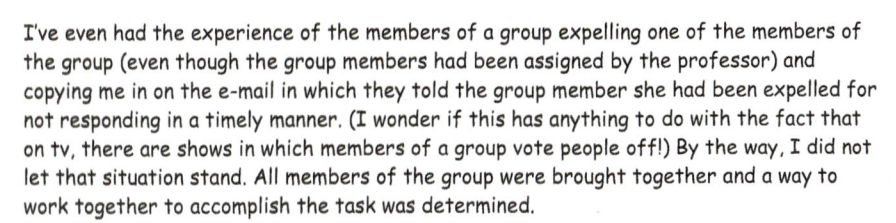

I've even had the experience of the members of a group expelling one of the members of the group (even though the group members had been assigned by the professor) and copying me in on the e-mail in which they told the group member she had been expelled for not responding in a timely manner. (I wonder if this has anything to do with the fact that on tv, there are shows in which members of a group vote people off!) By the way, I did not let that situation stand. All members of the group were brought together and a way to work together to accomplish the task was determined.

Collaboration among teachers is extremely important, and cooperative learning among students is one of the most valuable ways of learning. Thus, collaboration is a skill that teacher candidates should embrace and develop within themselves so that they can teach and model it to their students once they are in the classroom.

In this chapter, we will start with the collaboration among teachers and the rationale for why it is important. We will then move to discussing cooperative learning for students. Finally, we will consider the options for creating groups and for grading cooperative learning activities.

## *COLLABORATION AMONG TEACHERS*

According to Inger (1993), when teachers work together in a school, they see substantial improvements in student achievement, behavior, and attitude. He postulates that students can sense the program coherence and a consistency of expectations and that that leads to the improved achievement and behavior. In addition, he believes that the collegiality that comes with collaboration breaks the isolation teachers sometimes feel being the only grownup in the classroom, and thus, it can bring career rewards and daily satisfactions. He also determined that teachers who work together on curriculum and instruction find they are better equipped to teach. "Teacher collegiality avoids the sink-or-swim, trial-and-error mode that beginning teachers usually face. It brings experienced and beginning teachers closer together to reinforce the competence and confidence of the beginners" (paragraph 7).

Shachar and Shmuelevitz (1997) did a study with 121 junior high school teachers to determine if teacher collaboration had an effect on teacher efficacy. They found that the teachers who reported a higher level of collaboration with colleagues expressed a higher level of general teaching efficacy as well as in their ability to enhance students' social relations than the teachers who reported a lower level of collaboration. In addition, they found that the highly collaborative teachers implemented more cooperative learning activities in the classroom.

> **FROM THE PRINCIPAL'S DESK**
>
> There once was a time, before high-stakes assessment, when a teacher might expect to go into the classroom, close the door, and spend the day building a fantasy land with the children. But those days are long gone.
>
> In those simpler times much less was expected of the schools. Parents expected their children to be cared for and taught, but it was fully expected that about one third of children would not pass their coursework. Teachers taught. Students were expected to learn. But if they didn't, it was assumed that it was the student's fault, even if that student never had even one good teacher. But as the decades passed, more and more children were being left behind. Teachers and parents began to realize that more needed to be done. They realized that many of the children being left behind were capable of reaching higher standards, but in too many cases, were never asked to.
>
> Today, under high-stakes assessment, teachers are increasingly looking to professional collaboration as an effective means for meeting the wide-ranging needs of their students.
>
> That's why, when hiring new teachers, today's principals look for educators who are excited about working together as members of a professional team.

Little (1987) indicates the importance of teacher collaboration:

> The complexities introduced by a new curriculum or by the need to refine an existing curriculum are challenging. Teacher teamwork makes these complex tasks more manageable, stimulates new ideas, and promotes coherence in a school's curriculum and instruction. Together, teachers have the organizational skills and resources to attempt innovations that would exhaust the energy, skill, or resources of an individual teacher. The conclusions that one draws from the experiences of closely orchestrated, task-oriented groups in schools are consistent with conclusions drawn from other studies of organization: The accomplishments of a proficient and well-organized group are widely considered to be greater than the accomplishments of isolated individuals. (p. 496)

The concept that the product of a group is greater than the individual contributions of the members totaled is called *synergy*. It develops because one person mentions an idea, another builds on that idea, and the first comes up with something she wouldn't have thought of at all had the second person not added her part.

In order for collaboration to work, there are some key components that need to be in place (Inger, 1993):

1) Value has to be placed on the collaboration experience.
2) Authority has to encourage it (and sometimes assign it).
3) The groups need to be small enough (approximately three to six members) so that all members can have a voice.
4) Teachers (or teacher candidates) have to have some latitude in the scope of the work.
5) Teachers (or teacher candidates) need to be provided with training or assistance in collaboration if the group needs it.
6) Time needs to be made available so the collaboration can occur.
7) A concrete product (even if it is simply an oral report) needs to be the ultimate goal of the collaboration.

While it would be unfathomable that a teacher candidate could make it through an entire teacher education program without having participated in some collaborative experiences, it cannot be assumed that every candidate embraced the collaboration or saw its importance. Therefore, discussing the importance of collaboration, how it works, and its value is sometimes necessary in order for the experience to go smoothly, and to prepare the candidate to become a collegial and effective member of the faculty once she is placed in a school.

Inger (1993) concludes that schools benefit from teacher collaboration in four important ways [emphasis mine]:

> 1) Through formal and informal training sessions, study groups, and conversations about teaching, teachers and administrators get the opportunity to **get smarter** together.
> 2) Teachers are better prepared to support one another's strengths and accommodate weaknesses. Working together, they **reduce their individual planning time** while greatly increasing the available pool of ideas and materials.
> 3) Schools become **better prepared and organized to examine new ideas**, methods and materials. The faculty becomes adaptable and self-reliant.
> 4) Teachers are organized to **ease the strain of staff turnover**, both by providing systematic professional assistance to beginners and by explicitly socializing all newcomers, including veteran teachers, to staff values, traditions, and resources.

Teacher candidates in teacher education programs must not only be exposed to opportunities to learn together and to create products together, but they must be encouraged to embrace collaboration. It is simply one of the skills, and a disposition of mind, that a truly effective 21$^{st}$-Century teacher must have.

## *COOPERATIVE LEARNING*

Cooperative learning is an instructional method in which a group of students work together to complete a task (or tasks) with the ultimate goal being that the group members obtain a part of a knowledge base or a skill (or set of skills). In other words, they *cooperate* (work together) to *learn* something. While it often appears that the goal of most cooperative learning situations is the product (or presentation) that the group produces, the teacher should always remember that it's the learning that occurs that matters.

Since the mid-1980s, cooperative learning has been considered one of the strategies of best practices in the classroom. The largest value of cooperative learning comes from the fact that teamwork encourages students to engage in higher-level thinking skills including analyzing, explaining, synthesizing, and elaborating. Many researchers (e.g., Cohen, 1994; Johnson & Johnson, 1989; Kagan, 1993; Slavin, 1990) have also discovered positive effects on students' outcomes through cooperative learning. These can be in both the cognitive domain as well as the social domain. While sometimes cooperative learning involves simply two students working together, the more common usage involves a group of students.

When implemented appropriately, it has been determined that "cooperative learning improves acquisition and retention, higher-level thinking skills, interpersonal and communication skills, and self-confidence" (Kaufman, Felder, Fuller, 1999, paragraph 4).

The appropriate implementation of cooperative learning is key, of course. According to Johnson, Johnson, & Holubec (1993), there are five key elements that differentiate *actual* cooperative learning from simply putting students in groups to do a task. These are:

- A) Positive interdependence
- B) Individual and group accountability
- C) Face-to-face promotive interaction
- D) Interpersonal and small-group social skills
- E) Group processing

*Positive interdependence* involves the students recognizing that their success involves the entire group succeeding. This can be achieved through the delineation of shared goals, the dividing of the tasks among the members, and the sharing of materials. And often, the student's grade (or at least a part of it) is dependent on the performance of the other group members.

Encouraging a sense of group membership can also contribute to positive interdependence. For this reason, especially among elementary and middle school students, teachers will often have the group give themselves a name. While some groups will simply combine their first initials (e.g., JMT; the LNRers), others will be creative (e.g., Hot-Air Balloons), imitative of pop culture (e.g., Timbaland; Harry Potter), or even inspirational (e.g., TTG, The Top Group; Awesome!). However, the name is not as important as the fact that the students feel a part of something.

*Individual and group accountability* involves the concept that each person must pull his own weight and that the group members must believe that the group is only successful if all members participate. Most of us have had the experience of having a *hitchhiker* in a group. Just as a hitchhiker gets the benefit of traveling from one place to another without paying for a car, gas, insurance, etc., a hitchhiker in a group gets the benefit of the group (a shared grade, for instance) without doing his part. Individual accountability can be encouraged through various means of evaluation (which we will discuss later). In addition, it can be encouraged simply through the presence of the teacher as the group is working, and through the development of a classroom culture of intrinsic motivation that comes from valuing the experiences taking place in the classroom.

*Face-to-face promotive interaction* involves not only students meeting together but being responsible for helping (promoting) each other learn. With the advent of technology, sometimes cooperative learning takes place without the members being physically in the same place (meeting on a social network, using a webcam, etc.), but it is still important that a face-to-face (or pseudo-face-to-face) meeting take place so that the students can bounce ideas off one another. If there are six parts to a project, and three members of the group, sometimes they will each decide to simply *jigsaw* the work. This would involve each member simply doing two of the parts, and then one member combining them into a final project. This almost always results in an inferior product.

An important part of cooperative learning involves the cognitive activities that take place when one person makes a suggestion and another adds to it. So, while ultimately jigsawing may take place (particularly with secondary students who go off and do research individually), it is important that the group meet together initially to discuss the project, and again later, to discuss what they've found. (NOTE: Jigsaw II is a more formalized strategy and is described in the box.) In addition, the sharing with one another will result in the brain storing the information in more than one place. As the old adage states, *the best way to learn something is to teach it*. By sharing, a group member is teaching the material she has found. In addition, as students interact with one another, they develop a personal commitment to not only their own learning, but to that of the other group members as well.

> **JIGSAW II**
>
> The jigsaw strategy is used to develop the skills and expertise needed to participate effectively in group activities. It focuses on listening, speaking, cooperation, reflection, and problem-solving skills.
>
> - Listening - Students must listen actively in order to learn the required material and be able to teach it to others in their original groups.
> - Speaking - Students will be responsible for taking the knowledge gained from one group and repeating it to new listeners in their original groups.
> - Cooperation - All members of a group are responsible for the success of others in the group.
> - Reflective thinking - To successfully complete the activity in the original group, there must be reflective thinking at several levels about what was learned in the expert group.
> - Creative thinking - Groups must devise new ways of approaching, teaching and presenting material.
>
> Source: Muskingum Area Technical College (Zanesville, Ohio) Newsletter, September 14, 1994.

*Interpersonal and small group social skills*, while self-explanatory, are often overlooked by teachers when assigning group work. While a teacher will often spend a lot of time explaining the task(s) of the group, he sometimes fails to explain the importance of the teamwork and how it will be structured. The main social skills in cooperative learning involve allowing for leadership and followership, taking turns talking and listening, staying on task, using appropriate decision-making, building trust, communicating effectively, being respectful of each other, and being respectful of the other groups that are working in the vicinity.

The younger the group members, the more prescriptive the teacher needs to be in terms of delineating the behavior that is expected. For instance, if a group of three students are given a set of math manipulatives and told to figure out a problem using them, the teacher might have to tell the first-grade students that they are expected to take turns stacking the blocks, etc. Obviously, that would be offensive to seventh-grade students. However, those seventh-grade students might need to be instructed that the time spent on the problem-solving needs to be spent "on task and not discussing last night's tv show."

Teachers often set up expectations for cooperative learning during the first time or two that the students are placed in groups. During the next few experiences, the teacher may simply give a prompt of "good cooperative learning behavior is expected." After that, no verbal prompt may be required at all. However, she may occasionally need to quietly remind individual groups of the expected behavior when she notices they are not following the rules. Johnson and Johnson (1990) found that focusing on social skill development increased student achievement, and they postulated that that would enhance the students' employability, their interpersonal relationships, and their general psychological health.

*Group processing*, as Johnson and his colleagues (1993) describe it, involves taking time to analyze how well the group is functioning <u>as</u> it is performing the group work AND to debrief <u>at the end</u> to analyze how well it went. In doing this analysis, the group would look at both the success of their progress toward meeting the goal(s) of the project as well as their success in working as a team.

In addition to the five key elements of cooperative learning, there are some vital components a teacher must provide when giving a cooperative learning assignment. These include:

1) Assignment of roles within the group
2) Clear expectations of the expected product
3) Clear deadlines
4) Clear guidelines for evaluation

*Group roles.* Depending on the nature of the assignment, as well as the ages of the group members, the teacher may decide to assign roles within the group. Sometimes, it is appropriate for the teacher to actually assign who will serve in each role. Other times, the teacher may announce the roles he expects within each group and let the group members decide on who will fulfill each. And, still other times, no particular roles are required.

In the literature, there are various suggested roles for cooperative learning groups. Three of the most common are shown in the table below.

| Model 1 Roles | Model 2 Roles | Model 3 Roles |
|---|---|---|
| Leader | Leader | Assignment Coordinator |
| Timekeeper | Researcher 1 | Synthesis Coordinator |
| Recorder | Researcher 2 | |
| Presenter | Secretary | |
| Errand Monitor | Reporter | |

In the first model, each person has a role and the product is usually just a simple task that can be completed in a short time. In the second model, the task is probably more complex.

In the final model, everyone does a part, but the assignment coordinator makes sure everyone knows what they are expected to do, and the synthesis coordinator puts everything together once each person has done his/her part.

Some teachers use the "ticket-in" method of establishing groups. This method requires students to work individually (usually outside of class) on some aspect of a group assignment (e.g., completing a worksheet, finding answers to some questions, doing research on a particular animal). This work serves as their "ticket in" to participate in a group. Students who do not do the work are put together in a group, and they begin their work behind the others of course, and they often create an inferior product. The "ticket in" approach has been found by many teachers to encourage students to do the work so they can be in a group of their own choosing, or at least, a group where others have also done the work.

When I have groups of students working on group problem-solving or the creation of a project that lasts less than a single class period (with reporting at the end), I often announce just before the reporting that the person who spoke the least during the discussion will be the reporter. The groups then determine who that was. That encourages full participation by all members in future group activities.

*Clear expectations of the expected product.* As previously mentioned, learning by all the group members is the ultimate outcome we are striving for in cooperative learning. However, getting to that outcome often involves the creation of a product (or a presentation). Being very clear up front with the students about what is expected will increase focus for the group, and if well thought out by the teacher, will enable the creation of the product to actually result in the desired learning. Including a rubric on how the product will be graded is usually a good idea. Of course, if the rubric itself would give away the answer(s) that were expected or the research that would ultimately be found, obviously the teacher would not include one with the directions.

Because students, by their very nature, are young, and may not have the requisite skills, it is often good for a teacher to teach the groups about some general operating guidelines for accomplishing a task. These include:

| GENERAL OPERATING GUIDELINES FOR YOUNG GROUPS |
| --- |
| • Decide on specific activities and roles to accomplish the task. |
| • Decide on specific time allocations for each of the activities and set deadlines. |
| • Decide when the group will meet again to complete the next steps, or compile the final project. |
| • Evaluate the project prior to submission and review the group processes for having accomplished it. |

*Clear deadlines.* One of the most common areas of conflict involves difference of opinion, or difference of habit, among the group members concerning *when* the various tasks will be accomplished. Some students like to begin immediately as soon as an assignment is given. Others prefer to put it off until closer to the time it is due. The teacher can help mediate this problem by giving intermediate deadlines. For instance, she may require a progress report (or simply a log) to be presented to her (possibly even just orally) at the end of each week of a three-week project.

*Clear guidelines for evaluation.* Evaluation of the product is important for any assignment that is given. However, it is doubly important for cooperative learning activities. Just as there can be conflict between a teacher and a student about what was expected on a certain assignment, that conflict can increase exponentially when several students are discussing what they each *thought they heard* the teacher say.

Written guidelines are usually the best. However, the teacher needs to really think out the assignment herself before putting it in writing. And, if it is put in writing, she may simply have to accept the assignments she gets the first time through without that key part she thought was obvious if she failed to include it in the written directions. (She can fix it for the next time she gives the assignment.) Often, as teachers, we know what we meant to say, but sometimes, we don't realize what we failed to include until our students, with their creative minds, put their spin on it.

## CREATING COOPERATIVE LEARNING GROUPS

There are three basic ways to create cooperative learning groups. These are:

- A) teacher- selected based on criteria
- B) random assignment
- C) student-selected

Interestingly, research has shown that teacher-assigned groups often have fewer conflicts than do student-selected groups (Emerson, et. al, 1997). Also, if the teacher chooses the groups, he can decide to make the groups homogeneous or heterogeneous based on a variety of characteristics. This allows the teacher to create learning opportunities that random or student-selected groups do not. For instance, when students self-select, they often create homogeneous groups in terms of ability. In other words, the students who are good at math will often work together on a math puzzle, and the students with lesser ability in math will also choose to work together. A teacher can select the groups and make them heterogeneous in ability. Sometimes, the lesser-ability student can actually add to the group learning because he requires the group to do more explaining.

> In my personal experience, I have found that it is good to have heterogeneous groups in terms of gender as well. While same-gender groups tend to get the work done more efficiently, the mixed-gender groups often have a more varied, and creative, product. This is anecdotal on my part, but it has held true throughout my years of teaching at various grade levels.

As for the optimum size of cooperative-learning groups, that depends on the objectives of the activity. For a simple problem-solving activity in the classroom, the teacher may simply have the students pair off with their neighbors. For a classroom activity that requires brainstorming or a result that involves divergent thinking, a group of at least three or four is best. For a formal group that will be working together over an extended period of time, the **optimal size ranges from three to five**. Having more than five people in a group will often result in only a couple of the people doing the work while the others observe. Obviously, this defeats the purpose of cooperative learning.

## GRADING GROUP WORK

The chief question I receive from teachers when I do professional development on this topic involves how to grade cooperative learning projects. Petrulis (n.d.) puts the conflict very succinctly:

> Grading students' group work has controversial aspects. There is an ethic prevalent in academe and in American society at large which holds that students should be evaluated on the basis of their own individual work, and not that of others. This sensibility is challenged when students are evaluated on the basis of their interaction in a group, or the quality of a jointly-created product. In addition, students are understandably hesitant to place a portion-however small-of their educational fates in the hands of their peers until bonds of trust have formed.
>
> When students are asked to work collaboratively and to submit group products for a grade, instructors must confront inevitable differences among students and the conflicts that often erupt. Highly motivated students often resent being grouped with less committed peers. (paragraphs 25-26)

Some teachers simply require participation, and the quality of the project is graded. For those cases, there is no consideration of how the students work together, who does what parts of the work, who puts it together, and who does the actual submission.

On the other hand, some teachers include evaluation of not only the project, but also the process that took place while the project was being created. In other words, they assess both the *taskwork* and the *teamwork*. If the teamwork is being assessed, there are several ways it can be done. It can be assessed by the teacher, by the individual within the group, or by the peers within the group. If the teacher is assessing the group, she often does it by simply monitoring the group as they are doing the work in the classroom. Even a teacher sitting at her desk can direct her attention to each group for a few moments and determine who's on task and who's *hitchhiking*.

However, for more complex group work, the teacher is often not present, and much of the work is done individually anyway, and often away from the classroom. A teacher can use a self-assessment form like the one below to allow the individuals to confidentially report on the contributions of the members of the group.

### Group Work Individual/Peer Assessment

Circle the appropriate rating for yourself as well as your group members in terms of participation in the group work.

| Name | Excellent participation | Very good participation | Good participation | Some participation | Little or no participation |
|---|---|---|---|---|---|
| Billy | 5 | 4 | 3 | 2 | 1 |
| Krista | 5 | 4 | 3 | 2 | 1 |
| Leo | 5 | 4 | 3 | 2 | 1 |
| Nancy | 5 | 4 | 3 | 2 | 1 |
| Sean | 5 | 4 | 3 | 2 | 1 |

Circle the appropriate rating for yourself as well as your group members in terms of cooperation in the group work.

| Name | Excellent participation | Very good participation | Good participation | Some participation | Little or no participation |
|---|---|---|---|---|---|
| Billy | 5 | 4 | 3 | 2 | 1 |
| Krista | 5 | 4 | 3 | 2 | 1 |
| Leo | 5 | 4 | 3 | 2 | 1 |
| Nancy | 5 | 4 | 3 | 2 | 1 |
| Sean | 5 | 4 | 3 | 2 | 1 |

The teacher can then average the grades from the various ratings the individual as well as his peers gave him to determine how many of the 10 points for teamwork he is to receive. It is a good idea to allow the student himself to evaluate himself as well as his peers. In my experience, I have seen that often the student may not fully grade himself down if he didn't do as much as was expected, but he will grade himself down some. So, while the other students are giving him 2s or 3s, he'll give the others 5s and himself a 4.

Do keep in mind that it is best to average the scores given to the students rather than adding the total to the project. For instance, if the project itself were worth 50 points, you might then average the points for participation (for a total of 5 points maximum) and for cooperation (for a total of 5 points maximum). Therefore, the project itself would be worth 50 points, and the process points would be worth 10. Sometimes, the process itself would warrant being worth more than a few points, and sometimes there are specific criteria. In that case, you may want to create a form that involves using a Likert scale that the participants once again fill out, like the one shown below:

| Jenelle | Strongly Disagree | Disagree | Neutral | Agree | Strongly Agree |
|---|---|---|---|---|---|
| participated fully in the planning of the project | | X | | | |
| did his/her part on the research | | | X | | |
| assisted with the editing of the final product | | | | X | |
| contributed adequately to the reference list | | | | X | |
| fully cooperated with the group members | | X | | | |

| Amber | Strongly Disagree | Disagree | Neutral | Agree | Strongly Agree |
|---|---|---|---|---|---|
| participated fully in the planning of the project | | | | | X |
| did his/her part on the research | | | | | X |
| assisted with the editing of the final product | | | | | X |
| contributed adequately to the reference list | | | | | X |
| fully cooperated with the group members | | | | | X |

| Devon | Strongly Disagree | Disagree | Neutral | Agree | Strongly Agree |
|---|---|---|---|---|---|
| participated fully in the planning of the project | | X | | | |
| did his/her part on the research | X | | | | |
| assisted with the editing of the final product | | | | X | |
| contributed adequately to the reference list | | X | | | |
| fully cooperated with the group members | | X | | | |

| Max | Strongly Disagree | Disagree | Neutral | Agree | Strongly Agree |
|---|---|---|---|---|---|
| participated fully in the planning of the project | | | | | X |
| did his/her part on the research | | | | X | |
| assisted with the editing of the final product | | | | | X |
| contributed adequately to the reference list | | | | X | |
| fully cooperated with the group members | | | | | X |

As the teacher, you could assign point values of 1 for strongly disagree, 2 for agree, 3 for neutral, 4 for agree, and 5 for strongly agree. Thus, let's consider that Max filled out this sheet. Jenelle would receive 15 (based on 2 + 3 + 4 + 4 + 2) while Amber would receive 25, Devon would receive 11, and Max would receive 23 from Max's assessment of the group. Since all four students would be filling out the form, you might then average the numbers each student received from all four forms (including the number he gave himself). Possibly, the project itself might be worth 75 points and the other 25 points would come from the average of the peer reviews of the process.

Since technology is often readily available for students in 21$^{st}$-Century classrooms, you can sometimes allow the technology to provide you, the teacher, with a snapshot of how much each student participated. For instance, the use of a wiki, where students can edit on a shared document, will typically have a log that shows when the edits were done, and by whom. Some teachers look at the log and determine a participation grade.

In my experience, the rankings for students tend to come out about the same for each student (in other words, if one student gives a student a 2, often her other peers will also give her a 2). By knowing in advance that a teamwork grade will be given, by encouraging honesty in a classroom (and the teacher maintaining a certain amount of *withitness*) so that a group would have trouble conspiring against a single student, strong participation usually occurs and *hitchhiking* is avoided.

Do keep in mind that a teacher does not necessarily have to grade for teamwork. As the class coalesces into a learning community, teachers often find that they can simply grade the group based on the actual work that is done. This is also true for mature students. In college classrooms, many professors simply expect students to show their maturity and find a way to work together.

A single group work grade is often assigned to the project, with each group member receiving the identical grade. However, sometimes, if the objectives of the activity warrant it, a group work grade is given (e.g., for the presentation as a whole) and an individual grade is given for each student's part. And, sometimes, group work is not graded at all. In that case, the experience of simply working together to gain some knowledge is the goal. Thus, what the teacher hopes the students will gain from the experience will dictate which grading scheme, if any, is used. And, coming to an understanding with the students <u>at the beginning</u> of the experience about the expectations for the product (presentation, etc.) and the way it will be assessed is probably the most important aspect of how group work should be graded.

## BASIC CONCEPTS IN CHAPTER 3

A) Teachers in 21st-Century classrooms will be expected to collaborate with one another, with other educators, and with their students.

B) There are benefits to collaboration including synergy.

C) The size of the group is dictated by the task, but ideally, small groups of 3-5 members are best.

D) Cooperative learning is a strategy teachers use in classroom to encourage students to work together to accomplish a task and gain some knowledge.

E) Group work can be graded in a variety of ways including sometimes grading for the process as well as for the product.

NOTES:

# CHAPTER 4

# *You Mean I Gotta Teach That?*

**Curriculum Standards & Assessment**

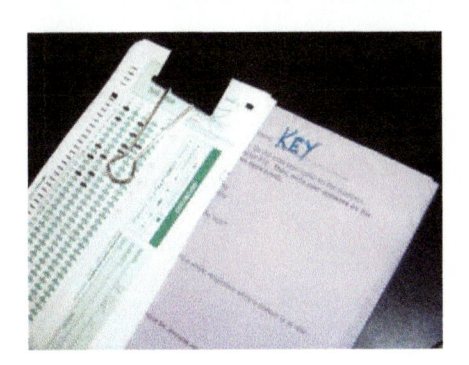

***KEY CONCEPTS:***
**Standards**
**New Common Core Standards**
**Creating a Unit**
**Writing Objectives**

*Learn why the world wags and what wags it. That is the only thing which the mind can never exhaust, never alienate, never be tortured by, never fear or distrust, and never dream of regretting. Learning is the only thing for you. Look what a lot of things there are to learn.*
 --T.H. White in *The Once and Future King*

The idea of "curriculum standards" is as old as education itself. This is because before someone can teach something, he has to decide what it is he is going to teach. This was true even when education was less formalized (e.g., if a man wanted to teach his son how to farm, he would determine that first he needed to teach him to clear the land, then prepare the soil, then plant the seeds, then till the soil around the plants, harvest the crop, etc.). Even in primitive schools, a teacher would determine what needed to be taught. In other words, he would establish the "curriculum" that he would teach for the year. Later, when one-room schoolhouses became two- or three-room schoolhouses with a "principal" teacher (the lead teacher), the principal teacher would set the curriculum. As school became more formalized, the more formalized the curriculum standards became. Eventually, in the 20$^{th}$ Century, virtually every local school "district" had a notebook containing the district curriculum.

If you are a public school teacher, what you teach in the classroom will be determined by the curriculum standards in your state. When you agree to teach in a public school, you are entering into a contract with the taxpayers of that state to provide the children in your classroom with an education that fits the curriculum the state has decided is appropriate for its citizens. Thus, it is your responsibility to provide that education to the children in your classroom. If your state has decided that the students should learn the multiplication tables in the third grade, and you are a third-grade teacher, you are expected to teach

> **FROM THE PRINCIPAL'S DESK**
>
> In 1986 I moved to Lexington, Kentucky, to accept my second principalship. I still recall visiting my new classrooms that fall. It was exciting to see how the teachers cared about the instructional environment they created for their students. But over the next few weeks, I began to notice something curious. Many of my teachers seemed to have the same "favorite units," and it did not seem to matter what grade they taught. I saw a beautiful lesson on dinosaurs taught in kindergarten. Then I walked down the hall and watched another lesson on dinosaurs being taught in second grade. I saw the same thing happening with rain forests, another favorite unit of my teachers.
>
> Clearly, something needed to change. A student going through our school needed to be exposed to an aligned curriculum that progressed and did not repeat the same information over and over again. Together, the teachers and I moved toward making that happen.
>
> Today 48 states have agreed to follow a national curriculum which assures that students will receive the content and skills they need throughout their educational experience.

the multiplication tables to your students. If a state has decided that students in a high school U.S. history class should learn about the writing of *The Star-Spangled Banner*, and you teach a high school U.S. history class, you need to include that in your course.

Often, the textbooks have already been aligned with your state standards, but not always. If your textbook includes six of the seven major areas included in the state standards, but not the seventh one, it is your responsibility as a teacher to include that seventh one anyway.

## COMMON CORE STANDARDS

Interestingly, many people believe that there has always been a national curriculum. And, in many developed countries, there is a national curriculum. However, that has not been the case in the United States because education, from the beginning of the establishment of the U.S. government, came under the jurisdiction of the states. There have been several attempts at establishing national standards, but until 2010, little actual progress was made. In 2010, a group of educators from throughout the United States developed the Common Core Standards (available at [corestandards.org](corestandards.org)) for the areas of English Language Arts and for Math. By 2011, 42 states had adopted them as their state standards. So, while they are not national standards *per se*, they are *de facto* national standards.

Thus, in the 21st-Century classrooms in at least those 42 states (as of 2011), teachers will be using the new standards for some areas, and their old state standards for other subjects. Common Core Standards for the areas of Social Studies and for Science are currently being developed and are expected to be available for review in the next few years.

## ORGANIZATION OF THE COMMON CORE STANDARDS

### English Language Arts Standards

The English Language Arts standards include standards in the five areas of:

  A) Reading Literature
  B) Reading Informational Text
  C) Writing
  D) Speaking and Listening
  E) Language

For each of those areas, there are *anchor standards*. These anchor standards are the same for grades kindergarten through twelfth grade, and there are ten or fewer for each of the five areas. The anchor standards for Reading are shown below.

| COMMON CORE READING ANCHOR STANDARDS |
| --- |
| 1. Read closely to determine what the text says explicitly and to make logical inferences from it; cite specific textual evidence when writing or speaking to support conclusions drawn from the text. |
| 2. Determine central ideas or themes of a text and analyze their development; summarize the key supporting details and ideas. |
| 3. Analyze how and why individuals, events, and ideas develop and interact over the course of a text. |
| 4. Interpret words and phrases as they are used in a text, including determining technical, connotative, and figurative meanings, and analyze how specific word choices shape meaning or tone. |
| 5. Analyze the structure of texts, including how specific sentences, paragraphs, and larger portions of the text (e.g., a section, chapter, scene, or stanza) relate to each other and the whole. |
| 6. Assess how point of view or purpose shapes the content and style of a text. |
| 7. Integrate and evaluate content presented in diverse media and formats, including visually and quantitatively, as well as in words. |
| 8. Delineate and evaluate the argument and specific claims in a text, including the validity of the reasoning as well as the relevance and sufficiency of the evidence. |
| 9. Analyze how two or more texts address similar themes or topics in order to build knowledge or to compare the approaches the authors take. |
| 10. Read and comprehend complex literary and informational texts independently and proficiently. |

Each of these anchor standards is expanded upon for each grade level.

| 6. Assess how point of view or purpose shapes the content and style of a text. | |
| --- | --- |
| Kindergarten: | With prompting and support, name the author and illustrator of a story and define the role of each in telling the story. |
| 1st grade: | Identify who is telling the story at various points in a text. |
| 2nd grade: | Acknowledge differences in the points of view of characters, including by speaking in a different voice for each character when reading dialogue aloud. |
| 3rd grade: | Distinguish their own point of view from that of the narrator or those of the characters. |
| 4th grade: | Compare and contrast the point of view from which different stories are narrated, including the difference between first- and third-person narrations. |
| 5th grade: | Describe how a narrator's or speaker's point of view influences how events are described. |
| 6th grade: | Explain how an author develops the point of view of the narrator or speaker in a text. |
| 7th grade: | Analyze how an author develops and contrasts the points of view of different characters or narrators in a text. |
| 8th grade: | Analyze how differences in the points of view of the characters and the audience or reader (e.g., created through the use of dramatic irony) create such effects as suspense or humor. |
| 9th/10th grade: | Analyze a particular point of view or cultural experience reflected in a work of literature from outside the United States, drawing on a wide reading of world literature. |
| 11th/12th grade: | Analyze a case in which grasping point of view requires distinguishing what is directly stated in a text from what is really meant (e.g., satire, sarcasm, irony, or understatement). |

As you can see, in kindergarten, the students learn that **someone wrote the story**. In first and second grade, they learn that different parts of a story can be told from the **point of view of various characters**. By middle school, they are analyzing **how point of view is developed**. As the grades progress, they learn more and more about point of view until they reach high school where they are taught to **read between the lines**. If teachers truly follow these new standards, and are not still just asking students in the ninth grade the same kind of questions they've been asking since early elementary, "Who's the narrator in this part of the story?", students should be able to be really excellent readers who can comprehend very complex text.

The same ten anchor standards that are used for *Reading Literature* are used for the broad area of *Reading Informational Text*. And, the progression (concerning that same sixth standard) increases in complexity as it moves from students recognizing that someone wrote the information through comparing their own point of view to that of the author. Then, in the upper grades, they eventually analyze the effectiveness of the ways that authors present their various points of view concerning issues.

There are also ten anchor standards for *Writing* (including the writing process, techniques, and audience), and there are six anchor standards for *Speaking and Listening* (concerning how to speak and how to analyze sources). The final area is called *Language*, and it includes six anchor standards related to using the conventions of grammar and usage, capitalization, punctuation, spelling, and vocabulary.

### *Math Standards*

Interestingly, the Common Core Math Standards are organized differently than the English Language Arts Standards. This is probably the result of disparate groups creating each of the sets of standards, but as these standards were developed for the purpose of being adopted across the nation (*de facto* national standards) and are precursors to further standards in the other subject areas, it has been surprising to many educators that they did not attempt to make the formatting consistent.

For the *Common Core Math Standards*, there are individual standards within domains and clusters for each of the grades kindergarten through eighth grade. For the high school areas, the domains, clusters, and standards are divided into what they call *conceptual categories*. Each grade level (or conceptual category) begins with an overview listing the domains and clusters, followed by the standards being spelled out.

The kindergarten overview includes:

---
**COMMON CORE STANDARDS: Kindergarten Math Overview**

**Counting and Cardinality** ←[domain]
    Know number names and the count sequence.
    Count to tell the number of objects.     } [cluster]
    Compare numbers.

**Operations and Algebraic Thinking**
    Understand addition as putting together and adding to, and understand subtraction as taking apart and taking from.

**Number and Operations in Base Ten**
    Work with numbers 11–19 to gain foundations for place value.

**Measurement and Data**
    Describe and compare measurable attributes.
    Classify objects and count the number of objects in categories.

**Geometry**
    Identify and describe shapes.
    Analyze, compare, create, and compose shapes.

---

The standards themselves spell out the specifics more fully. For example, the *counting and cardinality* domain for kindergarten contains the following seven standards organized within the cluster identified above:

---
**Kindergarten Standards: Counting and Cardinality Domain**

Know number names and the count sequence.
    1. Count to 100 by ones and by tens.
    2. Count forward beginning from a given number within the known sequence (instead of having to begin at 1).
    3. Write numbers from 0 to 20. Represent a number of objects with a written numeral 0-20 (with 0 representing a count of no objects).

Count to tell the number of objects.
    4. Understand the relationship between numbers and quantities; connect counting to cardinality.
        a. When counting objects, say the number names in the standard order, pairing each object with one and only one number name and each number name with one and only one object.
        b. Understand that the last number name said tells the number of objects counted. The number of objects is the same regardless of their arrangement or the order in which they were counted.
        c. Understand that each successive number name refers to a quantity that is one larger.
    5. Count to answer "how many?" questions about as many as 20 things arranged in a line, a rectangular array, or a circle, or as many as 10 things in a scattered configuration; given a number from 1–20, count out that many objects.

Compare numbers.
    6. Identify whether the number of objects in one group is greater than, less than, or equal to the number of objects in another group, e.g., by using matching and counting strategies.
    7. Compare two numbers between 1 and 10 presented as written numerals.

---

There are similar standards for each of the other domains and clusters for kindergarten and for each of the grade levels through eighth. The domains remain fairly consistent throughout the elementary grades; they change somewhat in middle school, as shown below:

| Kinder | 1st-2nd | 3rd-4th-5th | 6th-7th | 8th |
|---|---|---|---|---|
| Counting and Cardinality | | | | |
| Operations and Algebraic Thinking | Operations and Algebraic Thinking | Operations and Algebraic Thinking | Ratio and Proportional Relationships | |
| | | | Expressions and Equations | Expressions and Equations |
| | | | | Functions |
| Number and Operations in Base Ten | Number and Operations in Base Ten | Number and Operations in Base Ten | The Number System | The Number System |
| | | Number and Operations—Fractions | | |
| Measurement and Data | Measurement and Data | Measurement and Data | | |
| Geometry | Geometry | Geometry | Geometry | Geometry |
| | | | Statistics and Probability | Statistics and Probability |

As you can see, there are only four or five domains for each grade. *Counting and cardinality* is expected to be mastered in kindergarten so it is not contained in the first-grade standards. *Fraction study* begins in the third grade, and is further emphasized in the fourth and should be mastered by the fifth grade. *Statistics and probability* is then taught in middle school.

The high school conceptual categories are:

       A) Number and Quantity
       B) Algebra
       C) Functions
       D) Modeling
       E) Geometry
       F) Statistics and Probability

For all of the conceptual categories except modeling, there are domains and clusters within which the standards reside similar to the K-8 ones. For modeling, there are no domains or clusters or even a listing of standards. Rather, there are standards within the other categories marked with an asterisk that indicate they represent modeling.

Within the *number and quantity* conceptual category, used in the secondary schools, the domains and clusters include:

| NUMBER AND QUANTITY Conceptual Category |
|---|
| **The Real Number System** |
|     Extend the properties of exponents to rational exponents |
|     Use properties of rational and irrational numbers. |
| **Quantities** |
|     Reason quantitatively and use units to solve problems |
| **The Complex Number System** |
|     Perform arithmetic operations with complex numbers |
|     Represent complex numbers and their operations on the complex plane |
|     Use complex numbers in polynomial identities and equations |
| **Vector and Matrix Quantities** |
|     Represent and model with vector quantities. |
|     Perform operations on vectors. |
|     Perform operations on matrices and use matrices in applications. |

Just as with the elementary and middle school standards, the standards themselves are found within the clusters, as exemplified with *number and quantity*'s first domain (*The Real Number System*) shown below.

| The Real Number System |
|---|
| Extend the properties of exponents to rational exponents |
|     1. Explain how the definition of the meaning of rational exponents follows from extending the properties of integer exponents to those values, allowing for a notation for radicals in terms of rational exponents. *For example, we define $5^{1/3}$ to be the cube root of 5 because we want $(5^{1/3})^3 = 5^{(1/3)3}$ to hold, so $(5^{1/3})^3$ must equal 5.* |
|     2. Rewrite expressions involving radicals and rational exponents using the properties of exponents. |
| Use properties of rational and irrational numbers |
|     3. Explain why the sum or product of two rational numbers is rational; that the sum of a rational number and an irrational number is irrational; and that the product of a nonzero rational number and an irrational number is irrational. |

In addition, throughout the grade levels and high school conceptual categories, a separate set of eight overarching standards, which they call *Mathematical Practices*, are included. They are:

| MATHEMATICAL PRACTICES | 1. Make sense of problems and persevere in solving them.<br>2. Reason abstractly and quantitatively.<br>3. Construct viable arguments and critique the reasoning of others.<br>4. Model with mathematics.<br>5. Use appropriate tools strategically.<br>6. Attend to precision.<br>7. Look for and make use of structure.<br>8. Look for and express regularity in repeated reasoning. |
|---|---|

Unlike the English Language Arts standards that include 42 standards for each grade level, the number of standards per grade level varies. These range from 21 to 28 in the elementary grades, and 24 to 29 in middle school. The high school conceptual categories range from 27 to 43, with the largest number in geometry.

## CREATING A UNIT

Teachers typically create *units* in which they teach the concepts found in the standards. Sometimes, teachers base their units on the ones found in a textbook. However, in 21st-Century classrooms, students expect creativity that rivals what they see in the media (tv, computer) they digest daily. Therefore, many teachers figure out creative units that will engage the students while still teaching the concepts. For instance, three of the language standards for fourth grade are:

| | |
|---|---|
| CC.4.L.1a | Use relative pronouns (*who, whose, whom, which, that*) and relative adverbs (*where, when, why*). |
| CC.4.L.1c | Use modal auxiliaries (e.g., *can, may, must*) to convey various conditions. |
| CC.4.L.1e | Form and use prepositional phrases. |

Rather than calling the unit "relative pronouns, modal auxiliaries, and prepositional phrases" (which would not evoke student interest), a teacher might decide to do a unit called **"Batter Up!"** When the students walked into the classroom the first day of the unit, she would have a bulletin board decorated with a baseball theme.

She might then start the unit by having the students read the Abbott and Costello skit "Who's on First?" Then, as she explained relative pronouns, she would use sentences about baseball. Later, she would use baseball sentences to discuss when a student would use *may* versus *can*. Still later, she would discuss prepositional phrases while continuing the theme. So, while *educationally* the unit would be about using relative pronouns, modal auxiliaries, and prepositional phrases, student interest would be evoked by tying those concepts together into a unit about baseball. (Remember those three languages a teacher speaks!)

Typically, a unit is taught in a 2-3 week period of time, and a unit test is administered at the end as a summative assessment. After several units are taught (usually 3-4 in a marking period), sometimes an end-of-marking period test is administered that covers all the material in those units.

## WRITING OBJECTIVES

In order to make sure that the standards are met, a teacher must first determine what she wants the students to be able to DO once they have completed the unit. When writing an objective, it should meet the following conditions:

- A) It must contain an **action** verb.
- B) It must be **measurable**.
- C) It must be **succinct** and **straightforward**.

Sometimes, the standards themselves are written as measurable objectives, but sometimes they are not. Also, sometimes, the standards are too broad to be taught in a single unit. In that case, the teacher would break the standard into smaller objectives. For instance, consider the following kindergarten math standard:

| CC.K.CC.1 Count to 100 by ones and by tens. |

Obviously, a teacher would not teach a unit on counting to 100. Instead, she would start with a unit that involved counting to ten. Later, she would do another unit on the teens. Then, she would do a third unit on how the 20s, 30s, 40s, etc. involve a repeating pattern.

Thus, even with standards in place, a teacher needs to be able to write good objectives. She uses those objectives to direct her instruction. In fact, once she has her objectives, she will want to **deconstruct them** into the parts (knowledge, reasoning, skills, and products) as she plans her instruction. And, when she writes the unit assessment, she will look back at those objectives to direct what she puts on the test. If the instruction has been effective, and the assessment directly assesses the objectives, the students should do well on that assessment.

The most important part of an objective is the action verb. Objectives typically begin with the words *The student will be able to*. The verb that follows that phrase needs to be the action that you want the students to be able to DO once they have completed the unit. We often refer to it as your *power* verb. For instance, consider the following objective:

| POOR OBJECTIVE | The student will be able to: know the commutative property of addition |

*Know* is not an action. And, it's not measurable. In fact, you should never include the words *know, learn,* or *understand* in an objective. Also, do not include words like *demonstrate their knowledge of* or *show their understanding of*. Instead, use an action verb that you could measure that would show you that they knew or understood it.

Thus, you could replace that objective with:

| | |
|---|---|
| GOOD OBJECTIVE | The student will be able to: state the commutative property of addition |

However, even that is not the best objective. You don't simply want a student to be able to *state* that the commutative property of addition is $a + b = b + a$. What you actually want is for the commutative property to be a part of their ability to do math. So, your objective would be:

| | |
|---|---|
| BETTER OBJECTIVE | The student will be able to: use the commutative property of addition |

Objectives should also be written succinctly and in a straightforward manner. Include only what you ultimately want the students to be able to DO once they have completed the unit.

| | |
|---|---|
| POOR OBJECTIVE | The student will be able to: figure out what a metaphor (e.g., happiness is a warm puppy) is, find them in prose. They should also determine how they differ from similes (a cloud is like a soft pillow, etc.) |

Even though this objective includes measurable verbs (three of them, in fact) there are several things wrong with it. It is not succinct and it is not straightforward. An objective should be a single sentence, and it should include only what you ultimately want the students to be able to DO. Thus, this objective could be more succinctly written as:

| | |
|---|---|
| GOOD OBJECTIVE | The student will be able to: distinguish metaphors from similes |

Do keep in mind that students would need to be able to "figure out what a metaphor is" in order to distinguish metaphors from similes, so there can be some assumed steps within a good objective. (For instance, you would not include that students need to be able to identify numerals in an objective about multiplying two-digit numbers. However, students would have to be able to identify a 3 and a 7 in order to multiply 3 times 7.) Thus, in your deconstruction of the objectives into knowledge, reasoning, skills, and products that you'll use for instruction, you will include some of those assumed steps in your plans. However, your objectives themselves are what you want the student to be able to do once he has completed the unit. Think of it as something he would take forward into life.

Also, note that you do not put examples in an objective unless you include ALL the possibilities. Otherwise, simply don't put any. Therefore, you do not include "etc." in an objective.

| POOR OBJECTIVES | The student will be able to: identify the capital cities (Boston, Augusta, etc.) in the New England region |
|---|---|
| | The student will be able to: classify substances according to its state (e.g., liquid) of matter |

These should be written as:

| GOOD OBJECTIVES | The student will be able to: identify the capital cities in the New England region |
|---|---|
| | The student will be able to: classify substances according to its state (solid, liquid, gas) of matter |

Also, make sure when you are writing an objective that it is not merely a learning activity. For instance, don't indicate that a student will "practice rhyming words" or "write ten sentences containing metaphors". Instead, you ultimately want them to be able to "identify rhymes" or "use metaphors in their writing". Also, do not include learning activities or information about teaching that will take place in the classroom as a part of your objectives.

| POOR OBJECTIVES | *After extensive classroom discussion and research on the Internet*, the student will be able to create a bill in the format used by state senators. |
|---|---|
| | *Using the information discussed in class*, students will be able to write a short story. |

You don't want to limit students to the information they learned in class. Learning is about connecting new information with outside experiences, previously gained knowledge, etc. In addition, while teachers are often asked to classify objectives they have written into Bloom's levels (to assure that they are including *higher order thinking skills* in the unit, and not just teaching knowledge, comprehension, and application), you should not use the Bloom's verbs as your power verb in the objective. For instance, if your objective is that *students will be able to analyze a work of art*, the question would be analyze for what? That would be your power verb. If an objective was *students will be able to evaluate an article*, you would determine what characteristics they would be judging the value of (conciseness, clarity, facts to support their argument) and make that your power verb.

When writing an objective, think about the underlying knowledge you want the students to attain or a skill you want them to develop. Then, figure out a verb that will show you that they have that knowledge or skill.

## BASIC CONCEPTS IN CHAPTER 4

A) It is a public school teacher's responsibility to teach the curriculum standards mandated by the state.

B) The new Common Core Standards in English Language Arts and Math are not national standards *per se*, but they have been adopted as the state standards in those areas by the vast majority of the states.

C) A unit of study is usually completed in 2-3 weeks, should meet the state curriculum standards, and should evoke student interest.

D) Objectives must include a power verb that is measureable and be written in a straightforward and succinct manner.

E) The objectives should be deconstructed into knowledge, reasoning, skills, and products for the purpose of instruction.

F) The unit test should be aligned with the objectives, and if so, the student outcomes on it will inform the teacher of the effectiveness of the teaching.

NOTES:

# CHAPTER 5

## *Am I Getting Close to What You Want or What?*
### Formative Assessment

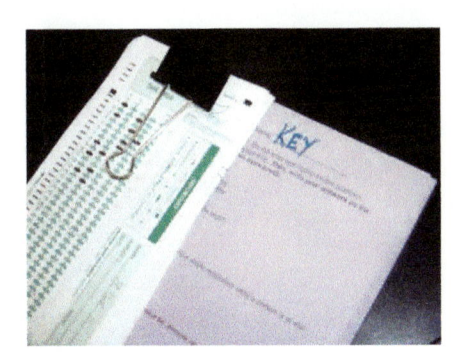

**KEY CONCEPTS:**
Historical Perspective
The Stiggins' Model
Types of Formative Assessments
Types of Formative Self-Assessment Tools
Formative Peer-Review Tools
Grading Formative Assessments

*The world does not pay for what a person knows. But it pays for what a person does with what he knows.*
—Laurence Lee

In recent years, Rick Stiggins, the director of the Assessment Training Institute in Portland, Oregon, has come to the forefront in the field of assessment concerning formative assessment. He states emphatically that it is important to balance assessment *for* learning with assessment *of* learning (Stiggins, et. al., 2008). However, while he is the latest researcher to study it extensively, he is certainly not the first.

## QUICK HISTORICAL PERSPECTIVE ON FORMATIVE ASSESSMENT

Scriven (1967) was the first to articulate the difference between *formative* and *summative* assessment. He basically considered it to be based on the point at which the assessment was done. If the assessment took place while the student was still *forming* his knowledge or skill base, it was formative. If the assessment took place after the final instruction in that particular area, it was considered summative.

In 1971, Benjamin Bloom, already famous for his *Taxonomy of Educational Objectives*, along with some colleagues, further expanded the definitions of formative and summative assessments by adding the dimension of purpose. They determined that formative assessment not only took place during the learning, but that its purpose was to determine how much of the knowledge base had been obtained at that point. In contrast, summative had as its purpose to determine how much (or at what level) the student had attained the knowledge or skill (Bloom, Hastings, & Madaus, 1971).

In 1983, an alarming report entitled *A Nation at Risk: The Imperative for Educational Reform* (National Commission on Excellence in Education) ushered in the era of the testing culture in America. It showed the American public that their school children were lagging behind school children in other parts of the world. In response, schools were encouraged to go "back to basics" and to check that the children were adept in those basics by placing lots of emphasis on achievement on standardized tests. Formative assessments became less important during this era, while schools began testing students more often, and awarding grades on most assignments (even those early in the learning process). This back-to-basics movement did improve education, so by the 1990s, again, the education establishment was looking for new methods.

A landmark meta-analysis was done by Black and William (1998) in the area of formative assessment. They analyzed several studies and further expanded the definition of formative assessment to involve the teachers changing their instruction based on it. In other words, a teacher could determine from a formative assessment that his students had mastered the content of a particular unit, and he would then decide to move on to the next unit (without completing the further activities he had planned). On the other hand, if toward the end of the unit, he saw through formative assessments that most of the students had *not* mastered the material, he could decide to add in more instruction and more opportunities for the students to interact with the material before giving the unit test (which is a summative assessment). In fact, the re-teaching aspect could have occurred at any point during the unit.

For years, good teachers had recognized that it was futile to move on to a next lesson that built upon the previous lesson if the students had not been successful on the first lesson. Unfortunately, some teachers (especially novices) simply trudged on through from Lesson 1 to Lesson 2 to Lesson 3, etc. Since people are taught from early in life to respect authority (first parents, then teachers) and to expect experts in a field to know better than you (if you're not an expert), those teachers may have felt that the textbooks and workbooks that had been developed by authorities and experts needed to be followed sequentially. Or, they may have been insecure about their own competence in the content, so they simply followed the pre-determined plan.

> **FROM THE PRINCIPAL'S DESK**
>
> The testing teachers do in their classrooms is an extremely important part of the teaching and learning process. Effective teachers know something about what their students already know before the lesson begins. To assure that the next lesson is presented at the appropriate level of difficulty, then, either formally or informally, they "test" the students to assure that they really did learn what the teacher intended to teach. And here's the most important part: once they know how their students performed, they change their instruction, and repeat as necessary, to make sure every child has achieved the standard. By this means, they remain focused on the success of each and every child.
>
> I used to tell my teachers, "If you're not willing to change your instruction based on the results of your assessments, then there's no need to waste time testing in the first place."

At the turn of the 21$^{st}$ Century, teachers were encouraged to recognize that they too were experts as they knew their individual students better than anyone! This gave them permission to adapt the materials to fit their students. As one educator stated, the *what* that is taught is in stone, but the *how* is left up to the individual teacher. This is the basis of the concept of *academic freedom*. The *what*, in this case, involves the curriculum standards that are set by the school, district, or state. So, while teachers are required to teach what the authorities have decided is appropriate in a particular subject at a specific grade level, they have the freedom to determine the methods that will best fit their students in attaining that knowledge and those skills.

## *FORMATIVE ASSESSMENT IN THE 21ST CENTURY: STIGGINS*

In the 21st Century, Stiggins (2006, 2008) expanded on the concept of formative assessment by including several aspects. These include expanding the purpose, informing the students of the learning targets, having students do self-assessment, and involving peers in the assessment process. While in previous years, teachers used formative assessments to make instructional decisions (whether to re-teach, give further practice, or to move on), Stiggins adds the aspect of having *the student* reflect on his work and do *self-assessment*.

This allows the purpose of formative assessment to expand to include having students determine:
- what's expected of them (the learning target)
- how close they are to the learning target
- what more they need to learn to reach the target
- what they've mastered, and
- even what more they may *want* to learn about the concept (beyond what the teacher set as the original objective)

In order for a student to do this, Stiggins advocates that teachers share their objectives with the students in advance. Teachers often need to break their objectives out into parts so that the student can see his progress toward reaching the overall objective. The parsed-out pieces of the objective are considered *learning targets* by Stiggins. In addition, having students reflect on their work helps the students to understand what success looks like, rather than simply defining success (or lack of) by the grades that are assigned to them. A further aspect of formative assessment that he suggests is the use of peer-to-peer assessment for the purpose of deepening the learning.

In contrast to formative assessment, Stiggins (2008) identifies the purposes of *summative* assessment, which he terms assessment *of* learning, as telling the student and others about her achievement, to verify her competence, and for gatekeeping. Examples of gatekeeping include using the summative assessments for promotion decisions, to determine college readiness, etc.

## *USING FORMATIVE ASSESSMENT FOR LEARNING*

In 21st-Century classrooms, assessment for learning can take place as:
   A) reflection by the teacher concerning how her students did on a formative assessment
   B) self-assessment by the student, and
   C) peer assessment

All are important components of the learning process. The learning needs to continue after the student turns in the work!

An example of how this might work is:

| Using Formative Assessments FOR Learning | |
| --- | --- |
| Who | Description |
| Teacher | Instructs |
| Student | Interacts with the material and submits the formative assessment |
| Teacher | Scores the assessment and gives feedback |
| Student | Reflects on the score and the feedback |
| Student/Peer | If a student can't figure out why he missed the points, he asks a peer |
| Student/Teacher | If the peer could not figure out why the points were missed, the student asks the teacher for clarification |
| Teacher | Decision is made about moving on or doing more work on the concept |

The decision possibilities include:

>A) Provide the student with more opportunities to interact with the concept if it was mostly misunderstood
>B) Provide the student with more opportunities to interact with the concept if it was somewhat understood, but more practice is obviously needed
>C) Move to the next new (possibly related) content if the material was mostly understood

The term *mostly understood* is used in the final possibility because full understanding of a concept usually does not occur until the concept is a part of a total knowledge base. For instance, if the concept of *nouns being defined as naming persons, places, things, or ideas* is introduced as the first lesson, and the students do well on the first formative assessment, the teacher may feel confident that she can move on to the next concept of *distinction between common and proper nouns*. However, the students probably won't have true understanding of nouns until they have learned about all the parts of speech.

The importance of students doing self-assessment is often overlooked. In fact, some students simply give a cursory look to the graded work, and then stuff the paper in their desk or notebook, or even throw it away. This is true for students all along the spectrum of achievement. Some students who got all or almost all of the items correct will not think it worth their time to reflect on the work. Likewise, many students who missed most of the items will quickly put away (or throw away) the graded assignment because it's painful to look at all their mistakes. By having students reflect on what parts they've mastered, and what parts they still need to master, students can mitigate those feelings of incompetence by recognizing that they simply haven't gained that information fully or mastered that particular skill YET. And, students at the top end of the achievement spectrum can have the opportunity to recognize that they have truly attained certain knowledge or mastered a certain skill, rather than just viewing it as having received a good grade.

---

*Tell me a story...*

As a college professor in a teacher education program at a large comprehensive university, I often encounter students who indicate that they "hate math" or "are not good at math."

I then ask the student, "If I were to ask you to change the oil in my car, could you do it?"

Most students say they couldn't. (If a student says he/she could do it, I change the request to *bake a soufflé* or *tailor a lined jacket so it fits me*.)

I then ask the student, "If I said I would pay you $10,000 to change my oil a week from now, could you do it?"

The answer is always an emphatic *yes*.

"How would that be possible?" I ask. The student of course indicates that he would find someone to teach him how to do it so he could get the $10,000.

*The purpose of this thought exercise is to help the student understand that knowledge and skills are attained, and that if they don't have that particular knowledge or skill yet, they can attain it. This is the underlying principle of having the students do self-assessment and reflection.*

---

Some teachers are resistant to the idea of having students discuss their graded work with their peers (Step 6). One stated to me that she feared that the students would think she was simply shirking her duties or not wanting to be confronted by students about the grade or feedback she had given. Another stated that she feared students would feel ashamed if they did worse on an assignment than a peer. However, there is great benefit to it, and if the teacher has fostered a sense of community in the classroom, there is usually little resistance. Obviously, as a part of fostering that sense of community, the teacher needs to remind the students that we are all on the same path, and that some are simply not as far along on the path.

The advantages of peer-to-peer assessment are many. Since the student is doing the work, and a peer is doing the same work, they can speak a common language that the teacher can't. While we hope that teachers have developed enough emotional intelligence, a concept expounded upon by psychologist and author Daniel Goleman in his groundbreaking book,

*Emotional Intelligence* (1995), to speak to the students in a language they can understand, it would be folly to believe that they can fully put themselves totally in the shoes of their students. However, peers are already in those shoes!

## TYPES OF FORMATIVE ASSESSMENTS

**Worksheets.** Historically, the most common type of formative assessment is a worksheet. Many curriculum materials include a workbook that accompanies the textbook. The worksheets in those workbooks are often good formative assessment tools. However, it is up to the teacher to determine the quality of the worksheet, and decide whether to use it or not. Sometimes, teachers will decide to use part of the worksheet (and tell the students to ignore another part of it). Other times, the teacher may adapt the worksheet to meet his needs. Teachers often create their own worksheets. And, increasingly, teachers are downloading worksheets from the Internet to use or adapt.

### What Makes a Good Worksheet

A) It evokes student interest with either a graphic, an interesting title, a story, or a question that draws the students in.

B) It fills the page appropriately with consistent spacing and good usage of the white space on the page. The title and the heading are appropriate.

C) An educator looking at the worksheet could quickly determine the objective that the worksheet would be assessing. That objective is educationally sound.

D) It includes clear directions so the students know exactly what to do.

E) It provides enough information so that the students can give the correct answers. This is particularly true for fill-in-the-blank items.

F) The items are grade-appropriate in terms of font size (larger for younger children; smaller for older but no smaller than size 10 or 11 for anyone) as well as complexity of the material.

G) It contains no more than three types of items. A common organization involves several items of one type (FITB, multiple choice, etc.) followed by a short answer or essay type item that requires the students to go more deeply with the information.

H) It is formatted professionally so it can be graded easily and consistently.

**Observations.** The second most common formative assessment involves the teacher simply observing the students as they discuss the concepts (such as determining the main causes of the conflict in the story) or perform an action (like using manipulatives to show three ways to make 35). The observations that she does can be formal in nature or informal. For instance, a teacher may walk around the room while the students are doing a science experiment and observe the appropriateness of techniques that are being used. She might correct the students verbally at that time (thus, doing an informal observation), or she might do a formal observation, in which she writes down the student's name, and fills out a checklist that she later shares with the student. The observations that a teacher does are varied and disparate. The same is true for what she records concerning them.

*Questioning.* Another common type of formative assessment involves asking questions. These can be either open or closed questions. They can be done during whole-group instruction, during small-group instruction, or individually. Students can respond orally or in writing. Sometimes, the teacher will collect the written responses, while other times, the teacher will simply go over the answers with the students aloud.

*"Home"-work.* Another type of formative assessment is the assignment of "home"-work. Obviously, homework can involve a variety of assignments or assessments (including summative assessments, such as creating a culminating project), but in this case, the emphasis is put on the *home* part of homework. It refers to something that cannot be accomplished in the classroom. Homework is often used to give the student the opportunity to reinforce, or practice, the concept or skill that has been taught, and "home"-work is excellent for this. The "home" aspect helps the student connect what he is learning to real life. For instance, if a lesson has been taught on figuring the circumference of a circle, the "home"-work can involve having the student take photographs (or draw pictures) of circular objects found in the home (like aspirin bottles, bowls, or clocks), measure the diameters of each, and figure the circumference of them.

*Journal entries.* Journals have become common tools for 21$^{st}$-Century students, and as formative assessment tools, students will often record information related to the concepts they've learned in them. For instance, a student may keep a learning log in her journal. In this, she writes down the main concepts she's learned that day. She may add a graphic organizer that displays the information in a way that shows how the various parts relate to one another. An important aspect that is often included in journal entries involves reflection. Having a student reflect on his learning has been shown to deepen that learning.

In the example on the next page, the teacher has given the students a prescribed format for their journal entries. It includes some particulars, but it also allows for divergent expression on the right-hand page.

### Journal Entry Serving as a Formative Assessment

*Child Dev.     Sept. 6*

*Main idea:* I learned about Piaget's theory today. It's about how children have to develop through certain stages in order to become able to learn. He has four levels.
*Something that surprised me:* Babies would not look for the ball.
*Example:* My brother is pre-operational. He likes to pretend.

*More:*

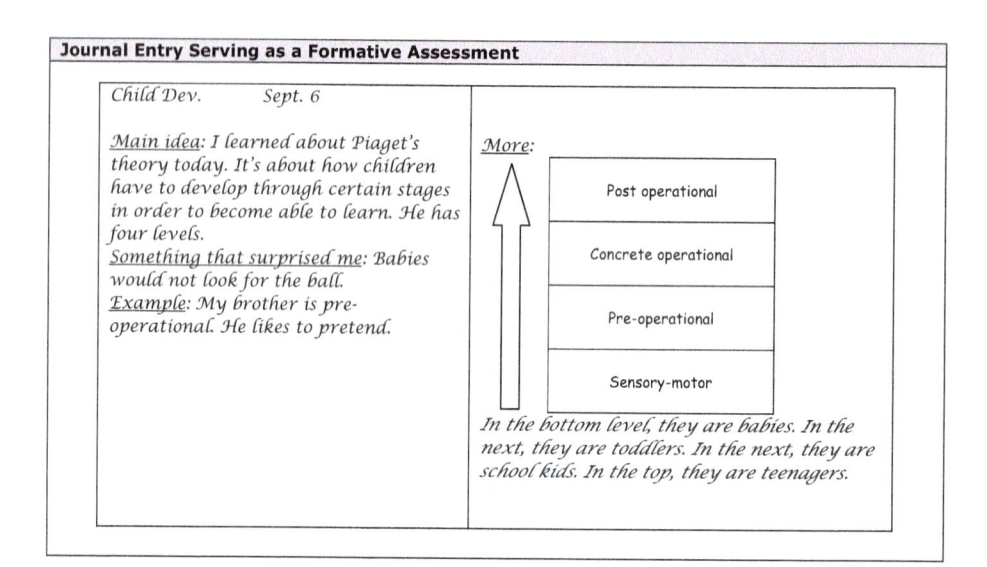

| Post operational |
| Concrete operational |
| Pre-operational |
| Sensory-motor |

*In the bottom level, they are babies. In the next, they are toddlers. In the next, they are school kids. In the top, they are teenagers.*

A teacher could then respond to the student's work as follows:

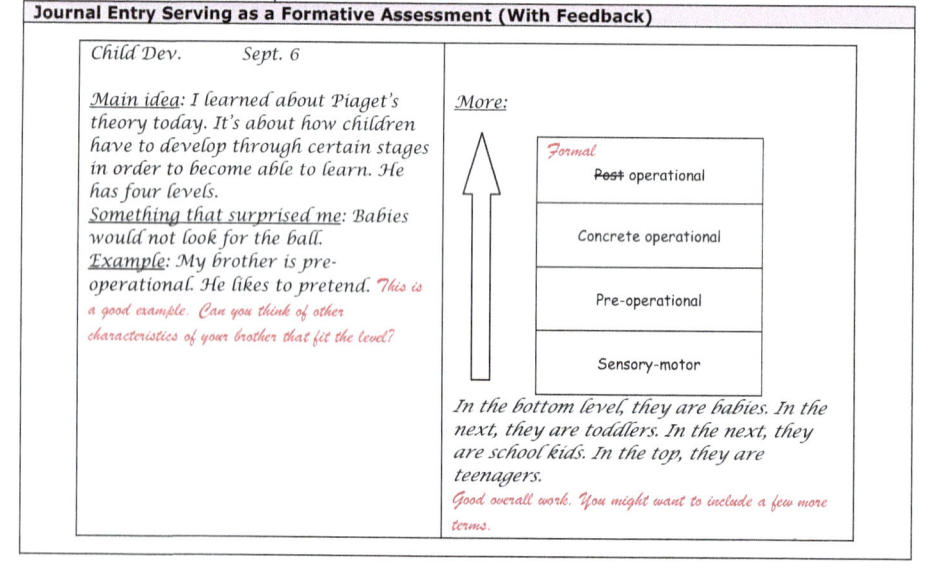

### Journal Entry Serving as a Formative Assessment (With Feedback)

*Child Dev.     Sept. 6*

*Main idea:* I learned about Piaget's theory today. It's about how children have to develop through certain stages in order to become able to learn. He has four levels.
*Something that surprised me:* Babies would not look for the ball.
*Example:* My brother is pre-operational. He likes to pretend. *This is a good example. Can you think of other characteristics of your brother that fit the level?*

*More:*

| Formal ~~Post~~ operational |
| Concrete operational |
| Pre-operational |
| Sensory-motor |

*In the bottom level, they are babies. In the next, they are toddlers. In the next, they are school kids. In the top, they are teenagers.*
*Good overall work. You might want to include a few more terms.*

***Exit slips.*** Journal entries are similar to exit slips that students fill out as formative assessments at the end of a lesson. Sometimes, the exit slip will simply ask the students to list concepts they learned from the lesson. This format can be completely generic and open-ended, and thereby used for a variety of subjects.

| Generic Open-Ended Exit Slip |
|---|
| *Name the five most important concepts covered in today's lesson:* |
| 1. |
| 2. |
| 3. |
| 4. |
| 5. |

On the other hand, an exit slip can be more prescriptive and created for a specific lesson.

| Prescriptive Exit Slip |||
|---|---|---|
| *List the four main causes of the Civil War:* |||
| 1. |||
| 2. |||
| 3. |||
| 4. |||
| *Identify the President of each during the Civil War:* |||
| THE UNION || THE CONFEDERACY |
|  ||  |

Sometimes an exit slip will contain selected-response items. A common type includes giving a student some characteristics or short scenarios for which they must circle the correct classification or word.

The following exit slip might be used by a teacher who had just concluded a lesson on words that are often confused:

### Exit Slip With Binary Choice Items

*Circle the correct term that would fit in the sentence.*

1. Surprisingly, some breeds of dogs actually weigh _____ than some breeds of cats.

    less        fewer

2. When the landlord got the electric bill, it was actually _____ than last month.

    less        fewer

3. Her training regiment included _____ miles and more strength training as the marathon grew closer.

    less        fewer

4. The Greatest Show on Earth, _____ was founded by P.T. Barnum in 1871, served as the precursor to America's obsession with entertainment.

    that        which

5. The event _____ moved the Cold War from the abstract to the concrete was the 1961 Bay of Pigs invasion.

    that        which

6. The _____ reason the protagonist fled was because she felt shame over her association with the antagonist of the story.

    principal        principle

7. Martin Luther started the Reformation because he disagreed with the basic _____ of the Catholic Church.

    principals        principles

Note that, in the above exit slip, the teacher is employing the concept of *teaching across the curriculum* by including other subjects (social science, literature) while assessing for her most recent grammar lesson.

Because students respond to items on exit slips quickly (and could possibly just guess), a teacher should be careful about assuming that they are full assessments of what the students have attained. Still, they do have their uses. For instance, in the binary choice one above, if most of the students got the items distinguishing *less/fewer* and *principal/principle* correct, but many did not get the *that/which* items correct, it could help inform the teacher that that concept was not as clearly understood as the others.

In recent years, teachers are beginning to include multiple choice items on exit slips. This is probably in response to the fact that multiple choice items tend to be the question type of choice on most standardized tests. An exit slip that includes multiple choice items is similar to a worksheet, but it is administered immediately after the lesson and collected before the students leave the room.

---

**Exit Slip With Multiple-Choice Items**

*Choose the best response to each item and write its corresponding letter in the blank in front of the number.*

_____ 1. In which branch of government is the Secretary of Education employed?
 A) Legislative
 B) Executive
 C) Judicial

_____ 2. Which of the following positions is not a part of the President's cabinet?
 A) Secretary of Defense
 B) Director of Homeland Security
 C) Speaker of the House
 D) Attorney General

_____ 3. The concept that was established in the U.S. Constitution that assured that no part of the government would become too powerful is known as
 A) the separation of church and state
 B) executive privilege
 C) checks and balances
 D) coordination of power

_____ 4. Bills related to spending are:
 A) the purview of the House of Representatives exclusively
 B) introduced in the Senate and approved by the House
 C) handled only by committees rather than Congress as a whole
 D) always introduced by the President

_____ 5. In terms of voting in the Senate, the Vice President:
 A) votes on every bill
 B) may vote on any bill, but usually does not
 C) is not allowed to vote
 D) only votes when there is a tie

The teacher could analyze the data she collects from the slips above to make a decision about what the next lesson should contain. Again, she needs to consider that, because it is an exit slip, student responses are quick responses, so this only represents their immediate responses (rather than more thoughtful ones that could occur on an assessment that allowed for more time). Still, if the majority of the students got answers 1, 2, and 5 correct, but many missed 3 and 4, she would know that she should definitely re-teach those concepts before moving on.

*Checklists.* Another formative assessment is a checklist. A teacher can create a list of the characteristics of a concept, individual aspects of a skill, steps in a process, or something similar that she then uses to determine if the student has attained those particular things. For instance, a Kindergarten teacher might use the following checklist:

**Checklist**

Name: *Damon*  Date: *Nov. 4*

| Consonant | States sound | Writes lower case | Writes upper case | Comments |
|---|---|---|---|---|
| B | X |  | X | Wrote LC backwards |
| T | X/2 | X | X | Sound took two tries |
| D | X | X | X | Noted it was beginning letter of his name |
| F | X | X | X |  |
| P | X | X |  | UC looked like a D |

Likewise, a high school chemistry teacher might use a checklist for quizzing the students on the Periodic Table. The teacher could fill in the first column with random elements and then call individual students to the desk and quiz them.

**Checklist**

Name: _____  Date: _____

| Element | Symbol | Atomic Number | Atomic Mass | Group<br>M  AM  TM  N-M  H  NG |
|---|---|---|---|---|
|  |  |  |  |  |
|  |  |  |  |  |
|  |  |  |  |  |
|  |  |  |  |  |

***Bell ringers.*** In recent years, the term bell ringer has become a part of teachers' jargon, but teachers have been using them for years. Basically, a bell ringer can be any short, quick activity that a teacher has the students do as soon as they arrive in the classroom (starting even before the bell rings). Because in many schools, students arrive at various times in the classroom, teachers have found that having something fun or interesting (and that's the key) related to either the previous day's work or to act to stimulate a student's interest in the new information or activity they will be dealing with that day is valuable.

Bell ringers are not usually graded. Often, they are puzzles, or riddles, or something that requires a student to create a quick drawing or graphic organizer. Sometimes, they are not paper-and-pencil based at all. For instance, teachers sometimes simply place manipulatives on the table with a prompt on the board. Other times, a teacher might have the first student who arrives in a group to come up with three questions from the previous day's lessons to ask his peers when the other members of his group arrive.

The purpose of bell ringers is three-fold:

      A) to help develop the habit of mind that the classroom is a place of learning
      B) to engage the student in the concepts being taught (either as an anticipatory set or a reminder to the student that he does indeed remember the concepts taught previously)
      C) to give the students something to do while the rest of the students are arriving

Teachers know that most mischief occurs during down-time, when the students are not engaged, so bell ringers change what can be some students simply waiting for their peers to arrive to an active engaged time. Do consider that the students will have varying amounts of time to complete the bell ringers, and that some students will not complete it at all (because, for instance, they arrived on the last bus). Thus, bell ringers are typically not collected or graded. Instead, they are used to increase student interest and get them engaged immediately in the teaching/learning process as soon as they enter the classroom.

***Other formative assessments.*** The formative assessments listed here are only the beginning. The teacher (or the student, for that matter) can be as creative as he wishes when creating formative assessments. The only restriction is that the formative assessment truly assess the objective that is trying to be fulfilled.

## TYPES OF FORMATIVE SELF-ASSESSMENT TOOLS

As previously mentioned, an important part of formative assessment involves the student doing a self-assessment or reflecting on the work he has done. He can do this self-assessment before submission of the work or after he has received the work back from the teacher (with her feedback on it). Like formative assessment tools, the variety of formative self-assessment tools is unlimited. However, there are a few common ones.

*Simple checklists*. Checklists that the students use for self-assessment are similar to the checklists that teachers use to assess the students. For a tool to fit in this category, the student should be able to mark the parts he has mastered with a checkmark or X, or have the opportunity to mark *yes* or *no*.

*Confidence questionnaires*. Stiggins (2008) suggests that these are excellent self-assessment tools that can encourage students to take control of their own learning. A confidence questionnaire asks the student questions about her ability to perform a skill or to respond to questions about information she has attained. Checklists of this type allow the student to identify where she is with particular concepts at a certain point in time. An example would be one in which a student assesses her ability to identify parts of speech in a sentence.

**Confidence Questionnaire**

Name _____   Date_____

| Part of Speech | Don't Understand These | Usually Just Guess | Sometimes Find Them | Always Find Them |
|---|---|---|---|---|
| Nouns | | | | |
| Pronouns | | | | |
| Verbs | | | | |
| Adjectives | | | | |
| Adverbs | | | | |
| Conjunctions | | | | |
| Prepositions | | | | |
| Interjections | | | | |

Other "levels" might be:
- don't get it, still hard for me, average, pretty good at it, mastered
- don't know it, usually miss it, can guess at it, know it
- 1 (being lowest in ability), 2, 3, 4, . . . 9, 10
- haven't learned it yet, can discuss it a little, can define and describe it, know a lot about it
- novice, apprentice, fellow, expert

If a class has recently learned about the caste systems of feudal England, the levels for a confidence questionnaire in another subject area even (for instance, math or science) might be:
- peasant, vassal, lord, knight, aristocrat, king

Or, if cause-and-effect had been taught using the game of chess, the levels might be:
- pawn, knight, bishop, rook, queen, king

Obviously, the levels can be as creative as you, or the student, choose them to be.

A confidence questionnaire can be open-ended as well. An example in the field of middle school mathematics follows.

---

**Open-Ended Confidence Questionnaire**

| 1. How you do feel about your ability to solve equations? |
|---|
| 2. How good are you at being able to write the correct equation needed to solve word problems? |
| 3. If given a formula, how good are you at solving the problem using the formula? |
| 4. What formulas do you still need to master? What ones are you confident with? |

---

***Reflections.*** While all self-assessments involve the student reflecting, this type of self-assessment involves the student actually writing his perception of his knowledge of a concept or ability to do a skill. This reflection can include the spectrum from a single sentence or phrase to several paragraphs or even pages. In it the student writes aspects of the information or skill that he understands, is still finding challenging, etc. as well as his feelings related to working with the material.

***CQ + Reflection Form.*** You can combine a confidence questionnaire with a reflection and format it in such a manner that it allows the student not only to consider his skill or knowledge level, but also the kinds of things he's doing that's resulting in the outcomes he currently has. An example is on the following two pages.

## CONFIDENCE QUESTIONNAIRE + REFLECTION FORM

# Self-Reflection Form

## PART 1: *How I'm Doing*

For each of the chapters, fill in the columns based on the information listed at the top of each. An example would be:

| Chapter | Major concepts I learned | Percentage earned (show work) | Reasons I lost points |
|---|---|---|---|
| 1 | Globe orientation<br>Latitude/longitude<br>Tropics of Capricorn/Cancer | 50/62 = 81% | I submitted one item late.(2 points)<br>I made computation errors. (6 points)<br>I didn't understand two of the questions on the quiz. (4 points) |

| Chapter | Major concepts I learned | Percentage earned (show work) | Reasons I lost points |
|---|---|---|---|
| 1 | | | |
| 2 | | | |
| 3 | | | |
| 4 | | | |

How are my percentages trending? Place an X in the box that most closely fits.

| They are going down | They are all over the place | They are consistent, but not as good as I'd like them to be | They are going up | They are consistent, and at a level I am satisfied with |
|---|---|---|---|---|
| | | | | |

**The percentage I have in geography so far is (show work):**

_____%

## PART 2: *What I Know*

Geographic terms I now know and can define are:

## PART 3: *What I'm Doing*

In terms of the **PPTs** available, which describes my interaction with them? Place an X in its box.

| I pretty much ignored them | When I needed some information, I skimmed through them | I listened to them | I listened closely and tried to understand the information being presented | I printed out the notetaking guides and took notes on them while listening |
|---|---|---|---|---|
| | | | | |

In terms of the **readings in the book**, which describes my interaction with them? Place an X in the box that correlates with the description.

| | I pretty much ignored them | When I needed some information, I skimmed through them | I read through it | I read through it and noted key points | I printed it out and read it; I highlighted as I read it and jotted down important ideas from it |
|---|---|---|---|---|---|
| Chapter 1 | | | | | |
| Chapter 2 | | | | | |
| Chapter 3 | | | | | |
| Chapter 4 | | | | | |

In terms of the **exercises**, which primarily describes my interaction with them?

| I didn't do them | I simply plowed through them without any preparation | I skimmed the reading and the practice exercises, but I then just went to doing the required work | I did the reading, and I did the practice exercises; then I did the required work | I did the reading, and I did the practice exercises; then I checked my work against the keys or with a peer on them; after that, I did the required work and checked it with a peer before submitting it (or doing the stats assessment online) |
|---|---|---|---|---|
| | | | | |

In terms of the **using the GEOG ONLINE resource**, which primarily describes my interaction with it?

| It's baffling to me | I tried to use it a little bit | I've practiced using it some | I used it quite a bit and I'm feeling somewhat confident about it | I feel like I can do pretty much what I need to using it |
|---|---|---|---|---|
| | | | | |

**The grade I hope to attain in geography is:** _____

**In order to attain that grade, my plan is:**

By having the students fill out how they are doing, what they know, and what they are doing, it will enable them to make the connection between what they are doing and how that is resulting in the outcomes they are receiving. Remember, student self-assessment is for the purpose of having the student do the reflection as well as for the purpose of informing the teacher about the students' beliefs.

***Student-led conferences***. The student can lead a conference with the teacher, or with the teacher and the parents present. In this conference, the student shows her work and the progress she has made in a certain subject. In order for these to be successful, the students need to be trained in how to conduct them. Often this training takes place in the classroom as a role-playing exercise. First, the teacher can have two students come to the front of the room to play the role of "parent" and "teacher". The teacher herself then plays the role of "student" and leads the conference. Then, the students can get in groups of three and practice while the teacher observes, and guides as needed. (This is discussed further in the last chapter in this book.)

***Other tools***. Just as formative assessment tools are only limited by the creativity of the teacher, other self-assessment tools can be created by either the teacher or the student. The content to be self-assessed will of course dictate the tool to a certain extent.

## FORMATIVE PEER REVIEW TOOLS

There are various ways that a peer can assess a fellow student. Peer-to-peer assessment can occur before the student submits the formative assessment to the teacher for grading, or after the student has received the graded assignment back. The first one simply involves having the student show his work to a peer before submitting it and asking for the peer to look it over for mistakes. The student would then presumably fix the assignment (if he found the peer's suggestions valid) before submitting. The second instance, in that same vein, involves having the peer look over his *graded* assignment and help him understand why he missed points (in other words, what he did wrong) or clarify the feedback the teacher had given him. He might also help him figure out the correct answers. Likewise, the peer may have missed some points on the same assessment, and the first student can help her understand why she had those answers incorrect.

The key point of peer assessment is for it to go both ways. That of course will not happen on every assignment, but it should happen over time. Some teachers believe that it is best to pair students of varying abilities together (e.g., a student who usually does well in math with one who does not do as well), but others prefer to allow the students to find their own peer reviewer. Sometimes, students will choose someone of similar ability; sometimes, not.

Tools that can be used for peer review include:

- having the students interview each other concerning a concept or skill
- using a checklist to grade a peer's work (prior to submission or for clarification after)
- using a rubric to grade a peer's work (prior to submission or for clarification after)
- having partners compare their work and reconcile any differences
- having students combine their homework onto a chart

There are others of course, and again, they are only limited by the creativity of the teacher or the students.

It is important to teach students how to do peer assessment. Otherwise, they will very likely simply say "good job" to each other after giving the work a quick perusal. Therefore, initially, it is important for the teacher to provide the students with specifics. For example, if the students were writing an essay, a teacher might suggest that they first determine if the five-paragraph format (introduction, three-paragraph body, conclusion) is present. Then, they would be instructed to read the introduction to see if it follows the guidelines expressed in class (hook, thesis statement, delineation of main points). That way, the students are learning to peer grade for content and will avoid the "good job syndrome" that so often occurs with peer grading.

## GRADING FORMATIVE ASSESSMENTS

Teachers often disagree about whether formative assessments should be graded or not. Some feel students won't do the work if they don't receive a grade for it. However, giving a grade for work when the student is just learning how to do it doesn't seem fair either. Thus, there are a wide variety of ways to address the issue.

***No grade.*** This can be used as long as the students are doing the work, and at a high level. In some schools, the culture of the school simply embodies the idea that a student has membership in the school, and as a member, will live up to the duties required for that membership. Sometimes, students simply have intrinsic motivation to learn the material and do the work. If the school you work in does not have such a culture, teachers will sometimes have to employ other methods to ensure the students are doing the work that is necessary for learning. When no grade is assigned, the student should at least receive feedback about her work. Sometimes, this is simply done by the class going over the work together. Other times, the teacher might collect the work and give feedback on the individual papers.

***Student/teacher conferences.*** A student can simply be called to the teacher's desk to show or discuss his work. Teachers can then do a variety of things concerning the work. These include (but are not limited to):

- award him a grade
- simply praise his work or his attempt to do the work and guide him on what to do next
- give him a checkmark on the paper and in the gradebook
- make some notes about the student's progress

Although novice teachers may find these time consuming, veteran teachers have learned to glean a lot of information about the student's progress in very short little conferences, and they can be conducted while the other students are engaged in work that does not require her constant supervision.

***Draft grades.*** Sometimes, a teacher believes the students have learned the material or gained the skill, but discovers that is not true when he starts grading the papers. If after grading a half-dozen or so of the papers, the teacher determines that the same mistakes or misunderstandings are occurring, the teacher can simply stop grading the papers at that time. He can go back to the graded papers, place a big X over the grade he had written at the top, and write:

+5/draft
(This would be an appropriate number of points for a small assignment, worth 25 points or so. For a larger assignment, the teacher might award 10 draft points.)

On the rest of the papers (the ungraded ones), he would place the same indication. During the next class period, he would then explain to the students that he felt that they needed more work on the concepts before receiving an actual grade. He could then use the worksheet itself to re-teach the concepts. Once he felt that the students were ready to try again, he could then give them a new formative assessment over the same concepts. That one would be scored. The reason for giving the draft grade is to reward the students for attempting the work. If a student in the class did not do the work, she of course would not receive those five points. Using a draft grade should be done sparingly though because the teacher does not want to encourage half-hearted first attempts at the work.

***Weighting grades into a pre-set percentage.*** A common policy in many schools is to have the formative assessments graded and returned to the students with grades on them, but to then combine all of those grades together and have them account for only a small percentage of the overall grade in the subject area. For instance, a school (or teacher) may decide that the formative assessments should be worth only 25% of the grade. In that case, the teacher would combine all of the points earned on the formative assessments and divide that total by the number of points possible on those assignments. This percentage would then be multiplied by 0.25 to determine how many of those 25 percentage points the student would receive.

This is shown in the following example:

> A student has received 263 points of the 332 points possible on the various formative assessments in her biology class. This would give her a 79% on those assignments.
>
> On the summative assessments in the class (a unit test and a project), she received 223 of the 250 points possible. This gives her an 89% on summative assessments.
>
> Formative: 0.25 x 0.79 = 0.1975
>
> This rounds to 0.20 meaning that the student receives 20 of the 25 percentage points allowed for the formative assessments.
>
> Summative: 0.75 x 0.89 = 0.6675
>
> This rounds to 0.67 meaning that the student receives 67 of the 75 percentage points allowed for the summative assessments.
>
> 20 + 67 = 87 (Meaning the student received an 87%)
>
> Since the formative assessments only represent ¼ of the grade, the student's overall percentage in the class is mostly determined by her achievement on the summative assessments.

*Multiple attempts.* Another way to award grades for a formative assessment is to allow the student to do the assignment several times. The teacher can set a limit on the number of times, or he can simply set a deadline, and count the last attempt. This of course requires a lot of grading for the teacher, but the teacher can make it easier by having the students bring their work up for a quick grading (against a key the student doesn't see). He then puts the number correct at the top of the page. The student can then go back and figure out *the puzzle* of which ones he has right and which ones he has wrong. Technology can be used to do the grading as well and formative quizzes can be set up for the students to take multiple times (until they are satisfied with their grade, until a maximum number of times has been reached, or until a pre-set deadline).

***Front-loading points.*** Because students learn best by interacting with the material, an excellent way for students to gain the knowledge or skills in a certain area, even in the beginning of the learning, involves simply doing the work. A teacher can front-load the assignment by making sure that a student will receive most of the points if he simply attempts the work. For instance, if a student is assigned the task of drawing a map of the school to scale for 25 points, the teacher might grade it:

| Scaled Drawing of the School |||||
|---|---|---|---|---|
| Criteria || Pts. possible | Pts. achieved | Comments |
| Outside walls | Indicated | 3 | | |
| | Logical | 1 | | |
| Inside spaces drawn and labeled | Rooms | 5 | | |
| | Hallways | 3 | | |
| | Office | 1 | | |
| | Cafeteria | 1 | | |
| | Gym | 1 | | |
| Legend is included | Included | 3 | | |
| | Logical | 1 | | |
| Drawing is to scale || 4 | | |
| Neatness || 2 | | |
| **TOTAL** || 25 | | |

Using this rubric, the student will receive most of the points if he simply attempts the assignment and includes the elements that he's been told to include. Later in the process, after he's presumably gained more mastery of the concept, a further assignment can assign more points for quality and fewer *effort* points.

***Cutesy rewards or privileges.*** Sometimes, teachers will simply reward students with stickers, pencils, baseball cards, etc. for turning in formative assignments or achieving certain levels on them. Privileges, such as extra time on the computer or getting to line up first for lunch, are also sometimes awarded in lieu of grades. In those cases, the teacher would still give the student feedback on the work. It is important that this option be used rarely. We do not want students to do work simply based on extrinsic rewards. However, if a handful of students did not do the rough draft that was assigned, a teacher might allow the students who did the rough draft to have computer game time while the other students worked on their rough drafts.

## *CONCLUSION*

Formative assessment is an important part of the learning process. While summative assessments provide us with information about how much the students have learned ultimately concerning the concepts, and are typically used in large part to assign grades on the gradecard, formative assessments are an important part of the overall learning experience. Stiggins (2008) concludes that the ultimate purpose of formative assessment is to help students learn more, and get better over time.

## BASIC CONCEPTS IN CHAPTER FIVE

A) Formative assessment is not a new concept, but the emphasis on it in 21st-Century classrooms has been increased.

B) The Stiggins' Model of formative assessment adds in the important component of involving the students in their own assessments.

C) Formative assessment includes doing assessment *for* learning.

D) Typical formative assessments include:
      1) worksheets
      2) observations
      3) questioning
      4) "home"-work
      5) journal entries
      6) exit slips
      7) checklists
      8) bell ringers

E) Peer-to-peer assessments and self-assessments can help students figure out how close they are to the target.

F) Some formative assessments are graded; others are not.

G) There are ways to accommodate grading formative assessments including using weighting of grades.

NOTES:

# CHAPTER 6

# *Is This Gonna Be On The Test?*
## Summative Assessment

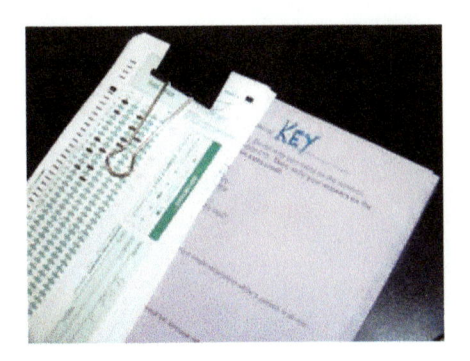

***KEY CONCEPTS:***
Description of Summative Assessment
Types
Usage
Face Validity
Use of Technology

> *Education's purpose is to replace an*
> *empty mind with an open one.*
> --Malcolm Forbes

Summative assessment is, as the term states, an assessment *in sum* (or *summary*) of what has been learned. "Summative assessments are done at the end of a period of learning (lessons, units, years) for the purpose of documenting student proficiency at the time of assessment" (McMillan, 2008, p. 10). This is of course in contrast to formative assessment which is done while students are *forming* their knowledge base or skills.

While formative assessment has become an emphasis in the 21$^{st}$ Century, summative assessment has always been the emphasis in schools. In contrast to formative assessment, which is assessing the students as they are learning the concepts, summative assessment involves the assessment that takes place after the learning has occurred. With formative assessment, the assumption is that more learning will continue, if needed, if the student being assessed has not accomplished meeting the target. With summative assessment, the assumption is that the learning has been completed, and now, the students will be showing to what extent they have mastered the content.

## PURPOSES OF SUMMATIVE ASSESSMENT

Summative assessment has three primary purposes.

| Primary Purposes of Summative Assessment |
|---|
| A) to determine how much the student has learned<br>B) to verify competence of the student against the standards that are in place<br>C) for gatekeeping |

The Organization for Economic Cooperation and Development (2008) expounds on this by stating that:
> Summative assessments are used to measure what students have learnt at the end of a unit, to promote students, to ensure they have met required standards on the way to earning certification for school completion or to enter certain occupations, or as a method for selecting students for entry into further education. (p. 1)

Once we have determined what the students have learned and how that learning fits within the standards that have been set, we then use that information to inform the **stakeholders** involved in the student's education. Direct stakeholders are those persons who are directly involved in the education of that particular student. The primary stakeholders are of course the student and his/her parents. Other stakeholders include the educators in the direct chain of that child's education. These include the teacher, support staff, counselors, and administrators. Other people who care about the education of that child are the members of the society in which he/she lives. A child who is educated will serve a very different role in society than one who is not educated. However, as a teacher, you can only communicate assessment information with the direct stakeholders. (The school in which you teach will have spokespersons to communicate information about school-wide assessments to the society.)

As we stated in the first chapter, the ultimate purpose of all assessment is to make educational decisions. In the case of many summative assessments, the decision that is made involves what we call **gatekeeping**. In other words, a summative assessment is often used to determine if a student can proceed through a certain gate. For instance, a student who successfully passes the Algebra I end-of-course exam is granted admission into Algebra II. Or, a student who is successful on the standardized tests for 4$^{th}$ grade is promoted to the 5$^{th}$ grade. Or, a student who reaches a particularly high level of success on an English exam is placed in the Honors English class.

## *PLANNING SUMMATIVE ASSESSMENTS*

Often when we plan summative assessments, we begin the planning with the end in mind.

| Taking the Hill! |
|---|
| Using a military metaphor, let's consider the concept of "taking the hill". In a military campaign, the commander determines the ultimate goal (to take the hill, where it is assumed the king is fortressed). |
| Before the army can capture the king, it must cross several barriers. Still, the planning starts with the fortress around the king. An evaluation is made of the final barriers protecting the king so that the army will arrive on the hill with the necessary equipment to *take the hill*. |
| Once the planners have determined what is needed at that point, they back down one level to determine what will be needed to cross the barrier prior to that one. For instance, there may be a set of guards posted at the bottom of the hill. Again, they assess what will be needed to cross that barrier successfully. |
| They then would look at the river lying between the encroaching army and the hill. Again, they would determine what was needed to successfully cross that river. They would then look at the forested area between them and the river. |
| The process continues until a full plan is in place from the beginning spot where the army will begin its campaign to it *taking the hill*. So, while they started in their planning with the end goal in mind, when they begin their actual plan of action, they begin from where they are currently located. |

In the classroom, we call this *backward design*. Wiggins and McTighe (1998) identified the steps of backward design as:

1) to identify the desired results,
2) determine what you will accept as evidence those results have been met, and
3) plan the learning experiences that would need to take place to gain that evidence.

Stiggins and Chappius (2011) further delineate this by asking what knowledge, what reasoning abilities, what skills, and what products would a student need to be involved with before they could create the evidence that would show that a student is ready to be given a summative assessment.

In the 21$^{st}$ Century, obviously key summative assessments are the standardized tests taken at the end of the school year in most schools. As a part of the 2002 mandate of *No Child Left Behind*, schools that received any form of federal funds had to provide an accountability system that proved that the students in that particular school were on grade level. Because virtually all public schools throughout the United States do receive federal funds, these accountability systems became ubiquitous. And, the accountability systems typically adopted were standardized tests that were aligned with the state curriculum standards.

Thus, the year-end standardized tests became the gold standard in terms of summative assessments. And, using this as the ultimate goal, schools often put in place a series of summative assessments that provided information to the schools throughout the year that would allow the teachers to know if the students had mastered material that would be on the standardized test at the end of the school year.

## TYPES OF SUMMATIVE ASSESSMENTS

Any assessment that demonstrates to what extent a student has learned a concept or gained a skill is a summative assessment. Because summative assessment "refers to the cumulative assessments, usually occurring at the end of a unit or topic coverage, that intend to capture what a student has learned, or the quality of the learning, and judge performance against some standards" (National Research Council, 2001, p. 39), there are numerous types of them. The common ones used in the classroom are discussed here.

*Chapter tests*. Because, even in the 21$^{st}$ Century, textbooks still dominate the curriculum in schools, and textbooks are arranged in chapters, a common summative assessment is a chapter test. Many chapters begin with a listing of major concepts that will be covered in the chapter as well as a summary at the end that restates what was covered concerning those major concepts. A chapter test will then test the students to determine if they can answer questions that assess that they have mastered those concepts.

*Unit tests*. Again, if we look at many K-12 textbooks, the chapters are grouped together into units. A unit is identified as a subject of study around a particular theme. For instance, a unit might be on map reading. In this case, the table of contents of the social studies textbook might state:

| FIRST TWO UNITS IN A SOCIAL STUDIES BOOK |
|---|
| Unit 1: Map Reading<br>        Chapter 1: Landforms and Bodies of Water<br>        Chapter 2: Latitude and Longitude<br>        Chapter 3: Legends, Keys, and Other Map Markings<br>Unit 2: Government<br>        Chapter 4: Local Government<br>        Chapter 5: State Government<br>        Chapter 6: Federal Government |

If the class covered the first chapter in two weeks, the teacher might then administer a chapter test (a summative assessment) at the end of the two weeks to determine to what extent each student had learned the information. During the next week, the students might engage in learning about latitude and longitude. The chapter test at the end of that time period would of course assess to what extent they had gained the skills related to that content.

Likewise, the following two weeks might involve the study in Chapter 3 related to reading legends and keys and other markings found on maps. At that point, another chapter test would be administered. Then, usually after a review of all the concepts related to map reading, a teacher would administer a unit test on map reading.

> Note: Some teachers do not administer the chapter test for the last chapter in the unit. Instead, they simply administer a unit test that includes assessment of that final chapter as well as the previous chapters. For example, using the social studies material above, the teacher might administer a chapter test over Chapter 1 at the end of two weeks, a chapter test over Chapter 2 at the end of the third week, and the unit test over Map Reading at the end of the fifth week.

*End-of-marking-period tests.* Most U.S. public schools involve a 180-day academic year. These 180 days are broken into 36 weeks, divided into two 18-week semesters. These are further divided into 9-week marking periods. In some schools, they are referred to as *quarters*. In other schools, they are simply referred to as *marking periods*. Some schools

require that an end-of-marking-period test be administered in each of the subject areas.
For instance, using the social studies example from the previous page, the two units shown might be covered in the first 9-week marking period. In that case, the end-of-marking-period social studies test would cover the two major themes of map reading and government.

***Semester tests.*** Many schools require semester tests rather than end-of-marking-period tests. Obviously, a semester is made up of two marking periods (which is of course one-half of a school year). In elementary and middle schools, these semester tests would simply be cumulative over the material covered in a particular subject for that particular grade level. In secondary schools, students sometimes take one subject (e.g., Family and Consumer Science) during the first semester of the school year, followed by a different subject (e.g., Marketing) during the second semester. In schools where block scheduling is in place, even the courses called solids (e.g., math, science, English, social studies) are only one semester long. In those cases, the end-of-semester test would actually serve as an end-of-course test. However, in many schools, secondary classes are a year long. In those situations, a semester test is sometimes administered at the end of the second marking period to determine to what extent each student has mastered the material at that point. Semester tests are sometimes administered at the end of the academic year as well, but more commonly, they are foregone for end-of-year or end-of-course exams.

> **FROM THE PRINCIPAL'S DESK**
>
> Unlike formative assessment, which provides immediate feedback for teachers which can then be used by the teacher to improve instruction, summative assessments can be thought of as a snapshot in time. The data produced by summative assessment is typically used in grading. It can also be useful for guiding decisions about the organization of courses in the school.
>
> In recent years, as tax conscious citizens and political leaders sought to implement statewide high-stakes accountability systems, summative assessments have taken on a new importance. They are not necessarily more important to the teaching and learning process, but certainly more important politically. High-stakes testing has caused many teachers to "teach to the test." Since teacher evaluation is often tied to student performance on these standardized achievement tests, and since principals are also evaluated on their schools' test scores, many teachers say they feel pressure to spend class time practicing for exams.
>
> But, at its best, summative assessment is an important part of the instructional process. It can inform classroom practice by providing the means to gauge, at a specific point in time, how students are learning relative to the content standards.

***End-of-year* or *end-of-course exams.*** At the end of the academic year, exams are often administered to determine to what extent the individual students can demonstrate their knowledge and skills in the subject areas for their grade level. It is becoming a much more common practice for these end-of-year exams to be **common exams**. This term refers to the concept of having all students in the school, irrespective of the classroom in which they received instruction, take the same exam. For instance, a common exam for 4$^{th}$-grade social studies might be administered. This exam is often created by the 4$^{th}$-grade teachers as a group and all have agreed upon its content. Of course, the content is aligned with the school's curriculum standards. In many secondary schools, end-of-course exams are becoming ubiquitous. These are similar in format to the comprehensive final exams administered at the end of most college courses. And, just as with elementary schools, more and more, the policy of administering a common exam throughout the secondary school (and sometimes the district or the state) is being adopted. Therefore, as a teacher, you may be called upon to participate in the creation of the common exam, and very likely, you will be required to administer that exam (whether you helped create it or not) to your students.

*Culminating projects.* While tests are the more common type of summative assessments, a culminating project is sometimes a good summative assessment as well. A culminating project is one in which the student demonstrates that he has obtained a set of skills or a body of knowledge (or more likely, both). A culminating project is typically designed at the Bloom's level of synthesis. And, that level requires that a new product is created using a variety of sources. Therefore, in order for a project to be a culminating project, the student must have gained a complete set of skills or body of knowledge. For instance, if a student is introduced to the concept of writing an acrostic poem, and then, he attempts to write one, that is not a culminating project (and it is not a summative assessment). However, if the student learns about types of poems, terminology used, acrostic poems, haikus, free verse, and refrains (including attempts at writing the various types as well as analysis of them), and then he creates a booklet of poetry (including those he writes as well as explanations of ones he chooses as good examples of the type), that would be a culminating project. And, it would be a good summative assessment of the student's knowledge base in the area of poetry.

*Portfolios.* "Although we often think of summative assessments as traditional objective tests, this need not be the case. For example, summative assessments could follow from an accumulation of evidence collected over time, as in a collection of student work" (National Research Council, 2001, p. 39). A portfolio is sometimes used as a summative assessment. This is particularly the case in situations where an exam would not provide a full picture of the student's knowledge base or skills. For instance, a final exam in the area of art might assess if students know the definitions of certain art terms and might even be able to assess if students can identify artistic methods and techniques. However, to truly assess if the students can employ the methods and techniques, a portfolio showing examples of their work with explanations (often called *reflection tags*) might be a better summative assessment. (Portfolios will be discussed further in a later chapter.)

*Standardized tests.* Standardized tests are tests that are administered, scored, and interpreted in a *standard* manner. This means that the administration, the scoring, and the interpretation is prescribed in advance and followed no matter where or when the testing takes place. Most 21$^{st}$-Century schools use standardized tests (either those created by national test development companies or state-developed ones) for demonstrating that their students are on grade level. The *No Child Left Behind Act* requires that schools that are receiving federal funds must have an accountability system in place to demonstrate that their students are either on grade level or working toward that goal.

A typical standardized test used for a school's accountability covers the basic material that is presumed to have been attained by a student in that particular grade level. They are often called achievement tests because they test to see to what extent a student has *achieved* the knowledge base and skills required.

While many schools do not use standardized tests for assigning grades to students, they do often use them to determine if the student is ready for the next grade level. Thus, sometimes they are used for promotion decisions. And, they are almost always used to evaluate the school's programs.

## THE USAGE OF SUMMATIVE ASSESSMENTS

Whereas occasionally <u>some</u> formative assessments are not recorded in the gradebook, virtually all summative assessments, except the standardized test scores, that occur in the classroom *are*. In $20^{th}$-Century classrooms, it was not uncommon for a teacher to base the student's grade only on summative assessments, and sometimes a single summative assessment.

In fact, I once taught at an institution that required comprehensive final exams, and the policy stated "If a student achieves an A on the final exam, the student must receive an A in the course." While that was a very controversial policy, and it led to many professors making their final exams exorbitantly difficult, the fact remains that, in many places, teachers often base the student's grade in a particular subject on how he does on the final exam. And, for some subjects, that makes total sense. For instance, if the goal is for students to be able to multiply one-digit numbers, the scores they received as they learned the multiplication tables are not terribly important. It is their ability to multiply that actually matters.

When I was first learning to drive a car, I was not terribly good at it. Thank goodness, those first tries were not taken into account when I applied for a driver's license. It was only my ability to drive on the day that I took the test that counted. For some school subjects, taking only the summative assessment into account may actually be the best policy.

But. . .
                              that, of course, is not always the case.

Let's consider another situation.

| | |
|---|---|
| Objective we want to assess: The student will be able to write effectively for a variety of situations. ||
| Possible Solution 1 | Have each student come to the front of the room, draw a slip out of a fishbowl with a situation and topic (e.g., write a letter to a company complaining about a defective product) written on it. The student could then return to his desk and demonstrate his ability to write for that situation. |

That single summative assessment would not necessarily be valid as the student who drew the complaint letter slip might not know how to write an effective complaint letter, but he might know how to do other effective writing. Likewise, he might be successful in writing the complaint letter, but it would not necessarily prove that he could write effectively in some other situations (e.g., a short story, a poem about a historical event).

Let's consider another possibility:

| | |
|---|---|
| Objective we want to assess: The student will be able to write effectively for a variety of situations. ||
| Possible Solution 2 | Have the student do snippets of writing in a variety of situations. For instance, he might be required to respond to three prompts. You might have him write one paragraph of that complaint letter, another three paragraphs in response to a prompt where he develops the setting and two characters to begin a short story, and a final prompt where he is asked to write a poem about the assassination of President McKinley. |

While the second situation may give the student more opportunity to demonstrate his ability, or lack thereof, to write effectively in a variety of situations, it still is probably not the best assessment to determine if indeed the student can write effectively in a variety of situations. Thus, a single summative assessment is not always the best way to assess a student's ability.

A final possibility might be:

| | |
|---|---|
| Objective we want to assess: The student will be able to write effectively for a variety of situations. ||
| Possible Solution 3 | Use both formative and summative assessments. This assessment would not be done in a single setting. It would take place over a period of time in the classroom. |
| | For instance, a teacher could have a student read several examples of short stories and analyze them. This analysis may simply take place in a classroom discussion, or it may be done in writing. However, in order for a student to be a good short story writer, he needs to have had the opportunity to see |

> what works in terms of creating good short stories. His involvement in those classroom discussions may be an important part in his development as a writer.
>
> Later, he will probably make a first attempt at writing a rough draft of a short story. The experience that takes place as he and the teacher, or he and a peer, discuss good and poor aspects of his first draft will definitely be valuable in the development of his ability to write an effective short story. His improvement of the short story is another important experience, so the teacher may want to take that "drafting" into consideration when assigning a grade.
>
> And, then, his final version of the short story would be submitted. While this final version could be considered a summative assessment, it would be a little unfair to base his grade simply on it because, while it does show his ability to write a short story at that point, it is still based on his FIRST ATTEMPT at writing a short story. He may ultimately write several short stories throughout the year. Some will be better than others. As he writes in other situations (for instance, complaint letters to a corporation), the process will be repeated. Therefore, a mixture of formative and so-called summative assessments (final drafts) may be included in the grade the teacher assigns for how well the student has achieved the ability to write effectively in a variety of situations.
>
> This set of experiences would then be repeated for other types of writing. Through the collection of this set of formative and summative assessments, the teacher could determine to what extent a student can actually *write effectively for a variety of situations*.

Often, summative assessments, particularly unit tests and end-of-course tests, are used as the largest basis for grades on a grade card. And, in many cases, this is a valid basis. If a teacher has covered three units in a marking period, and a student has achieved a grade of 82% on one unit test, an 85% on the second unit test, an 86% on the third unit test, and an 84% on the end-of-marking period test covering the three units, assigning the student an average of those grades, an 84% (which is a B in many schools), is probably valid.

However, for a social studies unit in which students participated in classroom discussions, wrote journal entries about concepts being discussed, and created a group bulletin board demonstrating how the concepts were interrelated, a student with those unit test and end-of-marking-period test grades might not have earned an 84% overall. If her participation in the discussions indicated that she fully grasped the complexity of the concepts, her journal entries were full of insights, and her contribution to the bulletin board created by her group was exemplary, an 84% might not be a good reflection of her knowledge and skills in those three units. Likewise, another student who did not participate in the discussions, whose journal entries were perfunctory, and who simply did the lettering for the bulletin board may have been able to answer approximately 84% of the answers on the test, but a B may not truly represent his knowledge and skills.

You might wonder how those two obviously different students would both come out with an 84% on the tests. And, if a teacher is an excellent test writer, most likely the insightful student would come out with a higher grade on the tests than would the less engaged student. However, if that is not the case, it is possible the test itself may be the issue. As a teacher becomes more adept at identifying exactly what needs to be assessed and being able to write assessments that truly are valid, the more that she can use summative assessments as the largest basis for assigning grades. Of course, as previously stated, for some subjects, it would be a project that might be a summative assessment. For others, it might be a collection of work.

But, let's not let the exceptions get in the way of the understanding of how summative assessment usually works. Let's return to the military metaphor. If we have planned well, our chapter tests will lead to success on unit tests. Our unit tests will lead to success on end-of-marking-period and end-of-course tests. And, those will have prepared our students to be successful on the standardized tests that purport to determine if a student is on grade level.

This is what is meant by: "Summative results, when embedded in the wider teaching and learning environment, are more likely to be used formatively" (Organisation for Economic Co-Operation and Development, 2008, p. 9). If your chapter and unit tests are truly valid summative assessments, they will be predictive of how the students will do on the standardized tests. That is the reason that teachers need to become experts in creating valid assessments, in analyzing already-created assessments for validity, and in aligning assessments with the curriculum standards they are used to assess.

## BASIC CONCEPTS IN CHAPTER 6

A) The primary purposes of summative assessment are:
    1) to determine how much a student has learned
    2) to verify competence
    3) for gatekeeping

B) Backward design allows a teacher to consider where he ultimately wants his students to be and to put steps in place to help them get there.

C) The main types of classroom summative assessments are:
    1) Chapter tests
    2) Unit tests
    3) End-of-marking-period tests
    4) End-of-course/semester tests
    5) End-of-year tests
    6) Culminating projects
    7) Portfolios

D) The primary usage of summative assessments involves giving grades and promotion to the next level (new unit, next course, next grade).

E) If summative assessments throughout the year are truly valid, the results on them will be predictive of how the students will do on the end-of-year standardized tests.

NOTES:

# CHAPTER 7

## *Stems, Distractors, and Other Confusing Words*
### Creating Selected-Response Items

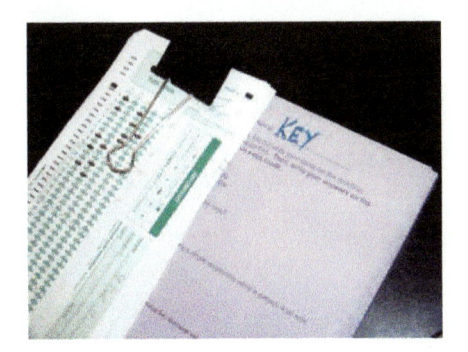

*KEY CONCEPTS:*
General Guidelines
Multiple Choice Items
Binary Choice Items
Matching

*The test of the artist does not lie in the will with which he goes to work, but in the excellence of the work he produces.*
--Thomas Aquinas

There was a time when we referred to multiple-choice, true/false, and matching items as "objective" items. However, the idea that anything is truly *objective* has been rejected for many years now. While the scoring of these items may be objective (meaning presumably no judgment is required since there is one correct answer on the key against which the test is graded), the writing of the items definitely includes a lot of *subjectivity* (Stiggins & Chappius, 2008). Because of that, we now refer to this type of items as selected-response items. This is obviously because the students *select* their *response* from the options provided by the test creator.

Selected-response items are popular because of their efficiency and reliability. Students can respond to a large amount of information in a prescribed amount of time, and their responses can be scored consistently by a variety of graders (or even a machine). There are, however, some disadvantages of them as well. These include the fact that selecting a response is not cognitively aligned with most things we do in life. Although we may choose among four options of Swiss cheese at the supermarket, the fact that we decided to buy cheese in the first place derived from a much more complex task than simply choosing among options. The other large criticisms of selected-response items are that they take time (and some measure of skill) to construct and they are susceptible to guessing.

## *GENERAL GUIDELINES*

There are general principles for writing good selected-response items (Popham, 2005; Kubiszyn & Borich, 2007; Miller, Linn, & Gronlund, 2009; Thorndike & Thorndike-Christ, 2010). The top ten include:

1) In order for an assessment to be valid, it needs to address the broad aspects of the content, not tiny details.
2) The content being assessed should be clear to the students.
3) There should be only one clearly defensible answer.
4) The directions should be directly stated, but succinct.
5) The test should contain good face validity.
6) Trick questions should not be included.
7) The items need to be written at a reading level appropriate to the students.
8) Unintended clues should not be included.
9) Absolutes, like *never* or *always*, should be used sparingly.
10) Negatives should be used with care, and the negative word should be formatted with emphasis (e.g., all caps or italicized).

*Assessment of the Broad Aspects*

Remember that you and the students are on a learning journey together. And, there is an agreement between you and the students that you will provide them with guidance in their learning, and that it is *that learning* that will be assessed. Thus, it is an important part of your job to be clear to the students about *what's important* in the learning that is taking place.

Every teacher has had a student raise his hand and say, "Is this gonna be on the test?" The reason that is annoying to the teacher is because it implies to the teacher that the students are only paying attention to those things that *will be* on the test. So, while I'm not suggesting you "teach to the test", I am stating that your tests should assess your objectives. And your objectives should not be about minutia.

If the items ask questions about tiny details in the reading rather than about the broad concepts, they may assess if the students can read for details, but it will not truly inform the teacher of the students' knowledge of the content. For instance, if a story is told in the text about a boy soldier in the Civil War who writes a letter home about being cold and hungry and homesick, a question on the test would need to be about the conditions under which members of the Union army fought, not about the name of the soldier.

*Clarity of Content Being Assessed*

In 21$^{st}$-Century classrooms, we let our students know the targets. We let them know what we expect them to learn. And, we let them know on what they can expect to be assessed. So, when they are taking a test, they should be able to determine what the item is assessing.

Let's consider an example:

| | |
|---|---|
| GENERAL GUIDELINES EXAMPLE A | _____ 18. In a bag, there are 17 red marbles, 3 white marbles, and 10 black marbles. What is the likelihood that a child will pull out a white marble if he sticks his hand in the bag and pulls out a marble without looking?<br>A) 1/10<br>B) 3/10<br>C) 17/3<br>D) 30/3 |

In this example, the student would know that he is being assessed on whether he can figure out the numbers he needs to use, and their correct placement, in a probability ratio.

*One Clearly Defensible Answer*

If an item includes more than one clearly defensible answer, but the teacher accepts only the answer she thought was the correct one, that item will not provide the teacher with accurate information about what her students know, or do not know, about the subject. Thus, every item needs to have one, and only one, clearly defensible answer. Otherwise, the item is not a valid test item. Let's consider another version of the previously stated item:

| GENERAL GUIDELINES EXAMPLE B (Poor) | _____ 18. In a bag, there are 17 red marbles, 3 white marbles, and 10 black marbles. What is the likelihood that a child will pull out a white marble if he sticks his hand in the bag and pulls out a marble without looking?<br>A) 1/10<br>B) 3/30<br>C) 17/3<br>D) 30/3 |
|---|---|

In this new version, both A and B are clearly defensible answers. If the teacher had taught the students that the formula for probability was that the numerator represented the number of items that fit the criteria being sought (in this case, white marbles) and the denominator represented the total of all possibilities (in this case, there are 30 marbles), many students might choose B. Even if the teacher had indicated that you then reduce the fraction to lowest terms when you write the ratio, in a testing situation, a student may see the 3/30 and choose it. So, while A is the better answer, some students would choose B. If a teacher wants to assess if her students can figure probability, having two clearly defensible answers will not provide her with a valid assessment.

*Clear Succinct Directions*

It is important that directions for each section of the test be included and that they be clear to the students. The previous example can be used again to illustrate the point:

| GENERAL GUIDELINES EXAMPLE B (Improved) | **Directions.** Choose the <u>best</u> response for each item below. Indicate your answer by writing the letter of that response in the blank in front of the number.<br><br>_____ 18. In a bag, there are 17 red marbles, 3 white marbles, and 10 black marbles. What is likelihood that a child will pull out a white marble if he sticks his hand in the bag and pulls out a marble without looking?<br>A) 1/10<br>B) 3/30<br>C) 17/3<br>D) 30/3 |
|---|---|

If the directions include the word "best" in them, and the teacher has indeed taught the students that a ratio is expressed in lowest terms, then there is only one *clearly defensible answer*.

Another way of clarifying the item so that the teacher is truly able to see if the students can figure ratios would be to include in the directions (or the individual item) that *all responses should be lowest terms*. As the teacher, it may seem completely obvious to you, but unless it's written on the test, it may not be as obvious to the students. For items in which, *all of the above* is the final option, if the directions do not include "best" in them, technically all of the answers are *clearly defensible answers*.

The directions also need to instruct the students about how to indicate their responses. An item that is formatted in the way Example B is would lead most test takers to automatically write the letter in the blank in front of the number. However, unless you state it, you will get a variety of methods by which your students provide their responses. Some students will circle the answer. Others will write it at the end of the stem (the "question" part of the item). Sometimes, students will circle one answer (say, B), but write another answer (say, A) in the blank. By indicating clearly how you want the response provided, it will make your grading easier. It will also help students organize their thinking as they are taking the test. In addition, if a student circles one answer, but puts another in the blank, the grading will be based on the directions. Do note that because circled answers are sometimes difficult to discern if the circle is not precisely around only one response, it will make your grading easier if you have students place the letter of their response in a blank in front of the numbered item. It is suggested that you use capital letters as your options because each is more distinctive from the other in a way that the handwritten lower case ones are not.

Do note that while you definitely need to be clear in the directions, they also need to be succinct. If the directions are too wordy and include too many criteria, students will simply ignore them. Therefore, it is important to include the necessary parts (what you want them to do and how you want them to do it), but not to include extraneous material that will distract or be ignored anyway.

*Good Face Validity*

Face validity refers to the idea that "the appearance of a test seems to coincide with the use to which the test is being put" (Popham, 2005, p. 68). In other words, the test appears, based on face value, to be a valid assessment. In addition to the fact that "what a test 'looks like' may be of importance in determining its acceptability and reasonableness to those who will be tested" (Thorndike & Thorndike-Christ, 2010, p. 167) as well as demonstrate the teacher's professionalism, face validity can actually have an impact on the outcomes on the test as well. A poorly organized test can cause confusion for the test takers. Students organize their thoughts as they work with the items. We do not want the test itself, and the way it's organized, to be a negative factor in assessing what a student knows.

As a part of this, the test should have a heading that is informative to the student. If the test covers the broad topic of The Civil War, that would be the title on the test. On the other hand, if the test is only covering the events leading up to the war and the initial volley tossed at Ft. Sumter, a better title would be "The Start of A Nation Divided: 1857-60" or something similar. The title should stand out by the use of bolding or increased font size, or both, and it should be written using title case or all caps.

In addition, items on the test should be organized into sections by item type (e.g., multiple choice, true/false, essay) and each section should have its own heading and set of directions. The section headings should use student-friendly language. For instance, while you can call the multiple-choice section *Multiple Choice* (as that is terminology familiar to the students), you would call the binary-choice section True/False (because binary-choice is not terminology that is familiar to students). For a contrasting-concept binary choice section, you would identify the section by the two concepts (e.g., Earth vs. Mars; George Washington or Thomas Jefferson). The section heading and the directions should be distinguishable from the items by the usage of a different font, italics or bolding, or a different color. This is shown in the example below:

| | **USING SIGNED NUMBERS** |
|---|---|
| GENERAL GUIDELINES EXAMPLE C | *Multiple Choice.* For each of the following items, choose the best answer and write its letter on the blank in front of the number. (2 points each) <br><br> _____ 1. When multiplying two signed numbers with the same sign, the answer will be: <br>     A) the larger number's sign <br>     B) positive <br>     C) negative <br>     D) sometimes positive, and sometimes negative |

Another part of face validity involves the professionalism of the test. Miller, Linn, and Gronlund (2009) indicate that face validity is defined by the following question: *Based on a superficial examination of the tasks, does the assessment appear to be a reasonable measure?* (p. 76). I mention this because there may be an audience for your test that gives it only a quick look-through. The most common example is parents. I often tell my college students that they should expect that everything they write as a teacher (from notes home to comments on student work to newsletters) could end up on the principal's desk or the six o'clock news. Because it could! The same is true for tests you create.

Consistency of format, accurate grammar and spelling, numbering of the items that follows from section to section (rather than starting over with the numbering for each section) are all a part of good face validity.

### No Tricky Questions

Sometimes teachers think that including tricky questions invokes critical thinking in students and they use that as a justification for including them on the test. However, the purpose of a test is to determine to what extent the students know the information. Since some students will possibly see through the trick question, and answer it correctly, others may not. Therefore, the assessment will not inform you of whether the students knew the information or not.

### Appropriate Reading Level

The purpose of an assessment is to make an educational decision. If a test is difficult for a student to read or comprehend because of the usage of words they don't understand, it will not truly assess if they know the information. Popham (2005) explains this in an entertaining way:

> When writing educational assessment items, *you should eschew obfuscative verbiage*. In other words, almost *any* other words, use vocabulary suitable for the students who'll be taking your tests. Assessment time is not the occasion for you to trot out your best collection of polysyllabic terms or to secure thesaurus-induced thrills. (p. 133)

So, as a teacher, write the assessment at a level that your students can understand. For instance, if you wrote your senior honors thesis on the Civil War, and you use language from that thesis in the items on the test for your high-school students, the assessment may not provide you with *any information* about how much the students actually know about the Civil War. And if the difficult vocabulary occurs early in the test, the students' brains may perceive that they can't understand the items on the test. That is what we call a *mental block*. After that, even if the other items on the test are easy to read and understand, the students may not think so. In that case, instead of trying to read and understand them, they may simply guess at the answers.

## No Unintended Clues

An *unintended clue* involves providing students with something within the item that either leads them *to the correct answer* or *away from the incorrect answers* even if they do not know the information. It is an offense that novice test writers commit at a much greater rate than that of veteran test writers. The more experience you have creating tests, the less likely you will commit this offense. In other words, you can grow out of it.

Let's consider an example:

| GENERAL GUIDELINES EXAMPLE D (Poor) | _____ 4. If a word indicates to whom or to what the action of the verb is being directed, that word is serving as an:<br>A) subject<br>B) predicate<br>C) indirect object<br>D) direct object |
|---|---|

Even if a student didn't know the information, he might easily choose C because it's the only one that sounds right. The *an* at the end of the stem guides the student to the correct answer. This is known as a grammatical incongruity. If the teacher provides the students with such a grammatical clue, "the result is decreased test validity. Students can answer items correctly because of knowledge of grammar, not content" (Kubiszyn & Borich, 2007, p. 117).

That particular item could be fixed easily as follows:

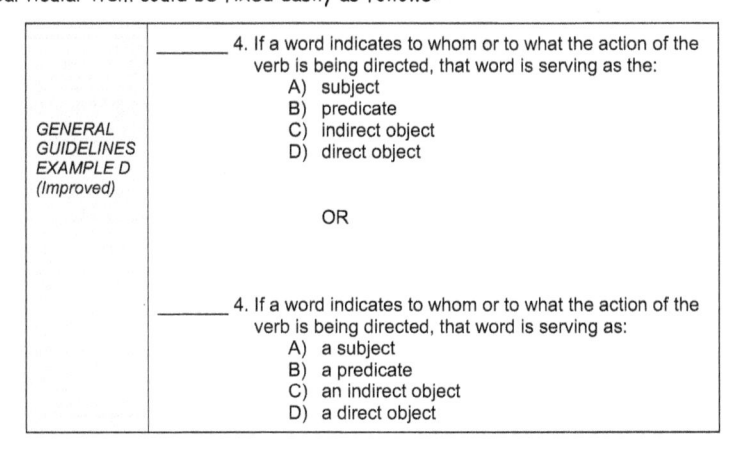

| GENERAL GUIDELINES EXAMPLE D (Improved) | _____ 4. If a word indicates to whom or to what the action of the verb is being directed, that word is serving as the:<br>A) subject<br>B) predicate<br>C) indirect object<br>D) direct object<br><br>OR<br><br>_____ 4. If a word indicates to whom or to what the action of the verb is being directed, that word is serving as:<br>A) a subject<br>B) a predicate<br>C) an indirect object<br>D) a direct object |
|---|---|

Simply by changing *an* to *the*, or by moving the article from the stem to the options, you have removed the unintentional clue.

I used this simplistic *grammatical incongruity* to demonstrate the concept, but it is a common error among test creators. It occurs because the test creator knows the right answer when she's creating the test. So, the stem and the correct answer are automatically grammatically lined up in her mind. However, unless the teacher is actually thinking about it, she may not line up the distractors (the incorrect answers) with the stem.

Let's consider another example:

| GENERAL GUIDELINES EXAMPLE E (Poor) | _____ 7. The author of "A Bird Came Down the Walk", who is known for her usage of near-rhymes, is:<br>A) Alfred, Lord Tennyson<br>B) Emily Dickinson<br>C) Carl Sandburg<br>D) William Blake |
|---|---|

Again, a student who didn't know the answer, and possibly had never read the poem mentioned, could find the correct response. The usage of the gender pronoun *her* directs the student to B because she is the only poet listed who is female. It could easily be improved removing the pronoun and restricting the stem. The item would then read:

| GENERAL GUIDELINES EXAMPLE E (Improved) | _____ 7. Known for usage of near-rhymes, the author of "A Bird Came Down the Walk" is the poet:<br>A) Alfred, Lord Tennyson<br>B) Emily Dickinson<br>C) Carl Sandburg<br>D) William Blake |
|---|---|

On the other side of the coin, sometimes a teacher can accidentally include a grammatical incongruity, or other unintended clue, that will lead a student *away* from a correct answer. For example:

| GENERAL GUIDELINES EXAMPLE F (Poor) | _____ 7. The explorer(s) who mapped out the Louisiana Purchase was:<br>A) Kit Carson<br>B) Meriwether Lewis and William Clark<br>C) David Livingstone and Henry Stanley<br>D) Zebulon Pike |
|---|---|

In this example, the correct answer is B. However, even though the teacher included the word *explorer(s)* to indicate the answer could be singular or plural, the usage of the verb *was* implies it is singular. A student who thought he knew the answer (Lewis and Clark) might actually be swayed away from it because of the grammatical incongruity.

This item could be improved by rewriting the item as a direct question:

| GENERAL GUIDELINES EXAMPLE F (Improved) | _____ 7. Who mapped out the Louisiana Purchase?<br>A) Kit Carson<br>B) Meriwether Lewis and William Clark<br>C) David Livingstone and Henry Stanley<br>D) Zebulon Pike |
|---|---|

Here's a more complex example that gives the students another form of an unintended clue:

| GENERAL GUIDELINES EXAMPLE G | _____ 11. Even though John Locke lived during a time when people were hostile to monarchies and he shared those political leanings, his writings<br>A) were not in favor of the kings and queens<br>B) can show how the monarchs are not fair<br>C) are long and classical<br>D) defended Queen Mary's right to rule |
|---|---|

In this example, the teacher knew that she wanted to make the distinction between Locke's personal beliefs and his writings. So, she wrote *Even though* in the stem. However, only Option D indicates something that is in opposition to being *hostile toward monarchies*. Thus, once again, even if the student wasn't familiar with Locke's works, his guess would probably be D because it is the only one that would logically fit.

Therefore, it is important that you check your tests after creating them to make sure you don't have any unintended clues that will either aid the students in finding the right answers or direct them away from them.

### *Rare Usage of Absolutes*

If you have ever attended a test prep seminar, you have probably been directed that if a multiple-choice option contains *never* or *always*, do not choose that one. Or, if a true/false item includes either of those words, it is typically false. As a teacher, you must be very careful when you use absolutes. In addition to providing the student with the ability to choose the correct response without actually knowing the information, the grading of those items can often be challenged by students as well.

Let's consider an example:

| GENERAL GUIDELINES EXAMPLE H | True/False:<br>_____ 9. The subject of a sentence is always either a noun or a pronoun. |
|---|---|

As the writer of the item, you may feel that it is true. However, a student could challenge that it is false because the subject of an imperative sentence (e.g., *Shut the door.*) is implied and therefore not a noun or pronoun. You obviously could argue back that the implied subject is actually an *implied you*, and therefore, a pronoun. However, the point of assessment is to determine if the student knows the information. That student who challenged your item may, or may not, have known the information.

Let's consider another example:

| GENERAL GUIDELINES EXAMPLE I | _____ 11. The Missouri Compromise was necessary because:<br>A) all of the slave states did not want the balance of power to change<br>B) more and more settlers were taking slaves north with them<br>C) the Missouri River was in dispute<br>D) Kansas and Missouri wanted to remain as territories, not states |
|---|---|

The answer you are seeking is A. However, because of the usage of the word *all*, a student could argue that not every one of the states argued for maintaining the power. In fact, it was primarily an argument of only a couple of strong senators from slave states. While the other answers are clearly not correct, the usage of an absolute could allow for this challenge. And, the student could correctly argue that there was *no* correct answer among the options.

This could easily be avoided by simply changing the item as follows:

| GENERAL GUIDELINES EXAMPLE I | _____ 11. The Missouri Compromise was necessary because:<br>A) some of the slave states did not want the balance of power to change<br>B) more and more settlers were taking slaves north with them<br>C) the Missouri River was in dispute<br>D) Kansas and Missouri wanted to remain as territories, not states |
|---|---|

In addition to the common absolutes of *never*, *always*, and *all*, other examples that you need to be careful in your usage of are: *every*, *entire*, *whole*, *must*, and *cannot*. There are of course others. A good rule of thumb is to rarely use absolutes in your items.

*Careful Usage of Negatives*

While teachers are discouraged from using absolutes in item writing, the usage of negative items is often necessary. Other times, it is a good way to assess if students truly know the information. Still, they need to be used with care and the word that makes the item negative needs to be shown with emphasis. Possible ways to indicate emphasis include italicizing the negative word, capitalizing all the letters in it, putting it in bold, or underlining it.

The following is a good example of the usage of a negative within an item:

| | |
|---|---|
| GENERAL GUIDELINES EXAMPLE J | _____ 11. Which of the following sentences is NOT an appropriate usage of a semi-colon:<br>A) The girls went to the movies; the boys went to the arcade.<br>B) Darla enjoyed three things; cookies, stuffed animals, and music.<br>C) The journal entries are optional; the reflections are not.<br>D) The possible dates include: Saturday, June 18; Sunday, July 15; or, Friday, August 4. |

This item allows you to assess three things.

First, that semi-colons *can be used* to connect two independent highly related clauses (as shown in A and C).

Second, that they can be used to separate items in a series that contain commas within each item (as shown in D).

And third, that they *cannot be used* to separate the premise from items in a series (as shown in B).

Thus, it is an excellent usage of a negative in a test item.

However, having said that, do not overdo the usage of negative items. For primary-aged students, a negative item would *seldom* be used. An example where it is sometimes used with young children is in *Which one does NOT belong?* type items. The students then choose the picture or word that does not have the same characteristics as the others.

For older students, you will have more opportunity to include negative items. However, still they should not dominate the test. If you have more than that, you may want to go back and look at each of those items and determine which of them could be written in the positive. The reason for this has to do with the way a student's brain orients to answering test items. For instance, in a multiple choice item, the brain is expecting to look for a *correct* answer. In a negative item, like the one shown in Example J, the brain must re-orient to looking for an *incorrect* answer (in other words, the one that is NOT an accurate usage of the semi-colon). To assist the students, emphasizing the word will help them with this re-orientation. Still, while negative items have their place on your assessments, they should be used sparingly. A good rule of thumb is that no more than approximately ten percent of the items on a summative assessment would be written in the negative.

### *MAJOR TYPES OF SELECTED-RESPONSE ITEMS*

The primary types of selected-response items are *multiple-choice, binary-choice,* and *matching.* In addition, *fill-in-the-blank items with a word bank or options provided* are also selected-response.

*Multiple-Choice Items*

According to Popham (2005) multiple-choice items have dominated achievement testing in the United States and many other nations for several decades. Because of that, they are ubiquitous in our schools, including on most teacher-made tests. A multiple choice (MC) item includes either a direct question or an incomplete statement in its **stem** (the first part of the item). This is followed by *multiple* **options** from which the students *choose* either the correct answer (for direct-question ones) or a word or phrase that completes the sentence (for the statement-completion ones). The options, which are sometimes called *response alternatives*, include the correct response along with some incorrect responses. The incorrect responses are called **distractors**. *(Note that it is spelled with an o, in contrast to the word distracter that is used in other settings.)*

| Best Practices for Multiple Choice Items |
|---|
| A) The stem is longer than the options and includes enough information that the student could think of the answer prior to seeing the options. |
| B) When there are words that would be repeated in each option, they should be moved to the stem. |
| C) The options should be homogenous in nature. |
| D) The options should be arranged in logical order (alphabetical, chronological, ascending or descending) unless that order would give away the answer. |
| E) The options should be of the same approximate length. |
| F) The number of options usually ranges from three to five, but can vary according to the content. |

Let's consider each more fully.

*What to include in the stem.* The stem will either include a question to be answered or an incomplete sentence that is to be completed with one of the options.

An example of a sentence-completion MC item would be:

| MC EXAMPLE A | 2. An object that has three sides is a:<br>A) square<br>B) rectangle<br>C) triangle |
|---|---|

For young children, the direct-question type of MC items is easier for them to answer than the statement-completion type. So, if an MC item can be changed to a direct-question format instead of a sentence-completion format, it is good to use that for kindergarten and first-grade students.

The previous example could simply be changed to:

| | |
|---|---|
| MC<br>EXAMPLE A<br>(Improved) | 2. What object has three sides?<br>A) square<br>B) rectangle<br>C) triangle |

However, some items, even for young children, are best formatted using the statement-completion type. For instance:

| | |
|---|---|
| MC<br>EXAMPLE B | **Directions.** Circle the word or phrase that best complete the following early American proverbs.<br><br>1. A penny saved is a penny:<br>   A) earned<br>   B) shown<br>   C) hidden<br><br>2. The grass is always greener:<br>   A) over the hillside<br>   B) on the other side<br>   C) down in the valley<br><br>3. Early to bed, early to rise, makes a man:<br>   A) fanned, with land, and tanned<br>   B) healthy, wealthy, and wise<br>   C) happy, and unable to tell lies |

Typically, the stem should include enough information that the student would be able to answer it even before they look at the possible responses. It reminds me of the popular television show *Who Wants to Be a Millionaire?* On that show, a question pops up first, and for a moment or two while the host is reading the question aloud, the responses are not showing. I have watched that show with friends and family members who would call out the answer before the options were showing. Thus, if at all possible, you should write the stems for your items with enough information in them that the students would be able to respond to them even if they covered up the options with their hands. And, you should write distractors that reinforce that they know the information rather than distractors that confuse them.

| | |
|---|---|
| *Important Note!* | Do not capitalize the first word of the options in a sentence-completion item because that would put a capital letter in the middle of a sentence for no reason.<br><br>            Teachers are always modeling for students! |

Most MC items will have stems that are longer than the options. For instance, the following would not be a good item:

| MC EXAMPLE C (Poor) | _____ 12. The patriots:<br>A) wore red uniforms and lived in the homes of the settlers<br>B) used stamps and objected to the high price of them<br>C) were farmers and businessmen as well as soldiers<br>D) asked the king to help them with the problems they were having |
|---|---|

Obviously a student could not cover up the responses with her hand and be able to respond to the item. That would be a first clue to you as a novice item writer that it may not be a high-quality item. A further problem with the item is that the amount of information in the options allows for too many variables to come into play. Therefore, it's a little difficult to determine what the item is trying to assess. Let's assume that the objective was that students would be able to *contrast the colonial and English soldiers*. In that case, we could probably assume that we could rule out A. However, B, C, and D are all possible correct responses. While C is the desired response and D is less likely than the others, students could clearly defend all of them. By moving more of the information to the stem, you are more likely to be able to truly assess the objective. This is shown in the improved example:

| MC EXAMPLE C (Improved) | _____ 12. The patriot soldiers were different from soldiers who were loyal to the English king in that they :<br>A) were quartered in the homes of the settlers<br>B) wore red uniforms<br>C) were farmers and businessmen as well as soldiers<br>D) depended on the king for supplies |
|---|---|

While in most cases, the stem is longer than the options, there are times when the options are longer than the stem. An example would be:

| MC EXAMPLE D | _____ 12. Which best describes the relationship between the main characters in *The Darling Triplets*?<br>A) The oldest daughter was the protagonist but she did not like being in the leadership role.<br>B) The middle child was the antagonist and was constantly serving in the peacemaker role.<br>C) The triplets were all protagonists in the story and they had little conflict among the three of them.<br>D) The antagonist was the new stepmother and she was hated by the protagonist who was the youngest of the triplets. |
|---|---|

In that example, the objective involves not only having the students be able to determine who played the role of the protagonist and the antagonist, but also how the characters interacted. This is a complicated test item, but it is appropriately written. Veteran item writers are often able to write this type of item after years of practicing item writing. As a new test creator, it's probably best to stick with having the stem be longer than the options and having the item assess only one straightforward concept.

*Lack of repetition.* As a teacher, you want to make the assessment as straightforward, and as uncomplicated, as possible. Therefore, if some identical information would be included in every option, move that information to the stem. For example:

| | |
|---|---|
| MC EXAMPLE E (Poor) | _____ 7. Women's suffrage was established by<br>A) the U.S. Constitution's seventh amendment<br>B) the nineteenth amendment of the U.S. Constitution<br>C) Amendment 14 of the U.S. Constitution<br>D) the 20<sup>th</sup> U.S. Constitutional amendment |

The teacher may think that he is making sure the student actually knows the information by mixing up the manner in which he creates the responses, but in doing so, he may invalidate the item. If the item is intended to determine if the student knows which amendment addressed the concept of women receiving the right to vote, moving the repeated information from the options to the stem will allow the item to be directly focused on that.

| | |
|---|---|
| MC EXAMPLE E (Improved) | _____ 7. Which amendment to the U.S. Constitution established women's suffrage?<br>A) seventh<br>B) nineteenth<br>C) fourteenth<br>D) twentieth |

Sometimes, an item can be simplified, and more focused, simply by moving the front parts of the options to the end of the stem. An example is:

| | |
|---|---|
| MC EXAMPLE F | _____ 22. The stain that played such a pivotal role in solving the mystery was:<br>A) on the boy's shirt collar<br>B) on the boy's shirt sleeve<br>C) on the boy's coat pocket<br>D) on the boy's belt buckle<br><br>*Improve by:*<br><br>_____ 22. The stain that played such a pivotal role in solving the mystery was on the boy's:<br>A) shirt collar<br>B) shirt sleeve<br>C) coat pocket<br>D) belt buckle |

Not only will this save room on the test, it will help you as the teacher to focus the test item on exactly what it is that you are assessing, and it will help the student be able to focus in on what he's being asked about. Remember, we want our 21$^{st}$-Century students to know the targets!

*Homogeneity.* The term *homogeneity* refers to things being *homogeneous* in nature. Items are homogeneous when they are alike in format, characteristics, content, nature, etc. In a multiple-choice item, homogeneity means that *all of the options are plausible responses* for the item. A simplistic example is:

| MC EXAMPLE G (Poor) | _____ 4. Which food contains the fewest calories?<br>A) ice cream<br>B) chili<br>C) carrots<br>D) chair |
|---|---|

While most teachers would never consider including a non-food item among the list of possible options, it does happen. And, the more complicated the items on an assessment, the more likely it is to happen. For instance:

| MC EXAMPLE H (Poor) | _____ 11. What does Plato establish in his prototype of a society in *The Republic*?<br>A) Justice is a compromise between the state and the people.<br>B) Class structures are fluid and individuals can move between them.<br>C) People often act like sheep once a leader has been elected.<br>D) He believes that people cannot be trusted and must therefore be shepherded. |
|---|---|

In this example, the fourth option is clearly different in format from the others. Thus, it lacks homogeneity. Just as the *chair* in the food example would not be chosen, Option D would not likely be chosen by most students in Example H.

The item could easily be improved:

| MC EXAMPLE H (Improved) | _____ 11. What does Plato establish in his prototype of a society in *The Republic*?<br>A) Justice is a compromise between the state and the people.<br>B) Class structures are fluid and individuals can move between them.<br>C) People often act like sheep once a leader has been elected.<br>D) People cannot be trusted and must therefore be shepherded. |
|---|---|

Now, Option D is on an equal footing with the other items in terms of being selected.

*Option arrangement.* For many multiple-choice items, there is no logical order for the options. For those items, you will simply want to assure that you have a variety of responses (e.g., A, B, C, D) throughout the test. A saying that is reported to have originated in the military is: *When in doubt, Charley out!* The meaning is that the best guess is C. The basis for this is that as teachers are creating test questions, they write the stem first. They then need to write some distractors. Then, they need to include the correct answer before they forget and leave it out. So, C becomes the most common response.

Several years ago, I had some of my tests evaluated for a variety of factors including the percentage of correct option choices. Interestingly, 40% of my responses were B. I was surprised, but I'm guessing that my students wouldn't have been. They probably had figured out the pattern and adjusted their guessing for items they were unsure of accordingly.

A teacher should have approximately 25% of each of the four responses (A, B, C, D) for four-option item tests, or approximately 33% of each for three-option item tests, or approximately 20% of each for five-option item tests. It doesn't have to be exact. However, if a single response (e.g., A) is not used throughout the test, or if a response (e.g., C) is used too often, it would be wise to change the position of some of the correct answers.

For some items though, the options should follow a logical order. This is particularly true in math. For example:

| MC EXAMPLE I (Poor) | _____ 28. If a factory produces 18 pallets per hour, and the factory is in production 10 hours a day, how many pallets per five-day work week would the factory be able to produce?<br>A) 90<br>B) 9000<br>C) 900<br>D) .90 |
|---|---|

In that example, the options should be placed in a logical order (from smallest to largest) so that the student could quickly locate the response he had calculated:

| MC EXAMPLE I (Improved) | _____ 28. If a factory produces 18 pallets per hour, and the factory is in production 10 hours a day, how many pallets per five-day work week would the factory be able to produce?<br>A) .90<br>B) 90<br>C) 900<br>D) 9000 |
|---|---|

Another possible logical order for items is alphabetical. An example would be:

| MC EXAMPLE J | _____ 7. Which New England state has the smallest land area?<br>A) Connecticut<br>B) Massachusetts<br>C) Rhode Island<br>D) Vermont |
|---|---|

When dates are involved, a logical order is chronological:

| | |
|---|---|
| MC EXAMPLE K | _____ 21. In which year did the Louisiana Purchase occur?<br>A) 1776<br>B) 1787<br>C) 1803<br>D) 1812 |

However, even in math, this rule <u>sometimes</u> would not be followed. For instance:

| | |
|---|---|
| MC EXAMPLE L | _____ 13. Which of the following fractions would represent the *greatest* portion of a pizza?<br>A) 1/5<br>B) 1/4<br>C) 1/3<br>D) 1/2 |

In that example, placing the options in order would give away the answer. However, unless there is a good reason not to do so, place the options in what would occur in the students' brains to be a logical order.

*Option length.* Test creators, particularly novice ones, tend to put more information in the correct option than in the incorrect ones. Therefore, one of the first "secrets" that you will learn at a test-prep seminar is, *when in doubt, choose the longest option*. To avoid providing students with this unintended clue, keep all the option lengths in a single item approximately the same, if possible. I say *if possible* because there are situations in which they might not be the same length. If you want to distinguish between two concepts and one is long, but the other short, you can still include both options, but also include one short distractor and one long distractor.

This is shown in the following example:

| | |
|---|---|
| MC EXAMPLE M | _____ 6. What was Monty's reaction to the arrival of the letter that the neighbor brought over?<br>A) He jumped up and down, grabbed it, and tore it open looking for the secret clue.<br>B) He stormed out of the room.<br>C) He quietly thanked the neighbor.<br>D) He was upset by it because an earlier letter had brought news of his grandpa's illness. |

In this example, the objective is for the student to be able to *relate events in the story to the characters' responses to them.* Thus, we want the student to determine which of Monty's reactions to the arrival of three different letters occurred when the neighbor brought the letter to the house. Since, two of his reactions were long (Option A and D), but was short (Option C), the teacher can include another short option (in this case, B—that may have occurred in the story, but not in reaction to the arrival of a letter) so that the student will actually need to know the information in order to respond correctly.

*Number of options.* Typically, four options are optimal. For children in kindergarten and first-grade, three-option items are sometimes included on assessments though. For most other grades, four-option items are preferred. For high school students in high-level content areas, especially where complicated material is being assessed (e.g., in an honors class), sometimes five options are included. And, in rare instances, the information being tested may dictate the number of logical options (e.g., the six levels of Bloom's). But for the most part, most tests you will create for your classroom will probably include four-option items.

*Binary-Choice Items*

Binary-choice items are written as statements, and students then have two options from which to choose. *Typical binary-choice* (T-BC) items are the true/false (T/F) type. The teacher provides a statement, and the student determines whether it is true or whether it is false. And, usually the options available are actually *true* and *false*. However, the options can also be *yes/no, correct/incorrect, right/wrong, describes it/doesn't describe it, fits the pattern/doesn't fit the pattern,* or any two similar options.

*Contrasting-concept binary-choice* (CC-BC) items also provide two options to the students, and just like the typical binary choice items, they are written as statements. However, in the case of CC-BC items, the options are two concepts that the students are *contrasting* (hence, the name). Examples would be: *meiosis/mitosis, Atlantic/Pacific, Dr. Jekyll/Mr. Hyde.* Of course, the possibilities are endless.

No matter the type of binary-choice items, there are some best practices to consider.

| Best Practices for Binary Choice Items on Summative Assessments |
| --- |
| A) They are written as statements and end with a period. B) Usually, only one concept is assessed in each item. C) They are written as a block and all have the same two possibilities. |

*Written as statements.* Because binary-choice items are written as statements, they end with a period. Novice test makers often put question marks at the end of binary-choice items. However, that is confusing to students. Consider the following examples:

| BC EXAMPLE A (Incorrect) | _____ 1. The composer of *The Magic Flute* was Mozart? |
| --- | --- |
| | _____ 2. Did Beethoven and Mozart live at the same time? |
| | _____ 3. Was the famous child prodigy composer Brahms? |

These items are NOT written in the correct binary-choice format. They should be changed so that they are straightforward statements:

| BC EXAMPLE A (Correct) | _____ 1. The composer of *The Magic Flute* was Mozart. |
| --- | --- |
| | _____ 2. Beethoven and Mozart were alive at the same time. |
| | _____ 3. The famous child prodigy composer was Brahms. |

Now, the items are can be determined to be either *true* or *false*.

*A full sentence.* For BC items, a full sentence is required as that will provide more clarity to the student. There is a temptation for novice test writers to create a contrasting-concept binary-choice section with phrases only as shown in this example:

| BC EXAMPLE B (Incorrect) | **Mexico** OR **Canada** |
| --- | --- |
| | _____ 1. North neighbor |
| | _____ 2. Spanish language |
| | _____ 3. Two borders with U.S. |

While Item 1 may seem clear to some students, others may have confusion about whether it means that the country is north of the U.S. or if U.S. *is* the neighbor to the north of it. Item 2 seems obvious to most people, but a student could defend an answer of Canada because there are of course some people who speak Spanish in both countries. The third item is the one that clearly exemplifies the need for a complete thought. Thus, this section will become a more valid assessment if the phrases are converted into complete sentences. Consider now the improved version:

| BC EXAMPLE B (Improved) | **Mexico** OR **Canada** |
| --- | --- |
| | _____ 1. This country is located north of the U.S. |
| | _____ 2. The Spanish language is spoken by most of its residents. |
| | _____ 3. This country has two separate borders with the U.S. |

Of course, to truly be a high-quality CC-BC section, clear directions would need to be included:

| | |
|---|---|
| BC<br>EXAMPLE B<br>(Correct) | **Mexico/Canada.** *Each of the following statements relates to either Mexico or Canada. Determine which country it applies to and write the name of that country on the line in front of the item.*<br>**Mexico**     OR     **Canada**<br>_____ 1. This country is located north of the U.S.<br>_____ 2. The Spanish language is spoken by most of its residents.<br>_____ 3. This country has two separate borders with the U.S. |

Note that the item section is named by the two concepts that are being contrasted. (Remember how we discussed that teachers speak three languages. When writing a test, speak the language of the students. Contrasting-concept binary choice items will make sense to you and your fellow educators. However, student-friendly language indicating what is being contrasted would make it clear to the students.)

Occasionally, a CC-BC section can have an additional option of *both*. Of course, if that is the case, it needs to be spelled out in the directions.

*A block of items.* When creating a test, determine the information that would lend itself best to binary-choice item types. For CC-BC types, all of the items must be about the same two options. For T-BC items, use a single format. In other words, do not have yes/no items intermingled with true/false ones.

Note: Sometimes, teachers have students cross out the part of the statement that makes the false items false, and correct the information above it. This can be used on formative assessments, but it makes the grading difficult, and sometimes inconsistent, on summative assessments so it should rarely be used on those.

### *Matching Items*

Matching items are probably the most difficult type of selected-response items to write for novice teachers. A matching exercise includes an initial list of items containing the *premises*, and a second list of items containing the *responses*. The student's task is to find a match among the responses for each premise.

There are best practices for writing matching exercises as well.

> **Best Practices for Matching Items on Summative Assessments**
>
> A) The lists must be homogeneous.
> B) The directions must include what is being matched as well as option usage.
> C) Items should be formatted into two columns on a single page.
> D) On summative assessments, past K-1, the number of items in each list needs to be unequal.

*Homogeneous lists.* In order for a matching exercise to be a valid summative assessment, the lists must be homogeneous. This means that every response must be a plausible possibility for every premise. Let's consider the following example:

|  | **Directions.** Match the items in one column to the other. | |
|---|---|---|
| MATCHING EXAMPLE A (Poor) | Abraham Lincoln | Born in the US makes you a citizen |
| | Fourteenth Amendment | Northerners who were opportunists |
| | Carpetbaggers | Outlaws slavery |
| | The Freedman's Bureau | Southerners who worked with the new state governments |
| | Scalawags | President in 1864 |
| | Andrew Johnson | Agency to assist former slaves |
| | Thirteenth Amendment | President in 1866 |
| | | Tobacco farmers |

This example shows the problem with lists that are not homogeneous. The student would look at the first premise, Abraham Lincoln. He would then look at the list of possible responses. Going down the list, his thinking might be:

> Born in the US makes you a citizen *(No; Abraham Lincoln sounds like a person and this describes a concept)*
> Northerners who were opportunists *(No; Lincoln is a person and this describes a group)*
> Outlaws slavery *(Maybe; this sounds like something a person could do)*
> Southerners who worked with the new state governments *(No ; again, this is a group)*
> President in 1864 *(Maybe; this is a person)*
> Agency to assist former slaves *(No ; a person can't be an agency)*
> President in 1866 *(Maybe; again, this is a person)*
> Tobacco farmers *(No; this is a group)*

Therefore, a student who didn't even know who Abraham Lincoln was would be able to simply rule out most of the possible responses.

Looking at the colors of the lines below, you will see that there are only a few plausible responses for each of the next two premises.

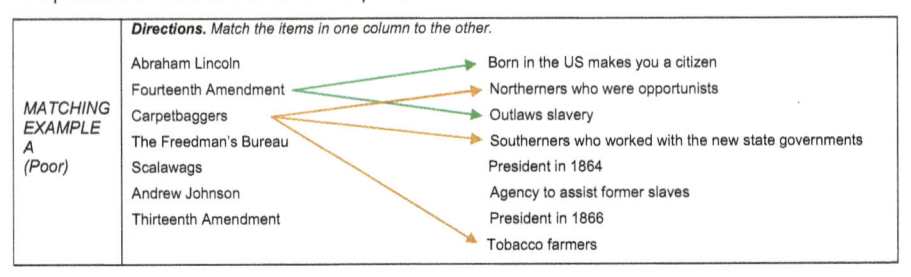

| | **Directions.** Match the items in one column to the other. | |
|---|---|---|
| MATCHING EXAMPLE A (Poor) | Abraham Lincoln<br>Fourteenth Amendment<br>Carpetbaggers<br>The Freedman's Bureau<br>Scalawags<br>Andrew Johnson<br>Thirteenth Amendment | Born in the US makes you a citizen<br>Northerners who were opportunists<br>Outlaws slavery<br>Southerners who worked with the new state governments<br>President in 1864<br>Agency to assist former slaves<br>President in 1866<br>Tobacco farmers |

Thus, the lack of homogeneity in each list leads to an assessment that is simpler than it attests is it (that each premise has the possibility of eight responses). Also, it is probably not clear to the students what objectives they are being assessed on. This leads to confusion. And, if a test is confusing to a student, the validity of that test comes into question.

Let's consider what a matching exercise containing homogeneous lists would look like:

| | **Directions.** The left-hand column contains special types of pronouns. The right-hand column contains sentences with pronouns <u>underlined</u>. Match the role the <u>underlined</u> pronoun has in the sentence with its type. Place its corresponding letter in the blank in front of the number. The sentences may be used only once and some will not be used at all. | |
|---|---|---|
| MATCHING EXAMPLE B | _B_ 1. possessive<br>_H_ 2. indefinite<br>_F_ 3. reflexive<br>_C_ 4. relative<br>_E_ 5. interrogative<br>_D_ 6. demonstrative | A) "That was the dress **she** chose," Ms. L announced.<br>B) "Serena can't have **my** dress!" Mariah replied.<br>C) "But, Serena was the one **who** saw it first."<br>D) "Serena is wearing the dress, and **that** is final."<br>E) "**Who** died and put you in charge?"<br>F) "Serena selected it **herself**," Ms. L defended.<br>G) "But I'm Mariah and I'm wearing **it**, and that's final!"<br>H) "**Nobody** is going to take that dress away from Serena!" |

The objective for this exercise is that the students will be able to *identify special types of pronouns in usage*. The teacher obviously had it in mind when she wrote the exercise, and the students would clearly be able to recognize the target they are being assessed on. One list contains the pronoun types, and the other list contains sentences exemplifying them. *Every* response is a *plausible possibility* for *every premise*. In other words, each of the sentences has a pronoun underlined in it that could possibly be that type of pronoun.

And, the student would need to actually know the pronoun types in order to figure out the correct matches. (Note: This is an example where a matching exercise assesses students in the higher-order thinking skill—HOTS—of analysis. Educators often believe that matching exercises can only be used to assess lower-level skills.)

*Matching directions.* While clear directions are important for every section of a test, they actually play a part *in the content* in a matching exercise. This is because you <u>must indicate</u> in the matching directions <u>what is being matched</u>. By having this as a requirement when you construct the exercise, you will assure that the lists are homogeneous. Thus, you do NOT simply state that students should *match the items in the first list with the items in the second list.* It's too vague. Even *match the terms with the descriptions* is too vague. If you cannot be more specific than that, it is very likely that your lists are not homogeneous. Look at the directions in *Matching Example A* versus the directions in *Matching Example B*. One tells the students what is being matched while the other is vague. And, the vague one does not contain homogeneous lists.

In addition, your directions need to include whether the responses can be used more than once, and if every response will be used or not. The importance of including the *option usage*, as this is called, is demonstrated in the example below:

| | **Directions.** Match the characteristics found in the right-hand column with the polygon types in the left-hand column by placing the letter of the characteristic in the blank in front of the number. The characteristics may be used only once and some will not be used at all. | |
|---|---|---|
| MATCHING EXAMPLE C | ____ 1. rhombus <br> ____ 2. octagon <br> ____ 3. square. <br> ____ 4. hexagon <br> ____ 5. pentagon <br> ____ 6. quadrilateral | A) created with exactly six sides <br> B) contains four 90-degree interior angles <br> C) has exactly eight sides, but not necessarily all of the same length <br> D) made up of two sets of parallels with all sides of equal length <br> E) its interior angles add up to exactly 180 degrees <br> F) made up of four sides which may or may be of equal length <br> G) contains nine equal sides <br> H) contains exactly five sides |

Without the directions *the characteristics may be used only once*, there are <u>two</u> clearly defensible responses for #3 and <u>three</u> clearly defensible responses for #6.

    A square:    contains four 90-degree interior angles (Option B)
                              is made up of two sets of parallels with all sides of equal length (Option D)

    A quadrilateral:   contains four 90-degree interior angles (Option B)
                                is made up of two sets of parallels with all sides of equal length (Option D)
                                is made up of four sides which may or may not be of equal length (Option F)

However, with the inclusion of those directions (that *each characteristic may be used only once*), Option D is the only response for a rhombus (#1). That leaves only Option B for the square (#3). With Option B and D already used, Option F is the only clearly defensible response for the quadrilateral (#6). Thus, you can see that the directions themselves become a part of the assessment of the content. (Note: This is an example of a matching exercise that truly invokes the Higher-Order Thinking Skill—HOTS—of *analysis*.)

Of course, as stated in the general guidelines, the directions need to include how you want the students to indicate their responses. Drawing lines between lists on summative assessments makes them hard to grade. In addition, beyond K-1, it indicates a lack of face validity. Thus, number the premises, and letter the responses, and have the students place the letters in blanks in front of the numbers.

*Formatting matching exercises.* While formatting is important throughout a test, it is doubly important for a matching exercise. A high-quality matching exercise begins with a set of directions that goes across the top of the exercise. The lists follow below in two columns, a left-hand one and a right-hand one. The premises are numbered on the left; the responses are lettered on the right. Blanks in front of the premise numbers are provided where students can place the letter of the corresponding match.

In order to assure that the spacing between each of the items in each list is appropriate, after the directions, insert a CONTINUOUS section break. After a couple of returns, insert a second such break. Between those two breaks, format that section into two columns. After writing the premises in a list, insert a COLUMN break. That will put your cursor at the top of the second column. Begin your first response across from the first premise.

This two-column method of formatting is considered best practices for matching exercises. This is because our brains are oriented to match items horizontally, rather than vertically. Because we want the formatting of our tests to aid the student in showing us what they know, this will allow the assessment to assist the student in that process. Other formats of matching exercises can actually confuse the students and invalidate the assessment.

*Number of items.* On summative assessments, beyond K-1, the number of premises and responses should be unequal. Even in those first two grades, you *can* have an unequal number of items in the lists. Do make sure you include that fact in the directions of course though:

| | |
|---|---|
| MATCHING EXAMPLE D | **Directions.** Draw a line from the picture to the name of the shape. One shape will not be used.<br><br>1. square<br><br>2. triangle<br><br>3. rectangle |

Typically, there are more responses than premises, but there can be more premises than responses. In this case, the responses will need to be used more than once because every premise must have a response. An example would be:

| | |
|---|---|
| MATCHING EXAMPLE E | **Directions.** Match the instruments to the family to which it belongs. Place the letter of the family in the blank in front of the number. The families may be used more than once and all of the families will be used at least once.<br><br>\_\_\_\_ 1. violin<br>\_\_\_\_ 2. clarinet            A) strings<br>\_\_\_\_ 3. tuba                B) brass<br>\_\_\_\_ 4. triangle             C) percussion<br>\_\_\_\_ 5. oboe              D) woodwinds<br>\_\_\_\_ 6. trombone<br>\_\_\_\_ 7. snare drum<br>\_\_\_\_ 8. cello<br>\_\_\_\_ 9. flute<br>\_\_\_\_ 10. trumpet |

Note that when there are fewer responses than premises, often the responses are centered, or slightly above center, in their relationship to the premises in terms of their vertical placement.

Common errors that novice teachers make when creating matching exercises include:
    A) having the first premise and the first response match
    B) putting the extraneous responses at the end of the list
    C) failing to have a response for every premise (usually just forgetting to include it)

These errors can be avoided by using the section breaks and two-column format when creating the exercise. Then, use these steps:
> 1) put in the numbered premises in order in the left-hand column.
> 2) insert a column break
> 3) put the responses in the order that matches the premises in the right-hand column; do not include the letters at this time
> 4) add in the extra responses at the end
> 5) re-order the responses (in alphabetical order, possibly, or simply in a random order)
> 6) letter the responses

Note that sometimes, on formative assessments (particularly on things like bell ringers), the *putting-together-of-the-puzzle* through the process of matching lists with an equal number of premises and responses can be fun. However, for a summative assessment, that "puzzle" aspect can lead to invalidating an assessment as students who don't know some of the answers might be able to simply figure out the puzzle.

## *A FINAL WORD*

There is a misconception that a selected-response item is not as valuable an assessment tool as a constructed-response one. In fact, multiple-choice items have truly been disparaged as being low level in what they can assess, and it's even worse for binary-choice items and matching exercises. However, selected-response items can be written at a variety of levels of complexity. They can assess at all levels of Bloom's Taxonomy, although synthesis is challenging, and at all levels of DOKs. Still, since misconceptions often grow out of experience, there is truth in the fact that many selected-response items you will encounter in your career will be written to assess simple knowledge and comprehension. Thus, we do need to be careful when we write them that we don't fall into the trap of simply writing those type of items because they are indeed easier to write than ones that assess students' higher cognitive abilities.

## BASIC CONCEPTS IN CHAPTER 7

A) The three main types of selected-response items are:
    1) multiple choice
    2) binary choice
    3) matching

B) The items should be formatted clearly, written at an appropriate reading level, contain clear directions, be straightforward, and have only one clearly defensible answer.

C) The items should not include unintended clues or tricky parts.

D) Absolutes and negatives should be used sparingly.

E) The items should contain good face validity so the items themselves do not prevent students from showing what they know.

F) Each section of the test should be clearly identified using student-friendly language, and the directions should be distinguishable from the items.

G) Multiple-choice items are either written as questions or as sentence-completion items.

H) The options for multiple-choice items should be homogeneous.

I) Binary-choice items should be written as statements.

J) Matching items should be formatted in two columns, and both lists need to be homogeneous.

K) For all selected-response items, placing short blanks in front of the numbered items where students place their letter responses will make grading easier for the teacher.

NOTES:

# CHAPTER 8

# *I Wrote on the Front and the Back So Surely I'll Get Some Points*
## Creating Constructed-Response Items

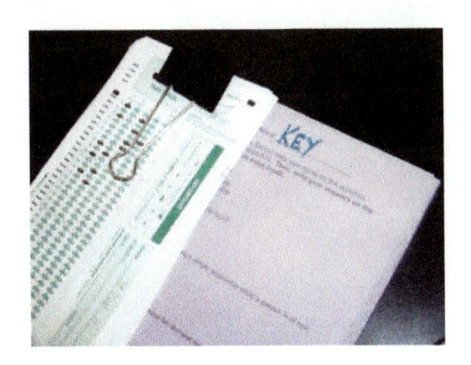

**KEY CONCEPTS:**
FITB Items (Without a Word Bank)
Listing Items
Short Answer Items
Essay Items
Writing Clear Directions
Creating A Key
Grading Selected-Response Items

*Education is not only not separate from life;
it is an instance of the process of living.*
--John Dewey

Just as the name implies, constructed-response items require the students to *construct* their responses. In contrast to selected-response items, where the answer is on the page and students select it, constructed-response items do not contain the answer. Students must respond by writing their answers. The main types of constructed-response items are:

A) fill-in-the-blank (without a word bank)
B) listing
C) short answer
D) essay

## FILL-IN-THE-BLANK ITEMS

If a set of fill-in-the-blank items contains a word bank, it is considered selected-response because the answers are provided on the page. If there is no word bank, FITB items become constructed-response. While FITB items with a word bank are fairly easy to construct, ones without a word bank are more complex. This is because the responses are not limited to the answers that you provide. Instead, they are limited by the words you include in the item. When writing FITB items, make sure to include enough information so that the item actually tests what you're setting out to assess.

| POOR EXAMPLE | 1. Hawaii became the _____ state in _____. |

Any of the following responses would technically be correct:

1. Hawaii became the *newest* state in *Washington, D.C.*
(That is, after all, where they signed the papers.)

1. Hawaii became the *prettiest* state in *history*.
(Few would disagree with that.)

1. Hawaii became the *last* state in *50*.
(It's technically correct.)

Since the teacher probably wanted to assess if the students knew that Hawaii was the 50th state and that it became a state in 1959, she would need to include enough information in the item to direct the students to provide those responses.

> **BETTER EXAMPLE** | 1. Delaware was the 1st state and Alaska became the ____ state in the year _____.

Another social studies item that could evoke wrong, but technically accurate, responses is:

> **POOR EXAMPLE** | 2. _____ is the last state.

While the teacher may have expected *Hawaii*, a student might have written *Wyoming* (thinking alphabetical) while another might have written *Rhode Island* (thinking geographic area). If the student had just had a lesson in science on the states of matter, she might even write *solid* if that was the last one she'd studied. The teacher could improve that item by stating:

> **BETTER EXAMPLE** | 2. _____ was the most recent state to be admitted to the Union.

Do however be careful not to include *too* much information so that the student is simply repeating in words you provided. I actually saw this item on a teacher-made science test:

> **POOR EXAMPLE** | 3. The *water* *cycle* _____ _____ is the continuous cycle of water on Earth.

Not only will this not assess if the students have gained the information, but really good students may assume that it can't be that simple and may actually overthink it and put wrong answers.

When writing directions for FITB items, keep them simple. Indicate that you want the student to fill in the blank with the correct word. If spelling will be assessed, indicate it. If not, there is no need to point it out. Do not state that spelling *and grammar* will be assessed as that will confuse students. Do not use the word *please* in directions for any item type as it implies a request rather than a requirement.

If the answer you desire is more than one word, provide individual blanks for each word. The lengths of the blanks should be long enough so that most students of that grade level will be able to write their answers in them. Some teachers think that it is best to have all blanks the same length, while others think they should be related to the length of the expected words. If you decide to follow the former guideline, rather than the latter, make sure the blank length you decide upon is long enough to accommodate the longest-word answer so the test will maintain face validity.

Don't try to assess more than two pieces of information in a single FITB item because, while you know what the completed sentence would look like, it may not be clear to the students.

| POOR EXAMPLE | 4. _____ _____ was the author from _____ who wrote _____ _____ which was a _____ novel. |
|---|---|

| BETTER EXAMPLE | 4. _____ _____ was the author from Louisville who wrote _____ _____ which was a *coming-of-age* novel. |
|---|---|

## LISTING ITEMS

Listing items require a student to provide examples for a specific criterion. Examples include asking students to identify *King Lear*'s three daughters, to state precipitating factors for the start of World War II, or to name the five literary elements. Typically, listing items are answered with words or simple phrases, although teachers do sometimes require complete sentences.

As with the FITB items, the directions should be simple, but clear, and the prompt should include enough information to elicit the responses that will demonstrate to you that the students have attained the knowledge you're assessing with that particular item.

A poor example would be:

| | |
|---|---|
| POOR EXAMPLE | 5. List the elements we discussed in class:<br>A)    C)<br>B)    D) |

This item does not determine if the students know anything about the particular elements that have been taught.

| | |
|---|---|
| BETTER EXAMPLE | 5. List four noble gases:<br>A)    C)<br>B)    D) |

To facilitate ease of grading, you should provide place indicators where the students will write their answers. For clarity, since items on a test are typically numbered, the use of letters or lines (instead of numbers) as guides is preferred.

When writing a listing item, you should be clear about what you're asking and provide enough information so that the lists received are specific to the content being assessed. You can't assume that students will answer based on the unit you've just spent the last two weeks covering! In addition, you should be specific about the number of items requested. Using *at least* or *some* can complicate the grading. If a student answers an *at-least-three* item with five answers, but two of them are inaccurate, should he receive the full points? Obviously, he has not mastered the concept if he is including wrong items. By being specific about the exact number desired, you will avoid those problems. These concepts are demonstrated below.

| POOR EXAMPLES | BETTER EXAMPLES |
|---|---|
| 6. Indicate some similes: | 6. Give four examples of similes:<br>A.<br>B.<br>C.<br>D. |
| 7. List the three main characters:<br>1.<br>2.<br>3. | 7. State the three main characters in Judy Blume's *Superfudge*:<br>_____<br>_____<br>_____ |

## SHORT-ANSWER ITEMS

Short-answer items (sometimes called direct constructed-response items) are similar to listing items, except that only one answer is needed. For an item to be classified as a short-answer item, the answer that is expected is usually just a word, a simple phrase, a single sentence, or even two or three sentences.

A short answer item requiring only a single-word answer is shown in the following example:

| *GOOD EXAMPLE* | 8. Who was the President of the United States during the Civil War? |

The answer that would be expected would simply be *Lincoln*.

An example that requires a phrase would be:

| *GOOD EXAMPLE* | 9. After the robbery, where did the character hide the stolen money? |

Students might answer *under the oak tree* or *buried in the backyard*.

A short answer item might require also require a more complex response. For instance, this one would require a single sentence:

| *GOOD EXAMPLE* | 10. Is Mars warmer or colder than the Earth? Why? |

It could be answered *Mars is colder than the Earth because it is further from the Sun.*

One requiring two or three sentences might be:

| *GOOD EXAMPLE* | 11. Use an example to explain how multiplication is related to addition. |

A student's response might be *Multiplication is a short-cut to adding repeating numbers. Five plus five plus five equals fifteen, but it would be quicker to multiply five times three.*

Directions for short answer items should include the expectations of the answer format (i.e., a word, a phrase, a complete sentence, a few sentences) and a notation that spelling will be counted (if it will). Grammar should only be mentioned (and counted) if complete sentences are required, and noted in the directions.

If all of the short-answer items are worth the same number of points, you often put that with the directions. However, typically point values vary according to the item, and in that case, are placed after the individual items. It is good to remind students that the number of points an item is worth is indicative of the amount of detail or depth required in the answer. For instance, an item worth seven points might require a more thorough answer than one worth two points.

## ESSAY ITEMS

Essay items continue the spectrum of complexity as they are more complex in their prompts and the expected responses than short answer items. There are two basic types of essay items, *restricted-response* and *extended-response*.

A restricted-response item asks the students to provide specific information in response to the prompt the teacher provides. For instance, a teacher might require a student to discuss Columbus' second journey to the New World in 1493. An extended-response item on the same topic might ask the student if he would have liked to been on that voyage or not and to give rationale for his answer.

| GOOD EXAMPLES | RESTRICTED | 12. Discuss Columbus' second journey to the New World in 1493. Include the purpose of the trip, the names of the ships, the locations that were visited, and the gains achieved from the trip. (15 pts.) |
|---|---|---|
| | EXTENDED | 13. Would you have liked to have been a crew member on one of the ships when Columbus made his second journey to the New World in 1493? Why or why not? (10 pts.) |

Another example of a restricted-response essay item might be:

| POOR EXAMPLE | 14. Compare the protagonist and antagonist in the story. (20 pts.) |
|---|---|

This is a restricted-response item because the teacher knows what he expects as an answer. However, he does not include enough details in the prompt, so there may be a large array of responses that would all technically have answered the item correctly.
A better prompt would include:

| FAIR EXAMPLE | 14. Compare the characteristics, behaviors, motivation, and outcomes of the protagonist and antagonist in the story. (20 pts.) |
|---|---|

In this example, the teacher knows exactly what he is expecting to be included in the answer. While he may not know exactly how the student will express it, he does know *the answer*.

Usually, a teacher will create either a simple scoring guide (that he simply jots down on a blank copy of the test, which then becomes his key) or a formal rubric. A teacher might write in the following simple scoring guide for the item on the previous page:

| | |
|---|---|
| **FAIR EXAMPLE** | 14. Compare the characteristics, behaviors, motivation, and outcomes of the protagonist and antagonist in the story. (20 pts.)<br><br>*Pro—Dahlia: sweet, kind, pretty; helped her neighbor; fed the dog<br>wanted to go to heaven; Lived a long life<br>Ant—Marvin: selfish, thrill-seeking, looked down on old people; yelled at the dog; scowled at kids; wanted an exciting life with "equals"; went bankrupt, died alone* |

The item as written, however, would not necessarily evoke the responses that the teacher expected. Note that the teacher has included the name of the characters in his key, and he has distinguished between the protagonist and the antagonist. While many students would answer the prompt as expected, not all of them would. And, a student would have a clear defense if she didn't.

An improvement on the prompt would be:

| | |
|---|---|
| **GOOD EXAMPLE** | 14. Identify the protagonist and the antagonist in the story. Describe the characteristics and behaviors of each. Compare the motivations and outcomes of each. (20 pts.)<br><br>*Pro—Dahlia: sweet, kind, pretty; helped her neighbor; fed the dog<br>wanted to go to heaven; Lived a long life<br>Ant—Marvin: selfish, thrill-seeking, looked down on old people; yelled at the dog; scowled at kids; wanted an exciting life with "equals"; went bankrupt, died alone* |

A possible rubric for that improved item would be:

| | | | |
|---|---|---|---|
| **FAIR EXAMPLE** | Protagonist | ID | 2 |
| | | Characteristics/behaviors | 3 |
| | | Motivation/outcomes | 5 |
| | Antagonist | ID | 2 |
| | | Characteristics/behaviors | 3 |
| | | Motivation/outcomes | 5 |
| | **TOTAL** | | **20** |

However, the above rubric does not actually inform the person grading the test about the correct answers. Sometimes, someone other than the teacher (e.g., an administrative assistant, a teacher's aide, a substitute teacher, etc.) may be grading the papers. Therefore a good rubric for a restricted-response item needs to include not only the requirements, but the actual expected answers as well.

An improved rubric for this restricted-response item would be:

| GOOD EXAMPLE | Protagonist | ID | Dahlia | 2 |
| --- | --- | --- | --- | --- |
| | | Characteristics/behaviors | Sweet, kind, pretty; helped neighbor, fed dog | 3 |
| | | Motivation/outcomes | Go to heaven; lived long life | 5 |
| | Antagonist | ID | Marvin | 2 |
| | | Characteristics/behaviors | Selfish, thrill-seeking, looked down on people; yelled at dog, scowled at kids | 3 |
| | | Motivation/outcomes | Exciting life with "equals"; bankrupt, died alone | 5 |
| | TOTAL | | | 20 |

For an extended response item, a good rubric obviously will not include the specifics. Instead, it will simply include the criteria.

| GOOD EXAMPLE | 13. Would you have liked to have been a crew member on one of the ships when Columbus made his second journey to the New World in 1493? Why or why not? (10 pts.) |
| --- | --- |

A rubric for the item above would be:

| GOOD EXAMPLE | Student's decision | States wanted or did not want to be on the journey | 1 |
| --- | --- | --- | --- |
| | Rationale | States why | 1 |
| | | Includes information related to the conditions of the journey | 3 |
| | | Response is logical | 2 |
| | Clarity of expression | | 2 |
| | Grammar/spelling | | 1 |
| | TOTAL | | 10 |

In this rubric, you will see that clarity of expression and grammar/spelling have been added as criteria. Obviously, clarity of expression is expected, so it doesn't have to be stated in the directions. However, if the teacher is going to grade for grammar and spelling, it must be stated in the directions for the essay section of the test. The awarding of points for the individual criterion is determined by what the teacher feels is the importance, in relationship to the others, of a particular criterion. In the above rubric, obviously the teacher wants the student to put himself in the position of the crew members and consider how they would feel. Therefore, she has awarded more points for the rationale than for other aspects.

Teachers often report that grading with rubrics, specifically analytic rubrics, improves the consistency of grading, efficiency of grading, and that they provide the students with quick, but thorough, feedback into the teacher's way of thinking as she was grading the papers.

Sometimes essay items are graded with holistic rubrics. Holistic rubrics allow you to look at the answer as a whole and award it a level of achievement for the entire answer (rather than for parts as indicated in an analytic one). Holistic rubrics have bands of criteria associated with a point value. There are usually either four or five bands. Some are generic in nature and can be used for a variety of tasks.

An example of a *generic* holistic rubric would be:

| GENERIC HOLISTIC RUBRIC ||
|---|---|
| 7 | Student answers all parts of the item thoroughly. The response is clear and the writing appropriate. |
| 5 | Student answers all parts of the item but the response lacks either thoroughness, clarity, or appropriate writing. |
| 3 | Student answers some parts of the item and/or the response lacks, thoroughness, clarity, or appropriate writing. |
| 1 | Student responds with an answer that does not answer the question or with an answer that is unable to be understood. |

A *specific* holistic rubric contains bands of criteria again, but within the bands, specifics or details related to the information in the prompt are included.

| GOOD EXAMPLE | 13. Would you have liked to have been a crew member on one of the ships when Columbus made his second journey to the New World in 1493? Why or why not? (10 pts.) |
|---|---|

For this item, a specific holistic rubric might be:

| SPECIFIC HOLISTIC RUBRIC ||
|---|---|
| 10 | The decision is expressed clearly and the rationale is thorough and logical and includes details demonstrating the student's familiarity with the journey. |
| 8 | The decision is expressed clearly and the rationale is provided and logical. A few details about the journey are included. |
| 6 | The decision is expressed, although it may lack clarity, and the rationale is brief with only a few details. It may also lack some logic. |
| 4 | The decision is not clear, the rationale is brief, non-existent, lacking in details, or illogical. |

A specific holistic rubric can also be used for a restricted-response essay item.

| GOOD EXAMPLE | 14. Identify the protagonist and the antagonist in the story. Describe the characteristics and behaviors of each. Compare the motivations and outcomes of each. (20 pts.) |
|---|---|

| SPECIFIC HOLISTIC RUBRIC ||
|---|---|
| 20 | The response includes the correct IDs, and a thorough discussion of the characteristics, behaviors, motivations, and outcomes, as well as a comparison of the two characters. Expression is clear. |
| 16 | The response includes the correct IDs, and the characteristics, behaviors, motivations, and outcomes of each. The expression is clear. |
| 12 | The response includes the correct IDs, but has gaps in the characteristics, behaviors, motivations, and outcomes. The expression is fairly clear. |
| 8 | The response includes the correct IDS, but only addresses some of the characteristics, behaviors, motivations, and outcomes. The expression lacks some clarity. |
| 4 | The response does not correctly identify the antagonist or the protagonist and provides few details related to them. The expression lacks clarity. |

The major advantage of grading with holistic rubrics is time-saving. Once they have been created, which does take some time, the grading can be completed fairly quickly. (Rubrics are again discussed in Chapter 10 and more further information concerning them is included there.)

## *WRITING GOOD DIRECTIONS*

Directions for constructed-response items are as important on a test as the test items themselves. Consider the following guidelines.

| GUIDELINES FOR WRITING DIRECTIONS FOR CONSTRUCTED-RESPONSE ITEMS |
|---|
| 1) Indicate the item type at the beginning of the section. |
| 2) Distinguish the directions from the items themselves by using bold, italics, a different font type, size, or color. |
| 3) Include the expectations for the answer (a word, a phrase, a complete sentence, a paragraph, a complete essay). |
| 4) Notify the student if spelling will be counted. |
| 5) Notify the student if grammar will be counted, but only indicate that if a requirement for complete sentences is also included. |
| 6) Do not use *please* in the directions as it implies the instructions are a request and not a requirement. |
| 7) If all of the items in the particular section will have the same point values, include them with the directions. If not, include the point values with each item. |
| 8) Do not repeat directions for the whole section within the items themselves. |
| 9) Write the directions using vocabulary that is appropriate to the grade level of the student. |

## CREATING A KEY

Teachers usually create a key by taking a blank copy of the test and write in the answers or simple scoring guide using a bright color ink (red and green are popular colors). In this electronic age, after a teacher creates the test, she will save a second copy of the test, and create a key using a different color font for the answers. She may also insert a rubric below the essay items that she will use for grading. In addition, she may highlight in yet another color the key words in the prompt to remind her (or another person doing the grading) of important things to look for in the student answers.

For items where answers may vary, but are restricted to a certain list, the teacher should include all the possibilities.

| GOOD EXAMPLE | 15. List three of the Great Lakes.  Any three of the following:<br>A) Huron          Ontario<br>B) Michigan       Erie<br>C) Superior |
|---|---|

If an item asks for examples, the possibilities may include too many options to list. In that case, the teacher should indicate that answers will vary, and then give a few possibilities.

| GOOD EXAMPLE | 16. List four rivers found in North America.  Answers will vary.<br>Possibilities include, but are not limited to:<br>A) Mississippi River    Missouri River<br>B) Rio Grande River    Colorado River<br>C)<br>D) |
|---|---|

As the teacher grades, she may update the key with notes that inform her about the nuances of the student answers and how she is addressing each. That will lead to consistency in her grading.

## BASIC CONCEPTS IN CHAPTER 8

A) Constructed-response items require the student to "construct" the response rather than select it from among the given information.

B) The main types of constructed-response items used on summative assessments are:
1) Fill-in-the-blank (without a word bank)
2) Listing
3) Short answer
4) Essay

C) The directions for constructed-response items need to be clear, include what is expected, and indicate if grammar/spelling will be counted.

D) When creating a key the constructed-response part of the test, include correct answers (in a different color), possible responses for items that will have varying responses, and a rubric for essay items.

E) When grading selected-response items, keep notes so that you will grade consistently across papers.

F) Because constructed-response items take longer to grade than selected-response items, use them judiciously.

NOTES:

# CHAPTER 9

## *You Mean This Test Could End Up on the Principal's Desk or the 6 o'clock News?*
### Creating A Professional Test

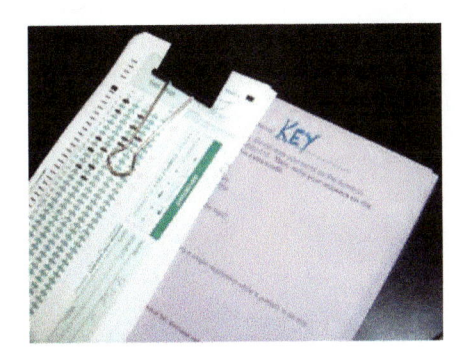

**KEY CONCEPTS:**
Test Blueprint
Formatting the Test for Good Face Validity
Organizing and Ordering Items

*He who fails to plan, plans to fail.*
--Anonymous

When creating a test, a teacher has to decide what will be covered on the test and how it will be organized. There is a special tool that a teacher uses for that purpose. It is called a test blueprint.

## TEST BLUEPRINTS

Just as a blueprint lays out the plan for a house, a **test blueprint** lays out the plan for a test. It is sometimes called a **table of specifications** because it is usually created in *table* format and *specifies* the content on the test, the degree to which each part of the content is tested, and usually, a breakdown of cognitive requirements. In other words:

A) what's on the test
B) how much of it is on the test, and
C) what's cognitively required

A blueprint for a house is created by an architect based on the homeowner's desires for certain parts of a house (e.g., kitchen, living areas, bedrooms, etc.), the size or number of each part (e.g., big kitchen, three bedrooms, etc.), and the quality of each part (e.g., granite countertops, separate living room and family room, on-suite bathroom in the master bedroom). A test blueprint is aptly named because it parallels those same concepts. A teacher determines that he is going to cover certain areas of content on the test as well as the extent of the coverage and depth he'll give to each area.

An example of a test blueprint is shown below:

| OCEANOGRAPHY | % of test | Knowledge | Comprehension | Application | Analysis | Synthesis | Evaluation |
|---|---|---|---|---|---|---|---|
| Ocean Water Properties | 10% | XX | XX | | X | | |
| Currents/Tides | 30% | XXXX | XX | XXX | XXXX | | XX |
| Ocean Floor | 20% | XXXXX | XXX | XX | | | |
| Ocean Life | 40% | XXXX | XXXXX | | XXXXXXXX | XX | X |

X = one item on the test

In the above example, the teacher knows that there is a fair amount of knowledge (terms like *salinity, currents, continental shelf*) that his middle school students need to know to have a good base in the area of oceanography. So, he has several test items at the knowledge level. There are other things they have to understand (e.g., the *Coriolis Effect*, the *moon's effect on the tides*). Thus, he thinks about how he will cover those things on the test. In addition, when it comes to ocean life, they have to consider the *intertidal zone*, the *neritic zone*, and the *open-ocean zone*, and analyze the various life that lives in each. Thus, in addition to having knowledge of the terms and understanding of their characteristics, he will want them to do some analysis related to the ocean life. To show full understanding, he'll have a couple of questions that requires them to synthesize information, and one where they evaluate (judge the value of) something related to ocean life.

By simply creating a simple blueprint, the teacher is able to more clearly think about what he will cover, to what extent, and *how*. The above blueprint would help guide him as he wrote the test. He certainly might move a few items on the blueprint as he wrote it (just as homeowners sometimes change things as the house is being built), but the blueprint at least acts as a basic foundation.

There is no agreed-upon *best format* for a test blueprint. In fact, some teachers simply start with a blank table like the one below:

| MC | BC | FITB | Short Answer | Essay |
|----|----|----|----|----|
|  |  |  |  |  |
|  |  |  |  |  |
|  |  |  |  |  |
|  |  |  |  |  |
|  |  |  |  |  |

They then think about what they have covered in the unit. For instance, a third-grade language arts teacher may have taught a unit that addressed the following standards:

| CC.3.L.2a-g<br><br>Demonstrate command of the conventions of standard English capitalization, punctuation, and spelling when writing. | a. Capitalize appropriate words in titles.<br>b. Use commas in addresses.<br>c. Use commas and quotation marks in dialogue.<br>d. Form and use possessives.<br>e. Use conventional spelling for high-frequency and other studied words and for adding suffixes to base words (e.g., *sitting, smiled, cries, happiness*).<br>f. Use spelling patterns and generalizations (e.g., word families, position-based spellings, syllable patterns, ending rules, meaningful word parts) in writing words.<br>g. Consult reference materials, including beginning dictionaries, as needed to check and correct spellings. |
|---|---|

Using the blank table, the teacher might fill it in with the content and number of items as on the table that follows.

| MC | BC | FITB | Short Answer | Essay |
|---|---|---|---|---|
| Title caps (3) | Possessives (2) | Spelling HF words (7) | Commas in address (1 item—2 pts.) | Dialogue (1 item—7 pts.) |
| Possessives (4) | Q-marks (1) | | Title caps (2 items—4 pts.) | Word families (2 items—20 pts.) |
| Q-marks (1) | Commas (2) | | | |
| Reference Materials (3) | Word parts (3) | | | |

The numbers in parentheses represent items on the test.

This is a simplistic way of doing it, but completely acceptable. Note that to be a true **table of specifications** though, it also needs to include the cognitive processes involved (i.e., DOKs, Bloom's levels). However, a simple *test blueprint* can take various formats, including the one above.

One way that teachers create a test blueprint is by looking at an outline of the content they have taught, and then, simply putting hash marks and item types (or cognitive levels) next to each part of the content. For instance, if a teacher taught a unit on biomes, she might have an outline that she based her instruction on, or a review sheet listing the content that she gave out to the students at the end of the unit. This is shown in the example on the next page.

## BIOME REVIEW SHEET

*In preparing for the test, make sure you review the following content. Make sure you can define the words and be able to give examples (if appropriate) of the items listed.*

Biome
Biosphere
Climate

| | |
|---|---|
| Tundra | Tropical rain forests |
|    Permafrost |    Canopy |
|    Animals of the tundra |    Floor |
| Coniferous forests |    Animals |
|    Coniferous trees | Grasslands |
|    Taiga |    Great Plains |
|    Animals |    Savanna |
| Deciduous forests |    Animals |
|    Deciduous trees | Deserts |
|    Animals |    Cactus |
| |    Animals |

A teacher might write her test looking at the review sheet, and then, after creating the initial test items, use it as a checklist to see what she's missing. After creating only the selected-response part of the test, it might look like:

## BIOME REVIEW SHEET

*In preparing for the test, make sure you review the following content. Make sure you can define the words and be able to give examples (if appropriate) of the items listed.*

Biome MC#1, #5, #11
Biosphere BC #16
Climate MC #2, #7

| | |
|---|---|
| Tundra MAT | Tropical rain forests MAT |
|    Permafrost MC #9 |    Canopy MC #4, #7 |
|    Animals of the tundra Polar Bear MAT |    Floor MC #8, #10 |
| Coniferous forests MC #12 MAT |    Animals Golden frog BC #22 Toucan MAT |
|    Coniferous trees MC #13 BC #18 #20CC-BC | Grasslands BC #21 MAT |
|    Taiga MC #2, #15 |    Great Plains |
|    Animals Prair. Dog BC #6 Beetles BC #17 Elk MAT |    Savanna MC #3 |
| Deciduous forests MAT |    Animals Bison MAT |
|    Deciduous trees BC #19 CC-BC | Deserts MAT |
|    Animals Black Bear MAT |    Cactus |
| |    Animals Nocturnal BC #16 Gila Monster MAT |

Based on this, the teacher had created 15 multiple choice items (#1-15), a typical binary choice section (#16-22), a contrasting concept binary choice section contrasting coniferous trees with deciduous trees, and a matching section with types of biomes as the premises and animals found in that biome as the responses.

With that much of the test created, and having done a checklist-type test blueprint, she can quickly see that she has given more emphasis to the coniferous forests and the tropical rain forests than she has to other content in the course. She may decide that is appropriate (if those are what she considers the most important aspects). Or, she may decide that she will change some of the items that covered those two areas to different items about some of the other content.

She may also notice that she has no questions yet about the *Great Plains* or about *cactus*. Since that is content that she felt was important enough to include on the review sheet, she will probably decide to include some further items that relate to them. In addition, since she has not yet created the constructed-response part of the test, but knows that she wants the students to compare two biomes (including the characteristics, plant life, and animals) in an essay item, she may see that it would be good to choose the *grasslands* and *desert* biomes since they are covered less on the test already.

Later, she might create an *actual* table of specifications that would also include the cognitive levels. Possibly, the MC items were worth 3 points each, the T-BC items worth 2, the CC-BC items worth 1, the short answer worth 3 each, and the essay item worth 10 points. Then, it might look like:

|  | # OF ITEMS (# OF PTS.) | % OF PTS. | KNOW | COMP | APP | ANALY | SYN | EVAL |
|---|---|---|---|---|---|---|---|---|
| Main definitions | 6 (16) | 13% | X | X | XX | XX |  |  |
| Tundra | 5 (11) | 9% | X | XXX |  |  |  | X |
| Conif. For. | 15 (30) | 24% | XXX | XXXXX | XX | XXXXX |  |  |
| Desid. For. | 10 (18) | 14% | X | XX | XX | XXXXX |  |  |
| Rain For. | 7 (19) | 15% | XX | XX | X | XX |  |  |
| Grasslands | 6 (18) | 14% | X | X |  | XX | X | X |
| Deserts | 4 (13) | 10% |  | X |  | XX | X |  |

She might be happy with the test at that point. Or, once again, she may decide to shift some of the items. For instance, since the CC-BC section contrasts the coniferous and deciduous trees, she might change one of the typical BC items about coniferous trees to be an item about plant life in the tundra. She might also increase the level of complexity in the item to move it from comprehension to analysis.

A test blueprint serves not only as a starting point for creating a test, but also as a tool that helps the teacher check to see if indeed the test she has written truly assesses the content as she intended. Sometimes, when writing a test, we *think* that we covered everything, and in the amount that matched the importance of the individual parts. However, when we actually put it on a test blueprint, we may see that some areas are in over-abundance while others have been slighted.

There is no actual requirement for the format of a test blueprint. Thus, I have provided you with several examples as follows:

## Test Blueprints Using Bloom's Taxonomy

### Figures of Speech Unit Test

| Content | Approx. Weight | Bloom's Levels (each X indicates the emphasis of the item) ||||||
|---|---|---|---|---|---|---|---|
| | | Knowledge | Comprehension | Application | Analysis | Synthesis | Evaluation |
| Similes | 25% | X | X | XX | XXXXX | X | |
| Metaphors | 25% | X | XXX | | XXXXX | X | |
| Hyperbole | 20% | | XXX | XX | XX | X | |
| Euphemisms | 10% | | XX | | | X | X |
| Irony | 10% | | XX | X | | X | |
| Personification | 10% | | X | X | | X | X |

### Figures of Speech Unit Test

| Content | Approx # of Items | Bloom's Levels ||||||
|---|---|---|---|---|---|---|---|
| | | Knowledge | Comprehension | Application | Analysis | Synthesis | Evaluation |
| Similes | 15 | | definition | compare with metaphors | | create paragraph using metaphors and similes and at least one of the other four | explain why the usage of the figures used in paragraph either added to it or detracted from it |
| Metaphors | 15 | | definition | compare with similes | | | |
| Hyperbole | 6 | | definition | | find in text | | |
| Euphemisms | 6 | | definition | | find in text | | |
| Irony | 2 | | definition | | find in text | | |
| Personification | 2 | | definition | | find in text | | |

## Test Blueprints Using DOKs

| Content | Level 1 Recall | Level 2 Basic Reasoning | Level 3 Strategic Thinking | Level 4 Extended Thinking | # of Items |
|---|---|---|---|---|---|
| Adding two-digit numbers | tens family | non-regrouped addition | | | 10 |
| Demonstrating regrouping (carrying) | | | showing the regrouped number to work the problem | | 5 |
| Working word problems | | pulling out numbers and solving | | | 5 |
| Creating word problems | | | | creating a word problem, showing strategy for solving | 1 |
| Reading graphs and adding two-digit numbers | | identifying amount and solving | drawing conclusions from the data | | 4 |

Two-Digit Addition

### Test Blueprint Using Straight Content

#### The First Five Presidents

| Content | Personal Characteristics | Basic Policy | Events | Approximate Weight |
|---|---|---|---|---|
| George Washington | Farmer Virginia Soldier | Limited government States' rights | Country's beginnings Constitutional Convention | 25% |
| John Adams | Lawyer Massachusetts Foreign diplomat Wife Abigail | Federalism | Alien and Sedition Acts Died July 4 | 20% |
| Thomas Jefferson | Renaissance Man Widowed Young Monticello Founded University of VA | Key author of Dec. of Ind. Anti-Federalism | Louisiana Purchase Embargo Act Died July 4 | 25% |
| James Madison | Short, serious Jefferson's mentee Virginia Wife Dolly | Father of Constitution Jeffersonian politician | War of 1812 | 15% |
| James Monroe | Lawyer Virginia | Jeffersonian politician | Monroe Doctrine Missouri Compromise | 15% |

The creation of a test blueprint (either before or after) is often an overlooked step in the test creation process. However, it doesn't have to be a long arduous task. It is very simple to create, and would typically cover a single sheet of paper. And, the effort involved pays enormous benefits because it can be very informative to the teacher.

## *FORMATTING THE TEST FOR GOOD FACE VALIDITY*

When formatting a test, it is important for it to appear professional. This is not only because you, as the teacher, never know where the test may end up, but because a professionally-formatted test will actually aid the students in orienting their brains toward being able to show what they know. As we discussed earlier, a test is valid if it tests what it purports to test. Face validity is a part of this. In other words, a test has good face validity if it "looks like" it is testing what it is supposed to be testing and if it appears to be a professional assessment.

Keep in mind that when a student sits down to take a test, there is a certain level of anxiety anyway. If you have done your job well, hopefully, the students will have an appropriate level of heightened awareness (that will allow them to do well) but not an inordinate amount of fear.

A good metaphor to use when talking with students about taking tests involves sports.

---

### IT'S THE GAME!

When a coach first meets with her team, she provides them with guidelines. She tells them about what will happen at practice, what equipment they should bring, etc. And, she announces when the first game with take place.

At the first few practices, the players work on developing individual skills. Then, they practice playing two-against-two or three-against-three in little mini-games. After awhile, a scrimmage is held in which the players divide into two teams and play a pretend partial game.

Watching from the sidelines, a parent will notice that the level of effort put forth by the children increases when a scrimmage is taking place as opposed to little two-on-two drills. And then. . .THE GAME.

The level of effort when the actual game occurs increases exponentially.

As the teacher, if you can help your students understand that the work they do in the classroom prepares them for the summative assessment—the game, if you will—it can reduce the anxiety. A coach tells her players at the beginning of the game, "Now, you can show the other team what you got!"

Likewise, when your students take a test, encourage them:
"Now, you can show what you know!"

Players entering a basketball court on game day would expect certain arrangements to be in place. The score board would be lit up, the benches for the teams set up on the sidelines, the announcers would be at the scoring desk, and there would be referees present.

Students taking a test have similar expectations. The test should have a heading that makes sense to them. The title should be in title case and should be larger than the rest of the test items. Then, the first section should begin with directions. If the entire test includes a single type of item (e.g., multiple choice), it may simply begin with the word *directions*. And, as mentioned previously, the section heading and the directions need to be distinguishable from the items themselves in terms of font size, emphasis, or color.

Sometimes, you may wish to include a place above the title for the name, date, and possibly even for scoring. This is shown in the example below.

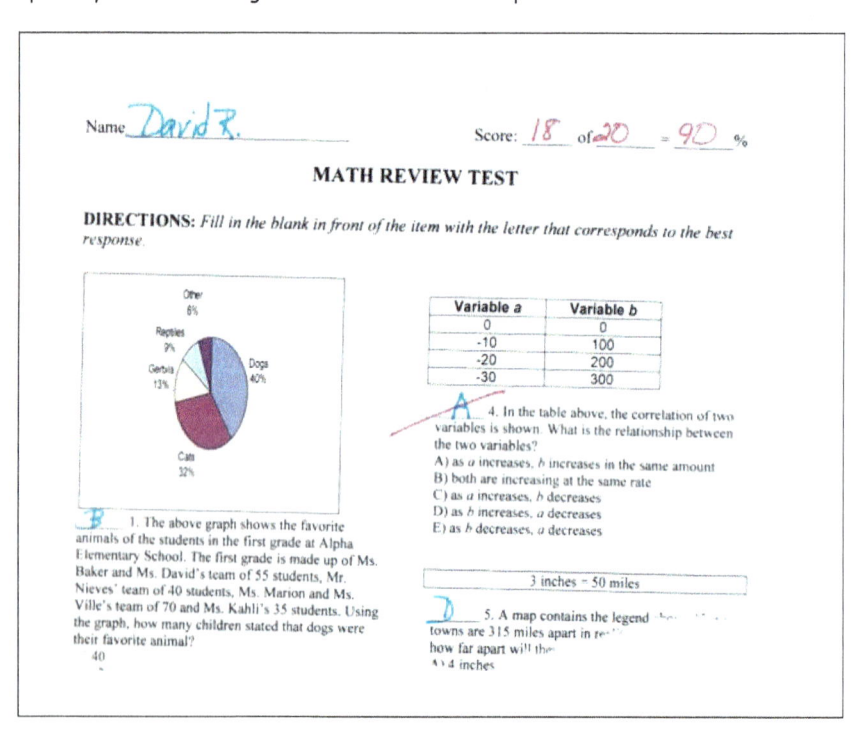

---

Name **David R.**          Score **18** of **20** = **90** %

### MATH REVIEW TEST

**DIRECTIONS:** Fill in the blank in front of the item with the letter that corresponds to the best response.

Pie chart: Other 8%, Reptiles 9%, Gerbils 13%, Dogs 40%, Cats 32%

| Variable a | Variable b |
|---|---|
| 0 | 0 |
| -10 | 100 |
| -20 | 200 |
| -30 | 300 |

**A** 4. In the table above, the correlation of two variables is shown. What is the relationship between the two variables?
A) as $a$ increases, $b$ increases in the same amount
B) both are increasing at the same rate
C) as $a$ increases, $b$ decreases
D) as $b$ increases, $a$ decreases
E) as $b$ decreases, $a$ decreases

**B** 1. The above graph shows the favorite animals of the students in the first grade at Alpha Elementary School. The first grade is made up of Ms. Baker and Ms. David's team of 55 students, Mr. Nieves' team of 40 students, Ms. Marion and Ms. Ville's team of 70 and Ms. Kahli's 35 students. Using the graph, how many children stated that dogs were their favorite animal?
40

3 inches = 50 miles

**D** 5. A map contains the legend ... towns are 315 miles apart in re... how far apart will the...
A) 4 inches

If there is more than one type of item, each section should be named, and there should be directions for each. All items of a single type (e.g., multiple choice, true/false) need to be together in a single block. There should be consistency of formatting throughout the test. And, there should not be extraneous "white space" on the test that would make the student wonder why it was there. In addition, graphics may be included on a test, but only if they relate to the test items. Sometimes, in an effort to evoke student interest, teachers will place a map of the US at the top of a page (or to fill in white space within the test). If it is not related to the test items themselves, it can distract the students.

Another important aspect of face validity involves professional grammar and spelling. Having improper grammar and spelling can distract the student, and thereby, prevent you, the teacher, from getting an accurate assessment of the student in that content.

An example of a well-constructed test can be found on the following pages.

# UNIT TEST: Shakespeare

Name:_____ Date:_____

**Multiple Choice.**
*Answer each question with the <u>BEST POSSIBLE CHOICE</u>. Indicate your answer by writing the capital letter of that option in the blank beside the question.*

_____ 1. In *Romeo and Juliet,* the characters of Tybalt and Benvolio have starkly opposite personalities (Benvolio is calm and reserved; Tybalt is impulsive and excitable). These characters exemplify what dramatic device?
   A. dramatic irony
   B. dramatic foil
   C. dramatic tension
   D. dramatic monologue

_____ 2. When Shakespeare's most famous soliloquy occurs in Act III, scene I of *Hamlet,* what is Hamlet trying to decide?
   A. to go to war or pursue peace
   B. to marry Ophelia or remain single
   C. to kill himself or continue living
   D. to become king or remain a prince

_____ 3. Shakespeare's sonnets were written using what poetic structure(s)?
   A. three quatrains
   B. one couplet
   C. iambic pentameter
   D. all of the above

_____ 4. What three categories can Shakespeare's plays generally be divided into?
   A. comedy, tragedy, or history
   B. instructive, entertaining, or poetic
   C. autobiography, fiction, or social commentary
   D. romance, adventure, or legend

**True/False.**
*Read each statement carefully to determine if the statement is true or false. Clearly write TRUE if the statement is true or FALSE if the statement is false in the blank beside the number.*

_____ 5. The first play Shakespeare wrote was *Romeo and Juliet*.

_____ 6. Shakespeare is credited with coining many popular English words and phrases.

_____ 7. Much of Shakespeare's work was first performed in the 18$^{th}$ Century.

_____ 8. All of Shakespeare's plays were divided into five acts.

**Which Play?**
*Circle the title of the play which each statement BEST describes.*

**9.** Some of the central characters of this play are Viola, Duke Orsino, Sebastian, and Malvolio.

    *Macbeth*        *Twelfth Night*

**10.** This play is considered a dramatic tragedy: many of the main characters die or suffer greatly in the course of the story.

    *Macbeth*        *Twelfth Night*

**11.** The event that sets the plot of this play into motion involves a prophecy revealed by three witches.

    *Macbeth*        *Twelfth Night*

**12.** This play uses cross-dressing to focus on gender roles and sexuality.

    *Macbeth*        *Twelfth Night*

**Short Answer.**
*Respond to the following prompt with 3-4 sentences. Grammar and spelling will be graded.*

**13.** Identify the Shakespearean character that you think is the most compelling. Explain why you chose that character.

(This test was adapted from one created by my students in my *Assessment in Education* course at Eastern Kentucky University, who gave me permission to use it as an example.)

## ORGANIZING AND ORDERING ITEMS

The most important thing to remember when organizing a test is that you don't want it to distract. The test itself is simply a vehicle by which you will be able to determine if the students have learned the information. You want it to be professional, sensible, and straightforward. That way, the students can concentrate on responding to the items rather than trying to figure out what they are supposed to do.

As previously mentioned, keep all items of a like type together in a group on a test. In addition, typically, you begin the test with the selected-response items, followed later by constructed-response items. If you include essay items, usually they are the final items on a test.

The types of items you have on a test are dictated by the content of the test, as well as by the testing situation. Also, a teacher has to be realistic about the amount of time she has to grade. For instance, a high school history teacher, who may have had some amazing discussions in class about the Industrial Revolution and how it changed America might want to have an essay exam in which each student answers ten essay items about the main concepts. However, if she has 125 students, that would take hours and hours and hours to grade. So, instead she would probably create a test that included several selected-response items because an important part of assessment involves providing students with feedback in a timely manner.

When ordering the items on a test, a good rule of thumb is to start with an item or two that are on the easier side. There is an unwritten agreement between teachers and students that certain concepts, considered basic information, will be on the test. For instance, if a history class had just studied a unit on the American Civil War, the students would expect that there would be a question on the test about who was president during that time (Abraham Lincoln). Putting those basic information items toward the beginning of the test can help students begin the test with confidence. Examples of basic information type items that you might put on the first page of the test include definitions, key figures, or a basic concept that has been reiterated throughout the learning experience.

On the other hand, if the hardest item on the test comes at the beginning, a student may suddenly doubt her knowledge of the topic. Even though she may actually know many of the answers for the other items on the test, she may not do as well on the test as she would have had the first item not been a very difficult one.

## BASIC CONCEPTS IN CHAPTER 9

A) A test blueprint is used by a teacher to create a test that directly correlates with the information that has been covered in the unit.

B) Test blueprints take on a variety of formats.

C) A table of specifications is a special type of test blueprint that includes not only the material being covered, the amount of coverage for each concept, and the cognitive level being used to assess it.

D) The most important aspect when organizing a test is that it should not distract.

E) When organizing items on a test, all items of a single type should be in a single section with the section identified and directions that are distinguishable from the items.

F) Typically, selected-response items precede the constructed-response items on the test.

G) Place basic information items at the beginning of the test; do not start with a very difficult item.

NOTES:

# CHAPTER 10

# *You Mean I Should Let The Students Know How I'm Going to Grade This?*

**Rubrics and Scoring Guides**

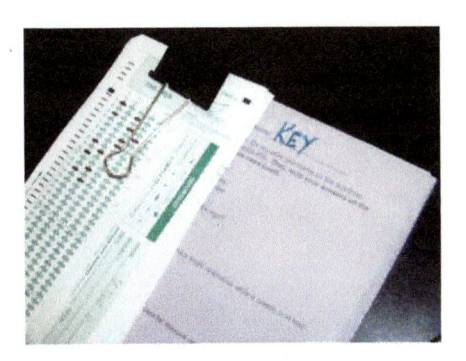

**KEY CONCEPTS:**
Holistic vs. Analytic Rubrics
Generic vs. Specific Rubrics
Grading Essay Items with Rubrics
Grading Performance Assessments with Rubrics
Peer Grading with Rubrics
Using Technology to Generate Rubrics

*If only I'd known then
what I know now...*
--Anonymous

When grading a product (or an answer to an essay item on a test), you as a teacher will often create a rubric. A rubric is simply a scoring guide.

> **THE NOT-SO-GOOD 'OLE DAYS**
>
> When I was a student and I would receive a graded paper back, I would often find that I had had a few points deducted because I hadn't included something in the paper that the teacher evidently expected. Rubrics were not widely used back then, and even when they were used, they were not provided to students in advance. So basically, you learned what the teacher wanted either by hearing it verbally from her, or by leaving it out and receiving points off.
>
> In 21st-Century classrooms, teachers often provide students with rubrics at the same time they provide them with the assignment. Sometimes, they are not written in rubric form *per se*, but students do receive written instructions with specifics that are then graded by the teacher using a rubric (that aligns perfectly with the information provided to the students).

A rubric itself, no matter what the type, must contain two things:

A) the criteria
B) levels

The **criteria** are the aspects of the product, answer, etc. that are expected. The **levels** are typically point values, but sometimes are described using such words as *poor, fair, good*, etc.

Rubrics can be used for a variety of grading in the classroom. They can be used to grade essay items on a test. They can be used to grade writing prompts for journal entries or lab write-ups in a science class. They can be used to grade performances, presentations, or speeches. They can be used to grade products. And, they can be used to grade portfolios.

## HOLISTIC VS. ANALYTIC RUBRICS

There are various ways to classify rubrics, but most people agree that there are basically two *general* types of rubrics: holistic and analytic. Holistic rubrics look at the product (performance, answer, etc.) as a whole while analytic rubrics look at the specific criteria expected. In addition, these two types of rubrics can further be classified as generic or specific. A generic rubric contains vague language that allows it to be used to grade a variety of products. A specific rubric is created to grade the individual product (performance, answer, etc.) and contains language specific to it.

A good way to think about these classifications is:

> Holistic
>     Generic
>     Specific
> Analytic
>     Generic (used rarely)
>     Specific

*Holistic rubrics.* A holistic rubric has bands of achievement listed on it. Using it, you look at the product (or answer on an essay item) as a whole. Then, you determine which of the bands is closest to describing it. An example of a holistic rubric is:

| | |
|---|---|
| 10 | The response is thorough, clear, and contains excellent grammar and spelling. |
| 8 | The response mostly answers the question, is mostly clear, and contains good grammar and spelling. |
| 6 | The response somewhat answers the question, lacks some clarity, and contains some grammar and spelling errors. |
| 4 | The response is incomplete, lacks clarity, and is poorly written. |

This holistic rubric is considered a *generic* rubric because it could be used for basically any prompt. For instance, it could be used to grade any of the following items on a test:

| Literature test: | Science test: | Government test: |
|---|---|---|
| 16. Why did the wedding planner get upset and did the father of the bride think her actions were justified? Explain. | 20. Explain the process of photosynthesis including the parts involved as well as the steps. | 31. State three examples that demonstrate the concept of checks and balances in the federal government. |

A specific holistic rubric is one that again contains bands, but the language on it is specific to the item being graded. For instance, a specific holistic rubric that would be used to grade the item on the literature test above would be:

| | |
|---|---|
| 10 | The answer fully explains that the wedding planner was upset because she was lied to as well as the fact that the father did not think her actions were justified. |
| 8 | The answer included some information about the wedding planner being upset about being lied to and the father not thinking the actions were justified. |
| 6 | The answer included either the fact that the wedding planner was upset about being lied to or the father not thinking the actions were justified, but not both. |
| 4 | The answer did not include either the reason for the wedding planner being upset or the father thinking she was not justified for her actions. |

In this rubric, the teacher would still be grading by looking at the item as a whole, and determining which band most clearly describes the answer shown, but the rubric itself is specific to the item as written.

*Analytic rubrics.* An analytic rubric includes various criteria with point values for each individual criterion. Let's consider the three items again:

| Literature test: | Science test: | Government test: |
|---|---|---|
| 16. Why did the wedding planner get upset and did the father of the bride think her actions were justified? Explain. | 20. Explain the process of photosynthesis including the parts involved as well as the steps. | 31. State three examples that demonstrate the concept of checks and balances in the federal government. |

Typically, an analytic rubric is specific in nature. For instance, to grade the first item, an analytic rubric might be:

| | | |
|---|---|---|
| Rationale for the wedding planner being upset | Didn't like being lied to | 3 |
| | Explains clearly | 2 |
| Father's feelings | Didn't think it was justified | 1 |
| | Explains that the ends (getting the site they wanted) justified the means | 3 |
| Grammar and spelling | | 1 |
| TOTAL | | 10 |

A generic analytic rubric (which is used rarely) that could be used for the above item would be:

| | | |
|---|---|---|
| Full explanation provided | Part 1 | 3 |
| | Part 2 | 3 |
| Accuracy | Part 1 | 1 |
| | Part 2 | 1 |
| Clarity of expression | Part 1 | 1 |
| | Part 2 | 1 |
| TOTAL | | 10 |

Do note that if you as the teacher are going to use an analytic rubric, it makes more sense to use a specific one. It will allow you to provide more feedback to the student. However, there are lots of generic rubrics, both of the holistic and the analytic types, that are available to you. And, keeping a notebook of ones that are useful to you will prove to be an excellent resource. Thus, I highly suggest it. After writing your test items, you may refer to your generic holistic rubrics and find one that perfectly fits. You may even find a generic analytic rubric that fits. In the second case, I'd suggest that you adapt the generic analytic one to fit the item as written. For instance, using the generic analytic rubric above to grade the literature question, you might adapt it to be a specific analytic rubric as follows:

| Full explanation provided | Planner's reaction | 3 |
|---|---|---|
|  | Father's thinking | 3 |
| Accuracy | Planner's reaction | 1 |
|  | Father's thinking | 1 |
| Clarity of expression | Planner's reaction | 1 |
|  | Father's thinking | 1 |
| **TOTAL** |  | **10** |

## USING RUBRICS TO GRADE ESSAY ITEMS

Above, we considered the different types of rubrics, and the examples were for grading essay items or writing prompts. Now, let's consider how you would actually do the grading using a rubric. An essay item that you might have on a social studies test would be:

> 17. President Andrew Johnson was impeached. Explain what is meant by the word impeached. Then, discuss why Andrew Johnson was impeached, the outcome of the impeachment, and the reason for the outcome. (10 points)

You could grade this item holistically, but without a rubric. In other words, by simply looking at the prompt, and then the student's response, you could determine how many of the 10 points you would award the student. To grade without a rubric, you need to determine what it is that you are ultimately trying to assess. In this prompt, the teacher wants to know if the student knows about Andrew Johnson's impeachment.

Keep in mind that a teacher *is grading* with a rubric when she's grading essay items, even if the rubric is only in her head. In the above prompt, she'd probably be thinking that she wants the student to state that impeachment means bringing charges to remove someone from office, that Johnson was impeached because he was interfering with reconstruction efforts, and that ultimately he was not removed

> **FROM THE PRINCIPAL'S DESK**
>
> When teachers develop grading criteria and communicate those criteria to their students through rubrics or other means it helps the teacher in several ways. A good, easy to use, rubric can save time in the grading process, and make grading more consistent which your students will see as more fair. Grading criteria also communicate your expectations to your students when they are shared in advance, as a part of formative assessment. Grading criteria help teachers decide how to teach and they help students understand how their work is graded.

from office when he agreed to stop doing that. Those individual criteria are what the teacher is grading for, even if she does not write out the rubric.

By actually writing down the rubric, possibly on an extra copy of the test that you as the teacher are making into the key, it will encourage more consistency in grading. Then, if students question why they received the points they did, you would be able to provide them with feedback that is clear and consistent. Do remember that students talk to one another. And, one of the things that students indicate they dislike the most is unfairness. A written out rubric, with clear delineation of the criteria that matches the prompt as written will assist you in grading fairly and providing consistent feedback to the students.

The rubrics veteran teachers create for items on a test are often simply jotted down in the space where the students write their answers on the key. However, novice teachers may make the mistake of not writing the rubrics out because it takes time. Eventually, it will come as second nature to you, but in the beginning it may feel like a bit of a task, and you may be tempted to skip over doing it. I encourage you not to do that as it will pay off in the consistency of your grading, and the ease with which you are able to provide feedback to the students. And, before long, you will find yourself being able to easily jot down the rubric for grading.

Most teachers find that there are three major advantages to having written rubrics. They are:

    A) they allow you to grade more quickly and efficiently
    B) they allow you to be more consistent in your grading
    C) they allow you to provide more consistent and detailed feedback to your students (especially when they ask questions about their grades)

On the next page, we have a holistic rubric and an analytic rubric that could be used to grade the prompt about Johnson's impeachment.

| HOLISTIC SPECIFIC RUBRIC ||
|---|---|
| 10 | The response includes a good accurate definition of impeachment, states that Johnson was impeached for the blocking reconstruction efforts, but that he was not removed from office because he ultimately agreed to no longer block the reconstruction efforts. The answer contains clarity of expression and excellent grammar and spelling. |
| 8 | The response includes an accurate definition of impeachment, mentions reconstruction, and discusses some aspects of the outcome. The answer contained some clarity. There were some grammar and spelling errors. |
| 6 | The response includes some, but not all, of the following three: a definition of impeachment, information about why Johnson was impeached, that he was not removed from office, and he agreed not to block reconstruction. The answer lacked some clarity. There were several grammar and spelling errors. |
| 4 | The response includes a brief response to some of the following: a definition of impeachment, information about why Johnson was impeached, the outcome, and the reason. The answer lacked clarity and contained poor grammar and spelling. |
| 2 | The response lacked clarity and did not address most parts of the prompt. |
| 0 | The response was missing or unreadable. |

| ANALYTIC SPECIFIC RUBRIC |||
|---|---|---|
| Definition of impeachment (bringing charges to remove someone from office) | Accurate | 2 |
| | Thorough | 1 |
| Reason for impeachment | Blocking reconstruction efforts | 2 |
| Outcome and rationale | Not removed from office | 2 |
| | Agreed to stop blocking efforts | 1 |
| Clarity of expression || 1 |
| Grammar/spelling || 1 |
| **TOTAL** || **10** |

Using the rubrics on the previous page, consider how you would grade the following student's response:

> *17. President Andrew Johnson was impeached. Explain what is meant by the word impeached. Then, discuss why Andrew Johnson was impeached, the outcome of the impeachment, and the reason for the outcome.*
>
> Impeachment means that charges are brought against an office holder indicating that he should be removed from office because he is not living up to his responsibility. President Johnson was impeached by Congress because he was blocking their attempts at Reconstruction of the country after the Civil War. In the trial, he agreed that he would stop blocking them so he was found not guilty and not removed from office.

Using either the holistic rubric or the analytic one, the student's response would probably be awarded 10 points.

Now, let's consider another response:

> 17. President Andrew Johnson was impeached. Explain what is meant by the word impeached. Then, discuss why Andrew Johnson was impeached, the outcome of the impeachment, and the reason for the outcome.
>
> Johnson was impeached by Congress. Because he didn't do what Congress want him to do. So they brought charges to remove him from office. They didn't get it done though because he said he wasn't doing that.

Looking at the holistic rubric, we can see that he would be awarded 6 points based on the parts that are highlighted below:

| | |
|---|---|
| 10 | The response includes a good accurate definition of impeachment, states that Johnson was impeached for the blocking reconstruction efforts, but that he was not removed from office because he ultimately agreed to no longer block the reconstruction efforts. The answer contains clarity of expression and excellent grammar and spelling. |
| 8 | The response includes an accurate definition of impeachment, mentions reconstruction, and discusses some aspects of the outcome. The answer contained some clarity. There were some grammar and spelling errors. |
| 6 | The response includes some, but not all, of the following three: a definition of impeachment, information about why Johnson was impeached, that he was not removed from office, and he agreed not to block reconstruction. The answer lacked some clarity. There were several grammar and spelling errors. |
| 4 | The response includes a brief response to some of the following: a definition of impeachment, information about why Johnson was impeached, the outcome, and the reason. The answer lacked clarity and contained poor grammar and spelling. |
| 2 | The response lacked clarity and did not address most parts of the prompt. |
| 0 | The response was missing or unreadable. |

Using the analytic rubric, he would be graded as:

| | | | |
|---|---|---|---|
| Definition of impeachment (bringing charges to remove someone from office) | Accurate | 2 | 1 |
| | Thorough | 1 | 0 |
| Reason for impeachment | Blocking reconstruction efforts | 2 | 1 |
| Outcome and rationale | Not removed from office | 2 | 2 |
| | Agreed to stop blocking efforts | 1 | 0 |
| Clarity of expression | | 1 | 1 |
| Grammar/spelling | | 1 | 0 |
| **TOTAL** | | **10** | **5** |

188

He did indicate that impeachment was removing someone from office, even though he didn't directly state that as the definition. Therefore, he could receive the points for his definition being somewhat accurate, but definitely not thorough. He also somewhat referred to the reason for impeachment, and he provided the outcome (that he was not removed from office). However, his reason for the outcome was not accurate. There were some grammar errors as well.

Using the holistic one, he received a 6, but using the analytic one, he received a 5. With a holistic rubric, the teacher is simply determining which of the bands *most closely* describes the answer. Typically, a teacher will <u>not</u> grade between the bands. Thus, she would award the student either a 10, an 8, a 6, a 4, a 2, or a 0. She would not award him a 5, for instance.

Sometimes, a student's response will not clearly fit one band. For instance, if a student answered all parts of the item but had poor grammar and spelling, typically, you would not award him the full points (the top band). Remember, with a holistic rubric, you are looking at the answer as a whole. Even though the bands will include descriptions of the criteria expected to guide you, the band you choose will be based on which description *most closely* describes the answer.

Do keep in mind that holistic rubrics allow for more rapid grading and is often used by teachers (or groups of teachers) when they need to grade a large number of items in a short time. For instance, if there is an on-demand writing experience that all fourth graders take three times a year, and the teachers grade them as a group during a two-hour period, most likely they will grade them using a holistic rubric. So, that is an advantage of a holistic rubric.

On the other hand, an advantage of an analytic rubric is that it can provide the student (and the teacher) with very specific feedback about the graded item. Over time, if a teacher (or a student) consistently loses points for grammar/spelling, or for failing to include a key piece of information, the analytic rubrics could be used to direct the student to work on improving his grammar/spelling or on his following the directions.

## USING RUBRICS TO GRADE PERFORMANCE ASSESSMENTS

A very common usage of rubrics is for grading performance assessments. Remember, performance assessments assess how well the student performs, but the performance may or may not take place in front of the teacher.

### Various formats

Rubrics can take on many formats. If an analytic rubric has four criteria, and all are of equal value, a 4X4 grid may be created. One for a speech is shown below.

**4X4 GRID WITH EACH CRITERIA WORTH THE SAME AMOUNT**

|  | 1 | 2 | 3 | 4 |
|---|---|---|---|---|
| Content | The content was unclear and contained inaccurate information. | The content lacked some clarity or contained some inaccuracies. | The content was somewhat clear and mostly accurate. | The content was clear and accurate. |
| Emphasis of Main Points | It was unclear what the main points were. | The main points were somewhat mentioned. | The main points were stated. | The main points were emphasized and repeated. |
| Topic Choice | The topic did not interest the audience. | The topic somewhat interested the audience. | The topic mostly interested the audience. | The topic kept the audience's attention. |
| Connection with Audience | The speaker did not connect with the audience. | A little eye contact was made with the audience and an attempt to connect with the audience occurred a few times. | Some eye contact was made with the audience and some connection with them was shown. | Eye contact was appropriate and the speaker showed interest in the audience while speaking. |

If there are three equal criteria, and there are three levels the teacher wants to assess, a 3X3 grid might be used for a presentation like the one below:

**3X3 GRID (All Criteria Equal)**

|  | Needs Improvement | Satisfactory | Excellent |
|---|---|---|---|
| Speech |  |  |  |
| Power Point |  |  |  |
| Handout |  |  |  |

Obviously, you can have grids of other types as well. You could have a 3X4 or a 4X5, or even a 10X3 (meaning ten criteria, with three levels for each). Sometimes the grids are filled in with words indicating what each level would look like (like the 4X4 example above), but sometimes they are not (like the 3X3 example shown).

Another format you may encounter involves horizontal holistic rubrics. While most holistic rubrics are written vertically, with the highest level at the top, they can also be written horizontally. Let's consider that you have the following essay item on a literature test:

> 22. In *The Mystery of the Purple Notes*, Rosie told Ethan there were two good reasons for telling "white lies". Name them. Then, give three examples of white lies they told.

A specific holistic rubric by which that item might be graded is shown below:

### HORIZONTAL HOLISTIC RUBRIC

| 2 | 4 | 6 | 8 |
|---|---|---|---|
| The response did not include accurate reasons or accurate examples. | The response included either one accurate reason or one accurate example, but not both. | The response included at least one accurate reason and at least one accurate example. | The response included two accurate reasons and three accurate examples. |

You can even combine types of rubrics to fit what you are trying to grade. If there are four criteria with equal values, and then you want to give an overall grade for another aspect, you might use the following format.

### MIXED FORMAT RUBRIC

| Content | Poor<br>1 | Fair<br>2 | Good<br>3 | Excellent<br>4 |
|---|---|---|---|---|
| Intro | | | | |
| Thesis Topic | | | | |
| Support | | | | |
| Conclusion | | | | |
| **Overall Presentation** ||||| 
| 10 | Professionally organized; excellent connection with audience; smooth transitions ||||
| 8 | Good organization; good connection with audience; good transitions ||||
| 6 | Somewhat organized; some connection with audience; some transitions ||||
| 4 | Fair organization; occasional connection with audience; awkward or few transitions ||||
| 2 | Unorganized; little connection with audience; no transitions ||||
| **TOTAL** | Content _____ / 16  +  Presentation _____ / 10  =  _____ / 26 ||||

A teacher would put Xs in the appropriate column for each of the content areas in the top part of the rubric, and then circle the number for the overall presentation. Those numbers would be added together and placed in the bottom box.

### USING TECHNOLOGY TO CREATE RUBRICS

There are rubric generators available on the Internet. Rather than endorse any particular site, I'm simply going to suggest that you type "rubric generator" into a search engine. You will find numerous sites that will allow you to put in the title of your project and the criteria. It will then "generate" a rubric for you to use.

Many of the rubric generators are quite useful, but it is important that you as the teacher do some serious thinking about the criteria and the points involved for each before inputting those. A rubric generator will organize the information into a usable format, but it is the information that you put in that will make the rubric valid to use for grading or not.

### PEER GRADING WITH RUBRICS

Sometimes, teachers will have the peers in the class grade a student's performance or product. The rationale for doing this is that the students will more pay attention during the presentation, speech, etc. (and learn the information) if they are grading it. In addition, they get the experience of critically thinking about the criteria by which the performance or product is being graded as well as varying levels of examples.

If you are going to have students peer grade using a rubric, it is very important that you go over the criteria with the students and explain what each level represents. However, a good teacher would have done that anyway when she first assigned the project.

## BASIC CONCEPTS IN CHAPTER 10

A) In 21st-Century classrooms, it is important to provide students with the teacher's expectations.

B) Rubrics are scoring guides containing the criteria by which something will be graded and the point values that each criterion will be worth.

C) Rubrics can assist teachers in being more efficient in their grading, being more consistent in their grading, and in providing better feedback to students.

C) The two general types of rubrics can be classified as holistic and analytic.

D) The chief advantage of a holistic rubric is that items can be graded more quickly using it.

E) The chief advantage of an analytic rubric is that it can provide more detailed feedback.

F) Rubrics can be created using a variety of formats

NOTES:

# CHAPTER 11

## *You Mean It's Not All About Tests?*
**Performance Assessments**

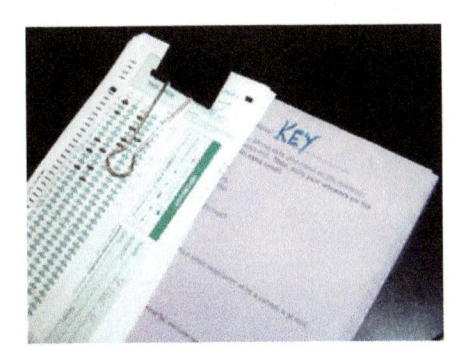

**KEY CONCEPTS:**
Definition of a Performance
Role of Ambiguity in Creativity
Performance Assessment Rubrics
The Importance of Modeling
The Importance of Engagement

*Education is not the filling of a pail,*
*but the lighting of a fire.*
--W. B. Yeats

What is a *performance assessment*? A performance, by definition, involves an action or a behavior, and it is often done in front of other people. The most typical actions one thinks of when discussing performances are singing, dancing, playing music, or acting *on a stage*. And certainly, those performances are often assessed (by critics, the audience, or financial backers).

While those assessments could indeed take place in a school setting, in a drama, dance, or music class, performances in a classroom do not typically take place *on a stage*. Sometimes, they take place in front of the classroom (in what one might consider to be a make-shift stage). Other times, they take place in a gymnasium (as in the case of a student running a 50-yard dash). Still other times, they might take place on a computer (where students might demonstrate their ability to navigate within a software program).

At one time, in order for something to be considered a performance assessment, it meant that the students actually performed in front of the teacher and the teacher assessed them as they were doing the performance, as in the examples above. Thus, performance assessments were usually limited to students:

      a) giving presentations or speeches
      b) performing on stage
      c) demonstrating a process (like doing an experiment), or
      d) exhibiting a skill (like doing a back flip)

However, with increased resources available to students and teachers, a performance assessment has come to include not only the above items, but also *products* created by a student. The thinking is that the student did indeed perform a certain action in the creation of the product and the product can be judged to determine if the student was able to perform the action. In addition, sometimes performances that in previous years would have taken place in person are now converted into a performance product (e.g., a DVD of student's speech or a narrated PowerPoint) that is graded asynchronously.

In order for a performance assessment to take place, an assignment has to be provided and students have to be allowed time to prepare for the performance (whether it will take place in front of the teacher or at home or in a work station, as in the case of creating a product). The instructions provided to the students are usually presented in writing, and usually in the form of a handout to which they can refer while they are preparing to perform. Often the assignment will include criteria that is required but in the context of student choice. For instance, students may be required to write a book report including delineated components, but each student gets to choose the book over which the report is done.

## *THE ROLE OF AMBIGUITY IN CREATIVITY*

Creativity has been found to be positively correlated with ambiguity (Tegano, 1990; Sternberg & Lubart, 1995; Urban, 2003). In other words, the more *ambiguous*, meaning less prescriptive, the assignment, the more creativity the students are likely to show. Conversely, the more prescriptive an assignment is (a detailed delineation of what is expected) the less creativity that will be expressed. Still, if student choice is allowed (thereby creating more ambiguity in what the teacher will receive), again the creativity can increase. This concept needs to be considered when a teacher is creating a performance assignment.

The amount of creativity desired by the teacher will of course be dictated by her objectives. If the performance assessment is simply for the purpose of the student demonstrating certain facts or knowledge, creativity may be less important. On the other hand, if the teacher wants the students to extend what they have learned and apply it in a different setting, obviously, creativity will be at the forefront.

Consider the following assignment:

| | |
|---|---|
| *UNAMBIGUOUS ASSIGNMENT* | Choose one of the 20$^{th}$-Century U.S. Presidents. Create a poster that includes a visual of the man, the dates of his term(s), and six highlights of his Presidency. |

The teacher giving that assignment was very prescriptive, and thus, she will know exactly what she expects to see. She of course will not know which of the Presidents the student will choose nor possibly the exact six highlights related to that President, but for the most part, the posters she receives to grade will be similar in nature. This is certainly a fine example of a performance assessment, especially if her objective is for the students to demonstrate their familiarity with the 20th-Century Presidents and the events associated with their terms.

However, if a teacher has an objective that the students will take their knowledge of the 20th-Century Presidents and expand upon it, her assignment might be more ambiguous:

| AMBIGUOUS ASSIGNMENT | Choose one of the 20th-Century U.S. Presidents and create a poster related to his term and how it affected the century. |
|---|---|

The teacher giving that assignment will receive a variety of posters with varying degrees of detail on many different topics. But, if the teacher's objective is for students to not only have familiarity with the Presidents but also to recognize the role his Presidency played in the century, then this ambiguous assignment might be better for assessing that. However, with an ambiguous assignment, a student may technically fulfill the assignment without really fully meeting the objective. For instance, if a student created a poster for Woodrow Wilson in which he used nice large lettering to write the word LEAGUE OF NATIONS and then has cut-outs of the original member nations as well as a cut-out of the U.S. with a big X through it (indicating he knew that while it was the brainchild of President Wilson, the U.S. did not join it), some teachers would consider the assignment fulfilled while others might not.

A more prescriptive assignment, but one that still allows for more creativity than the first assignment, might be:

| SOMEWHAT AMBIGUOUS ASSIGNMENT | Choose one of the 20th-Century U.S. Presidents and create a poster that <u>states</u> the *most important work* of that President as well as the *effect that work had on* the century. In addition, <u>illustrate</u> the work and its effect. |
|---|---|

No matter the amount of creativity the teacher wants to encourage, there still needs to be at least some guidelines describing what the teacher expects. Without those, many students will feel uneasy about doing the assignment. Students often try to lessen the ambiguity by asking the teacher for more specifics. Also, to make sure a student fulfills the objective, a teacher can require the student to have his/her ideas for the project pre-approved. Thus, when the student who created the League of Nations poster described it to the teacher, she could have instructed him that his idea partially fulfilled the assignment, but that further effects of the League of Nations needed to be explained or illustrated.

## PERFORMANCE ASSESSMENT RUBRICS

In addition to providing the students with the assignment, the teacher will often also provide them with the rubric by which it will be graded at the same time. Performance assessments can be graded using either analytic or holistic rubrics, and the rubrics can be specific or generic in nature.

*Analytic rubrics* indicate the various criteria over which the student's performance or product will be assessed and the point values that will be awarded to each. Analytic rubrics allow the teacher to determine what he considers to be important in the assignment, and through the designation of varying number of points to the individual criteria, the relative importance of each criterion to the others. For instance, if a speech teacher awards three points each for eye contact, fluency of speech, and appropriate gestures, but 18 points for the content of the speech, he is indicating that the words being spoken are twice as important as the speaking aspects. Another speech teacher might reverse those point values.

Analytic rubrics can be *specific* or *generic*. The example described above is a generic rubric that could be used by a teacher for a variety of speeches. In contrast, *specific* analytic rubrics include the exact criteria required for a particular assignment. If the speech teacher wanted to create a specific analytic rubric for a persuasive speech, he might include the speaking aspects of eye contact, fluency of speech, and appropriate gestures, but would probably include further delineation of the inclusion of a thesis statement, explanation of why the audience should care, suggested solution, evidence, and summary. This very specific rubric would not work for informative, demonstrative, or entertainment speeches, whereas the generic one would.

Holistic rubrics are used to grade the work as a whole. Typically, they include bands of achievement with generalized criteria described for each band. (Rubrics are explained in more detail in Chapter 10.) A generic holistic rubric for a speech class might include:

| | | |
|---|---|---|
| GENERIC HOLISTIC RUBRIC | 12 | Speech was excellent in organization, clarity of purpose, and delivery. |
| | 9 | Speech was appropriately organized, met the purpose, and delivered well. |
| | 6 | Speech was somewhat organized, met the purpose, and was delivered somewhat well. |
| | 3 | Speech lacked good organization, only minimally met the purpose, and was delivered poorly. |

Holistic rubrics can also be specific in nature. In that case, the specifics of the assignment are included in the various bands.

As we consider which type of rubric to use, let's consider the unambiguous assignment that stated:

| UNAMBIGUOUS ASSIGNMENT | Choose one of the 20$^{th}$-Century U.S. Presidents. Create a poster that includes a visual of the man, the dates of his term(s), and six highlights of his Presidency. |
|---|---|

For this assignment, a teacher might choose to use *analytic rubrics* for her grading. Two possibilities are shown below.

| | Criteria | Specifics | Pts. |
|---|---|---|---|
| SPECIFIC ANALYTIC RUBRIC | Choice of President | Name | 2 |
| | | Picture | 3 |
| | Dates of His Term | Included | 1 |
| | | Accurate | 2 |
| | Highlights of Presidency | Six are provided | 6 |
| | | Occurred in his term(s) | 6 |
| | | Accuracy of the events | 6 |
| | | Events were actually important | 3 |
| | Quality of the Poster | Neatness | 2 |
| | | Appropriate grammar/spelling and citations (if needed) | 2 |
| | | Aesthetic appeal | 3 |
| | **TOTAL** | | **36** |

| | Criteria | Pts. |
|---|---|---|
| GENERIC ANALYTIC RUBRIC | Appropriate Project Choice | 5 |
| | Components Included | 24 |
| | Visual Aspects | 5 |
| | Project Quality | 6 |
| | **TOTAL** | **40** |

However, the assignment could be also be graded with *holistic rubrics.*

| | | |
|---|---|---|
| **SPECIFIC HOLISTIC RUBRIC** | 25 | The poster is neat and the student's choice of President is illustrated with a visual. The term dates are accurate, and six actual highlights are accurately described or illustrated. |
| | 20 | The poster is neat and the student's choice of President is illustrated with a visual. The term dates are accurate, and most of the highlights are actual highlights and accurately described or illustrated. |
| | 15 | The poster is somewhat neat and the student's choice of President is identified. Either the term dates or some of the highlights are inappropriate or inaccurate or missing. |
| | 10 | The poster is somewhat messy and the student's choice of President is identified. The term dates may be wrong or missing. Most of the highlights are inappropriate or inaccurate or missing. |
| | 5 | The poster is messy. The name of the President, the visual, and/or the dates are missing. Most of the highlights are inappropriate or inaccurate or missing. |

| | | |
|---|---|---|
| **GENERIC HOLISTIC RUBRIC** | 25 | The project is aesthetically pleasing and includes all the required components. All aspects of the project are accurate. |
| | 20 | The project is somewhat aesthetically pleasing and includes most of the required components. Most aspects of the project are accurate. |
| | 15 | The project is somewhat aesthetically pleasing and includes most of the required components. Some aspects of the project are inaccurate. |
| | 10 | The project is only minimally aesthetically pleasing and one or more of the required components are missing. Some inaccuracies are present. |
| | 5 | The project is not aesthetically pleasing and only minimally meets the requirements. |

The points awarded for the assignment of course would be related to the teacher's decision about the importance of the assignment within her curriculum and grading scheme.

A more ambiguous assignment could also be graded with the various types of rubrics.

| AMBIGUOUS ASSIGNMENT | Choose one of the 20th-Century U.S. Presidents and create a poster related to his term and how it affected the century. |

For this assignment, the teacher could again use *analytic rubrics*. Because of the content, the specific one would probably include few specifics.

| SPECIFIC ANALYTIC RUBRIC | Criteria | Pts. |
|---|---|---|
| | Choice of President | 4 |
| | Includes Information Related to His Term | 10 |
| | Includes Effects of His Presidency | 8 |
| | Quality of the Poster | 6 |
| | TOTAL | 28 |

| GENERIC ANALYTIC RUBRIC | Criteria | Pts. |
|---|---|---|
| | Appropriate Project Choice | 5 |
| | Content Fulfills the Assignment | 15 |
| | Visual Aspects | 3 |
| | Project Quality | 7 |
| | TOTAL | 30 |

Likewise, it could be also be graded with *holistic rubrics*. And, because of the ambiguity of the assignment, these are more likely to be used.

| SPECIFIC HOLISTIC RUBRIC | 40 | The poster is neat and the student's choice of President evident and he was a 20th-Century President. The aspects of his term and its effect are accurately described or illustrated. |
|---|---|---|
| | 30 | The poster is neat and the student's choice of President evident and he was a 20th-Century President. The aspects of his term and its effect are included but are either not clear or contain inaccuracies. |
| | 20 | The poster is somewhat neat. The choice of President may or may not be accurate. The aspects of the term and its effects are either inaccurate or missing. |
| | 10 | The poster is not neat. There are inaccuracies in the Presidential choice, the term, and/or its effects. |

| GENERIC HOLISTIC RUBRIC | 25 | The project is aesthetically pleasing and includes all the required components. All aspects of the project are accurate. |
|---|---|---|
| | 20 | The project is somewhat aesthetically pleasing and includes most of the required components. Most aspects of the project are accurate. |
| | 15 | The project is somewhat aesthetically pleasing and includes most of the required components. Some aspects of the project are inaccurate. |
| | 10 | The project is only minimally aesthetically pleasing and one or more of the required components are missing. Some inaccuracies are present. |
| | 5 | The project is not aesthetically pleasing and only minimally meets the requirements. |

You will note that the *generic* rubrics are very similar or exactly the same as the ones used for the unambiguous assignment. This is because generic rubrics can be used for a variety of assignments. Wise teachers keep a number of generic rubrics available for easy access. Sometimes, teachers will use a generic rubric but adapt it with some specifics for a particular assignment. However, if a teacher uses a generic rubric, she should make sure all aspects of the generic rubric actually match the assignment.

When using a rubric, whether it is analytic or holistic, specific or generic, teacher-made, teacher-adapted, or from a stockpile of generic rubrics, the teacher needs to make sure that the rubric includes points for quality and accuracy. It should not be simply a checklist that records the presence or absence of components.

## THE IMPORTANCE OF MODELING

As early as the 1960s, researcher Albert Bandura identified the fact that modeled behavior, whether negative or positive, was imitated by pre-school children. He and other subsequent researchers (Singhal & Rogers, 1999; Milgram, 1974; Patterson et. al., 2008) determined that this same imitation occurs in older children as well as adults. It is part of the human condition. The teacher can take from this the importance of providing examples or performance models when giving an assignment. If the assignment allows for student choice, a teacher will often use an example created by a student in a previous term. For instance, if the assignment involves students creating a book box or cube that illustrates the literary elements of a book of the their choice, the teacher might either create an example, find a ready-made one, or ask the permission of a previous student to use his work for demonstration purposes. Whether the teacher creates the example or uses one created by someone else, the example should be one that students typically would not choose to do because the use of it as an example takes it out of the possible choices.

If the assignment is very prescriptive and does not provide for student choice, of course the teacher cannot provide an actual example of that exact assignment. For instance, in the field of literature, an assignment might be:

| | |
|---|---|
| UNAMBIGUOUS ASSIGNMENT | Create a poster including the name, author, setting, key characters and the roles they played, and theme found in Othello. |

Obviously, the teacher cannot create an *Othello* poster containing the elements required. However, he could create a similar example using another literary work and being careful to include the components listed in the assignment.

## THE IMPORTANCE OF ENGAGEMENT

As a teacher is thinking about creating the assignment, he of course wants his students to fully engage in the action they will be performing. Csikszentmihalyi (1990) identified the concept of *flow* which he described as the feeling of enjoyment that occurs when one is fully engrossed in the activity. He determined that almost any activity could become engaging for a person if the goals of the activity were reasonably challenging and clear and if frequent feedback was provided. Note that many video game developers have embraced Csikszentmihalyi's work.

In the classroom, if a performance requires many hours of preparation, it is important that intermediate goals are provided and feedback is given. However, the teacher does not have to be the one giving the feedback. Instead, peers can provide the feedback. Since the peer would presumably be creating a similar product or engaging in preparation for a similar performance, he/she might be able to provide even better feedback than the teacher. After all, the peer speaks the language of the student in a way the teacher does not.

There are limits however to the usage of peer feedback. For instance, if the performance assessment is very prescriptive and the products the teacher would be receiving from the students will be almost identical in nature, then peer feedback cannot be used. For example:

| UNAMBIGUOUS ASSIGNMENT | Create a map of the Tennessee Valley. Include the major landforms, bodies of water, population centers. Indicate major crops and industries and the primary locations where they take place. |
|---|---|

Obviously, for this assignment, having students doing intermediate peer reviews would not be appropriate. However, a teacher can do very quick intermediate reviews (e.g., two-minute interviews with each student) even if he has many students. Foregoing the intermediate feedback could mean that the student spent a lot of time and energy doing inaccurate work. Correcting the wrong path early in the process is important, and intermediate deadlines can assist in this.

In addition to creating an assignment that encourages *flow*, the teacher hopes that the student will become engaged in the process to the point that he/she sees the *intrinsic value* of performing the action, and thus, takes pride in his/her work.

Langer (1989) identified three aspects that have to occur for students to truly become *mindful* of the action they are doing and thereby seeing its intrinsic value. These include:

    1) loving the challenge,
    2) reveling in the accomplishment, and
    3) seeing the performance as being representative of his/her perception of self.

In other words, if the students feel the assignment is challenging, but something they have the knowledge and ability to do, it is a good assignment. It becomes a great assignment if the students feel that the product or performance truly expresses how they think of themselves.

Performance assessments are often called *authentic assessments* because they more closely resemble real-life experiences than do many other assessments. And, if the assignments are appropriately designed, they can encourage creativity and engage students to the point that they want to continue learning more about a particular subject.

## BASIC CONCEPTS IN CHAPTER 11

A) A performance is an action or behavior.

B) A performance assessment is an assessment of an act a student has performed, but it may or may not have been done in the presence of the teacher.

C) The more ambiguous an assignment, the more creativity is encouraged.

D) While a teacher wants to encourage creativity, he needs to make sure that the assignment does indeed assess the objectives of the course.

E) Performance assessments are usually graded with rubrics.

F) To assure good performances (whether synchronously or asynchronously), teachers need to provide good models of the expected performances.

G) Good learning resulting from the act of performing requires that students be fully engaged in the work.

NOTES:

# CHAPTER 12

# *Do We Have to Look At This Stuff A Second Time—I Already Graded It Once*
## Portfolio Assessment

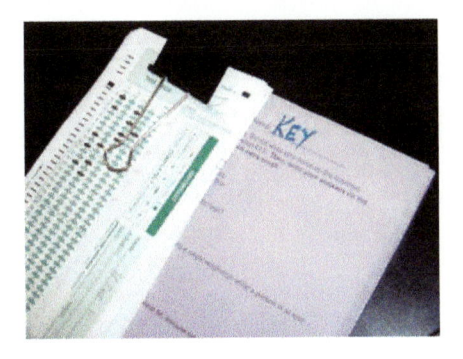

***KEY CONCEPTS:***
Portfolio Types
Portfolio Development
Scoring of Portfolios

*Creativity is allowing yourself to make mistakes.*
*Art is knowing which ones to keep.*
—Scott Adams

Portfolios have been around for more than a hundred years, but they did not become common in education until the 1990s. Prior to that time, cartoonists and artists had portfolios of their work that they carried with them, usually in three-feet-by-four-feet brown leather "folios" that were "portable" as they peddled their services to potential clients. Later, models and actors began developing portfolios with their pictures, letters of recommendation, movie posters, etc.

In the late 20$^{th}$ Century, portfolios entered the educational arena as educators recognized that tests did not always show an accurate picture, or at least not a complete one, of students' abilities, skills, or knowledge base. As educators began looking at a variety of student products and achievements, the portfolio was co-opted as a way to collect those "alternative" assessments.

A portfolio, whether it is a model's, actor's, artist's, or one in the education field, is a collection of one's work or evidence of work that has been done. Just as artists' and models' portfolios once simply showed the work they'd done, when portfolios entered the education field, they too were simply a collection. And, some portfolios that you as a teacher might employ are still simply that. Others might not include the actual work, but rather evidence of the work that has been done. Still others might include another aspect: that of improvement over time. A final type may be a complex portfolio that combines several aspects to demonstrate a "big picture."

### TYPE 1: Simple Collection of Work

In this simplest type of portfolio assessment, typically a student will simply collect his/her best work and place it in a three-ring binder or a scrapbook. The works that are contained are called *artifacts*. Even in this simple type, there is a wide variety of formats that the portfolio can take. Let's consider a five-entry writing portfolio.

A teacher could ask students to collect into a binder either:

    A) their five best writing pieces
    B) five pieces of writing that demonstrated different purposes (informative, persuasive, etc.)
    C) five short stories
    D) five different types of writing (poem, short story, expository article, etc.) about a particular topic (e.g., the Civil War, natural resources, etc.)
    E) five journal entries that they particularly enjoyed writing
    F) five book reviews

Obviously, the options are endless.

## TYPE 2: Collection of Evidence of Work

Sometimes it would not be either plausible or desirable to include the actual work in a portfolio. For instance, it not only would be difficult for an architect to include the dozens of pages of blueprints, permits, purchase orders, etc. related to his building projects, but it probably wouldn't be very informative to someone looking at such a portfolio. Instead, a portfolio that would be more valuable to her for showing potential clients her work would be to include a narrative, a simplified building plan, a cost analysis and timeline, and a picture of the finished building for each of three or four completed projects.

Likewise, in an educational setting, it might be more appropriate for a student to create a portfolio that includes evidence of his work rather than the work itself. For instance, students doing a two-month project related to natural resources might be involved in a bird count, a beach clean-up, a home recycling project, and three or four in-class experiments. A portfolio including photos, narratives, flyers, charts, etc. would allow students to show evidence of the work they did, and it would allow the teacher the opportunity to have a tangible product that she could grade.

## TYPE 3: Demonstration of Improvement over Time

Many educational portfolios today include not only a collection of materials but also the aspect of demonstrating growth over time. According to Kubiszyn & Borich (2010), the principal purpose of portfolio assessment is to "tell a story of a learner's growth in proficiency, long-term achievement, and significant accomplishments in a given academic area" (p. 205).

They further define portfolio achievement as:

> a planned collection of learner achievement that documents what a student has accomplished and the steps taken to get there. The collection represents a collaborative effort among teacher and learner, to decide on portfolio purpose, content, and evaluation criteria. (p. 205)

In a portfolio of this type, students include early "drafts" or early attempts at doing a skill. In addition, students often include a reflection tag (simply a short note about the entry) for each entry. These reflection tags lead the viewers of the portfolio through it so they can "see" the improvement. They act like the small narratives (called cutlines in print journalism) that appear below a picture in a newspaper or magazine.

| REFLECTION TAG | *This is my first attempt at writing a paragraph containing gerunds and appositives. I did pretty well on the appositives, but I identified words that I thought were gerunds but weren't.* |
|---|---|

In the next included work, she might attach this reflection tag:

| REFLECTION TAG | *This work contains actual gerunds. I also identified them well. The teacher noted that it was an improvement over the previous work. Again, I did well on including three appropriate appositives. At this point, I felt I did understand both concepts.* |
|---|---|

The portfolio might then include pieces of writing demonstrating various other concepts (e.g., figures of speech, active vs. passive voice, and foreshadowing). For each of those concepts, there would be papers demonstrating the student learning them. A final entry might be a culminating paper that demonstrated the student's abilities in all the concepts.

Often, a portfolio demonstrating improvement will include full reflections the student has written *while* doing the work as well as feedback from the teacher. Because the purpose of this type of portfolio is to demonstrate the learning process, these reflections by the student and the feedback from the teacher can be a good demonstration of that.

Even within this type or portfolio, there are variations. For instance, a portfolio could contain the entire writing process (from brainstorming to the final project) for a large research paper. That portfolio would show the student's refinement of her ideas, improvement of her writing across drafts, etc.

In contrast, a portfolio could simply show a student's increased ability in writing across time. Students could include two pieces of writing they did in September, two in October, two in November, and two in December. They could then include the reflection tags that pointed out how their work had become better throughout the semester.

A further variation of this would be for a student to create a portfolio of her science projects and the write-ups in her lab notebook. This would show not only her increased ability to write up the labs, but also would reflect the increased complexity in the science projects as the school year progressed.

*TYPE 4: Complex "Big Picture" Portfolio*

A complex portfolio includes various components (and can have entries from the other types of portfolios) that enable the viewers to see the "big picture" of a student's learning process, abilities, skills, or knowledge base. For instance, an elementary teacher might require the students to create a portfolio showing work in each of the four main subjects (language arts, math, social studies, science), write an introduction for each of the four areas, write reflection tags for each entry including what was learned in that assignment, and write a concluding paper about their learning during that school year.

A big picture portfolio in the area of high school art might include entries that defined certain terms, showed examples of each term found in work by professional artists (cited appropriately, of course), a reflection on the student's understanding of the term or his difficulty or ease in including that concept in his art pieces, and his attempt(s) at including that concept in a piece of art. The portfolio itself might conclude with a culminating product that included all the concepts described in the portfolio.

Complex "big picture" portfolios require students to deal deeply with concepts and provide entries and additional materials (reflection tags, descriptions, section dividers) that demonstrate that he has a deep understanding of the concept. It will also convey those concepts to the viewers of the portfolio, thereby allowing the student to possibly *teach* someone the concepts. And, it has long been assumed that the best way to learn something is to teach it!

## DEVELOPMENT OF A PORTFOLIO ASSESSMENT

In order for the creation of the portfolio to be a useful activity and the assessment to be valuable (actually assessing something the teacher feels is worth being assessed), the teacher first needs to determine what his purpose is in assigning the portfolio. Sometimes, teachers have students create portfolios so they can be on display for a parent's night. And while this is not a bad purpose, it certainly should not be the only goal you would have when deciding your students would create portfolios. In other words, what is it that you *actually* want the parents to see in those portfolios? That would be your actual purpose. Do you want the parents to observe the students' best work in all the concepts taught in the class? The students' best work in a single subject? The variety of ways in which a student dealt with a particular concept? A student's improvement over time? The possibilities are endless.

Thus, as with all assignments or assessments, your first step involves determining what it is you want the students to be able to do (the purpose), and then determining how you will assess that. Once you have determined that, you then need to make five further decisions. They are:

  a) who
  b) what
  c) when
  d) where/how

| | |
|---|---|
| REAL-LIFE CORRELATION | In real life, the who, what, when, where, and how is referred to as the 4Ws and an H. It is used in creating newspaper news stories or creating reports. The *4Ws and an H* assures that the writer provides the reader with the essential information needed for understanding. |

*Who.* As the teacher, you will need to determine who makes the decisions about what will be included. Sometimes, it's the teacher. Sometimes, it's the student. Sometimes, it's a combination. For instance, the teacher might state to the students that she wants them to choose five writing samples to include in the portfolio. In that case, the student would be making the decision.

On the other hand, if the teacher tells the students to include the report they wrote about the animal of their choice, the poem they created for Black History Month, two book reports, and the landfill editorial each had to create in their portfolios, the *who* is the teacher. If the teacher sets parameters, but the student still does the choosing, then it is a combination of the two. An example would be a teacher telling students to include six writing samples of their choice, but that two had to be expository, two had to be short fiction, and the other two could be any sort of writing.

*What.* This involves determining what you as the teacher want the students to include. The *what* could be not only the work to be included, but also how it is organized, and what auxiliary materials (reflection tags, table of contents, glossary, pictures, conclusion, etc.) are required.

*When.* This refers to not just the due date of the portfolio, but also to the parameters you as the teacher set in terms of when the items were created that the students can include.

*Where/How.* This refers to the format of the portfolio. In other words, where the students will compile the materials or how they will compile them.

### *RUBRICS FOR A PORTFOLIO*

As previously mentioned, rubrics can be classified into the two categories of *analytic* and *holistic*. Typically, for a portfolio, a set of rubrics is used, rather than a single rubric. For the various components of the portfolio, either analytic or holistic rubrics can be used. Those numbers awarded on each rubric is combined onto a portfolio score sheet and added to the points for the overall presentation of the portfolio itself.

For instance, if a math teacher gives the students an assignment to create a portfolio that includes:

    A) two math papers they are the most proud of with reflection tags for why they chose them
    B) a project that demonstrates knowledge of the key terms learned during that time
    C) a piece of art related to one or more of the math concepts learned with rationale
    D) a piece of writing related to some aspect of math
    E) an illustrated explanation of a math problem and how to solve it

She might also require them to have a cover page, a table of contents, and a concluding page that provides closure (e.g., "Thank you for viewing my project" or a quote that is related to the project).

After creating rubrics for each of the sections, she might then create a *portfolio scoring sheet* similar to the one below:

---

**MATH PORTFOLIO**

Name_____

Date_____

Cover Sheet:          _____ of 2 points
Table of Contents:   _____ of 4 points

| A) Math papers with reflections | _____ of 22 points | Comments: |
| B) Terms | _____ of 30 points | Comments: |
| C) Artwork | _____ of 15 points | Comments: |
| D) Writing piece | _____ of 18 points | Comments: |
| E) Solved problem | _____ of 28 points | Comments: |

Closure Sheet:     _____ of 1 points

Neatness:          _____ of 3 points
Overall Look:      _____ of 5 points

**TOTAL:** _____ **of 130**

The overall purpose of portfolio assessments is to have the student bring together his work and present it for viewing by others (always the teacher, but also often an audience beyond her). In doing so, it is hoped that he will organize the learning that took place in such a way that he chooses to internalize it. It also prepares him for similar activities (giving presentations, pulling together a project, building a house, organizing a store display, etc.) that he might do as an adult.

## BASIC CONCEPTS IN CHAPTER 12

A) A portfolio is a collection of works.

B) There are four basic types of portfolios used in education:
    1) Simple collection of work
    2) Evidence of work
    3) Improvement over time
    4) Complex "big picture" type

C) Reflection tags are often created by the students and attached to the artifacts in the portfolio to give a brief explanation to the viewer (or grader).

D) The development of the portfolio's requirements can be accomplished by various members of the educational community.

E) Portfolios are often graded by a series of rubrics or a long scoring guide.

NOTES:

# CHAPTER 13

## *Did I Pass?*
### Assigning Grades

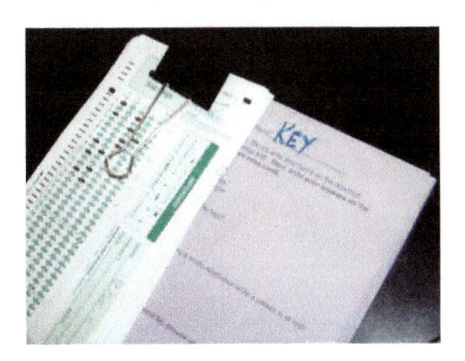

**KEY CONCEPTS:**
Grading
Determining Weights for Grades
Report Cards
Progress Reports and Portals

*There are advantages to being elected President.
The day after I was elected, I had my high school
grades classified Top Secret.*
                                            --Ronald Reagan

Something that will occur regularly as a part of your job as a teacher will be the assignment of grades. Sometimes, it is a part of a teacher's job that she does not like. However, it can become a part of your job that you actually enjoy. Consider the following story:

| Loving Those Fittings! |
|---|
| I once heard an Olympic ice skater being interviewed about what the worst part of being an Olympic athlete was. I was expecting to hear that it was the grueling practice schedule, the cold lonely rink in the early morning, etc. |
| Instead, she said, "It's all the fittings for the costumes. I hate doing those." |
| One of her team mates was sitting there and said, "I used to feel that way. But then, my mom told me that as long as I was in the sport, I would have to have costume fittings. She said that because it was part of the sport, I should simply decide that it was an enjoyable part. So now when I go to fittings, I look forward to seeing the new costumes, seeing the improved fit after an alteration, and I even get involved in some of the choices of fabric now." |

In addition, the grades you provide for the students can give you, the teacher, feedback about how you're doing in your job. Of course, you'd love it if all of your students achieved all of the work at a high level, and all could be awarded a grade of A. That's not realistic, we know, but still you can see the fruits of your labor, even for students whose grades are not as high as you would have hoped.

## DETERMINING WEIGHTS

When you figure grades, you will have to determine how much a particular assignment should affect a student's grade. Another way of saying this is to determine how much *weight* each assignment should carry. Obviously, some assignments will not be worth

> **FROM THE PRINCIPAL'S DESK**
>
> Grading students can be challenging to some teachers because grades can be used to evaluate student work and even determine who gets access to certain programs. It is important that grades are an accurate reflection of the quality of work the student is capable of producing and that those grades are assigned fairly. It is because grades are important that they produce anxiety in many students.
>
> Assigning grades in a fair and accurate manner takes time. Teachers must consider the different types of work they ask students to do and consider which aspects of the course should carry the most weight. That information is used in his grading criteria that must come directly from the curriculum standard being taught.
>
> In my opinion, the best teachers begin by fully understanding the content standard and then deciding what they will accept as evidence of their students understand or have met that standard. Only then did these teachers design the lesson they would present. This process is called "backward design" because it begins with the end in sight.

as much as others. For instance, a quick assignment done in a class period would not be worth as much as a research paper that the students worked on for three weeks. Also, depending on the subject, or the specific objectives for a single unit, the amount of weight given to a particular assignment or assessment would vary. Remember though, awarding points for assignments will often mean that the students will actually put in more effort, and that will result in more learning taking place. And, sometimes, awarding a larger number of points to an assignment is necessary to get the students to give it enough effort.

Thus, a teacher will be weighting grades. Sometimes, teachers don't think they are weighting grades *per se* because they are simply assigning point values to each assignment that reflect how much each should affect the overall grade. For instance, a daily journal entry might be worth 5 points each, and the unit test might be worth 100 points. Other assignments might include weekly checks worth 15 points each, group projects worth 25 points, homework assignments worth 15 points each, and a research paper might be worth 200 points. By assigning the most points to the research paper, the teacher is indicating that she believes it should carry the most weight. Likewise, by assigning smaller point values to the journal entries, she apparently believes that these smaller assignments should be worth less weight. This method is called *using a straight percentage*. However, teachers should not think that they are not weighting grades simply because they use this simple straight percentage method.

A second way to weight grades is to put various kinds of assessments into categories (e.g., quizzes, homework assignments, projects, exams, etc.) and then determine the weight that each category would be worth. For instance, a teacher might consider that she wants the quizzes to be worth 10% of the final grade, the homework worth 20%, the projects worth 30%, and the tests worth the final 40%. That way he can have any number of assignments in each of the categories. Then at the end, he will total the points in that category and multiply it by the percentage (e.g., 0.30 for the projects) of that category. This method is called *weighting grades by category*. Sometimes, a school will have guidelines a teacher must follow concerning the weighting of grades. For instance, a school may require that 33% of the students' grades must be based on formative assessments (done while students are *forming* their knowledge base and developing their skills) and 67% must be based on summative assessments (done after the learning to determine to what extent a student has learned the material). In a school where writing is emphasized, there may be school-wide guidelines that at least one-fourth of the students' grades must be based on writing assignments.

Thus, you should base their grading on:

1) your school's requirements
2) your objectives
3) what you feel shows the true assessment of your students

One thing you should not base your grading system on is *how* the students came out on the assessments. In other words, if a lot of your students didn't turn in their homework, you should not automatically make that worth less weight. Or, if the students did poorly on a unit exam, a teacher should not decide that it will be worth a lesser percentage. In fact, a teacher should make a decision in advance of figuring student grades about how the weighting would be determined.

Do note that veteran teachers are more adept about using straight percentages than novice teachers because they have experience for what assessments have truly shown them their students' abilities in fulfillment of the objectives. Novice teachers, on the other hand, often inadvertently award too many points to some assignments and too few points to others. Therefore, sometimes it is best for novice teachers to plan in advance the weight that each category will receive.

In this age of differentiated instruction, sometimes a student needs extra practice attempts to reach mastery of a concept. If a teacher knows that some of her students require more time (and attempts) to reach the level of understanding compared with other students, he may wisely make more attempts available to those students who need more practice. In that case, making that whole category of attempts worth a single percentage will work to not disadvantage those students who need a different number of attempts.

Also, it is important to recognize that a single weighting system does not have to be used for all your subjects. For instance, a teacher may decide that the true fulfillment of one objective would require a certain weighting system, but the fulfillment of another would require a completely different one. This can even happen within a subject area (e.g., giving more weight to lab write-ups because of the importance of students being able to discuss chemical solutions, but, having a balanced weighting for using the periodic table).

## FILLING OUT REPORT CARDS

Report cards, which are sometimes called gradecards, are provided to parents on a semi-regular basis. In 20th-Century classrooms, gradecards simply came out four times a year, at the end of each nine-week marking period. They were called grade*cards* because they were made of card stock. Sometimes, a single card was sent home at the end of the first quarter, with only the upper fourth of the card filled out. The parents had to sign it and return it. At the end of the second quarter, that same card went back home with the second quarter's grades included. Thus, when it went home for the last time at the end of the year, the parent would have a record of the student's grades throughout the year.

> **FROM THE PRINCIPAL'S DESK**
>
> One of the most enduring elements of the school experience is the time honored report card. Grades, and report cards, serve several important purposes. They serve as an evaluation of student work, a source of motivation to students, and as a way to mark transitions from one semester to another or one year to the next.
>
> Grading is also a means of communicating student performance to parents, universities, future employers, and the students themselves, about that student's current performance and potential for future success.

Later, individual cards for the marking period were created. Three examples are shown on the following pages.

### Secretariat Middle Schools
2000 Track Ave., Carnegie, KY 44444
### GRADECARD

Student Name _____   Marking Period _____

Teacher's Name _____   Subject _____

#### School-Wide Grading Scale

| | |
|---|---|
| 94-100 | A |
| 90-93 | A- |
| 87-89 | B+ |
| 83-86 | B |
| 80-82 | B- |
| 77-79 | C+ |
| 73-76 | C |
| 70-72 | C- |
| 67-69 | D+ |
| 63-66 | D |
| 60-62 | D- |
| Below 60 | F |

| Category | Student Percentage | Class Average For Category |
|---|---|---|
| Assignments | | |
| Quizzes | | |
| Projects | | |
| Unit Tests | | |
| Other | | |

| Student's Overall Percentage | Student's Letter Grade | Comments: |
|---|---|---|
| | | |

Teacher's Signature _____   Date _____

*Educating Tomorrow's Champions*

# TRI-COUNTY SCHOOLS
## Kindergarten REPORT CARD

Academic Year: _____-_____    Quarter: 1 2 3 4

Student's Name _____ Teacher _____

ATTENDANCE: _____ of _____ days

### SOUNDS ASSESSMENT
    Initial Sound Fluency
        Pre-Test _____      Post-Test _____
    Letter Naming Fluency
        Pre-Test _____      Post-Test _____

### LETTER ASSESSMENT
    Uppercase letters
        Pre-Test _____      Post-Test _____
    Lowercase letters
        Pre-Test _____      Post-Test _____

### COMPREHENSION
        Pre-Test _____      Post-Test _____

### MATH
    Rote counts to _____
    Identifies numerals to _____    Writes numerals to _____
    Recognizes number quality to _____
    Shows combinations    Sometimes    Usually    Always

### COLORS/SHAPES
        Pre-Test _____      Post-Test _____

COMMENTS:

Teacher Signature: _____    Date: _____

*Washington/Adams/Jefferson County Schools, 428 Presidential Circle, White House, SJ 01789 (555) 523-7272*

### SUNSHINE SECONDARY SCHOOL
212 Cloudless Ave., Nice Weather, ST 10101
Quarterly Report

Student _____

Subject _____

| Quarter | 1 | 2 | 3 | 4 |
|---|---|---|---|---|
| Date | | | | |
| Percentage | | | | |
| Letter Grade | | | | |

Teacher _____

Comments:

---

### SUNSHINE SECONDARY SCHOOL
212 Cloudless Ave., Nice Weather, ST 10101
Quarterly Report

Student _____

Subject _____

| Quarter | 1 | 2 | 3 | 4 |
|---|---|---|---|---|
| Date | | | | |
| Percentage | | | | |
| Letter Grade | | | | |

Teacher _____

Comments:

---

### SUNSHINE SECONDARY SCHOOL
212 Cloudless Ave., Nice Weather, ST 10101
Quarterly Report

Student _____

Subject _____

| Quarter | 1 | 2 | 3 | 4 |
|---|---|---|---|---|
| Date | | | | |
| Percentage | | | | |
| Letter Grade | | | | |

Teacher _____

Comments:

---

### SUNSHINE SECONDARY SCHOOL
212 Cloudless Ave., Nice Weather, ST 10101
Quarterly Report

Student _____

Subject _____

| Quarter | 1 | 2 | 3 | 4 |
|---|---|---|---|---|
| Date | | | | |
| Percentage | | | | |
| Letter Grade | | | | |

Teacher _____

Comments:

Remember, report cards are considered semi-legal documents. Therefore, it is not the place to inform a parent of issues unrelated to the student's performance in your classroom or course. Also, it is very important to be very careful with the spelling of the child's name, with the actual grades themselves, and with the date. Consider the following comments that a teacher might put on a grade card. The list on the left are comments that you would not put on a grade card. The list on the right would be appropriate comments.

| Do Not Include on a Grade Card | Appropriate Comments |
| --- | --- |
| Jamal does not live up to his potential. | Jamal participates in class, but has failed to hand in four homework assignments. |
| Michael has the top grades in my class this year. | Michael's grades are among the top grades in my class during this marking period. |
| Patti is an excellent student. | Patti has performed excellently in this course. |
| If Suzanna would simply study harder, I am sure she would be an A student. | Suzanna's highest grades in the course were on her two projects. |
| It looks like Charles' father really spent a lot of time working with him on his science project. | Charles' project on the Amazon Rainforests showed good creativity. |
| Thanks for FINALLY filling out those forms so Kathy could use the computer lab with the other students. | Kathy was unable to complete some of the work required in computer lab during the first part of the semester. |
| Charles continues to disrupt class and spends more time in the Principal's Office than he actually does in class. | |

When filling out a report card, it is completely possible to leave the comments section blank. If behavior has been a problem, it would rarely be addressed in the comment section of a report card. Sometimes, however, a report card will actually have a behavior section. An example is shown below:

| Classroom Behavior | | | | |
| --- | --- | --- | --- | --- |
| | Needs Improvement | Fair | Good | Excellent |
| Use of shared materials | | | | |
| Cooperation with peers | | | | |
| Listening skills | | | | |
| Respect | | | | |

A teacher would then have the opportunity to check a box for each criterion. Having behavior as a part of a report card is more common in the lower grades than in the upper ones. And, even if it is a part of the report card, extreme situations that require parental input should have been dealt with at the time they occurred. A report card is not the place for a parent to find out for the first time that his/her child is having a severe behavior problem in the class.

## PROGRESS REPORTS AND PORTALS

Some schools require that progress reports be sent home at regular intervals. Sometimes, they are sent mid-way through the marking period, sometimes they are sent monthly, and sometimes they are sent as needed. Often, they contain no more than a comment, but they may include either a percentage or a letter grade as well. Three examples are shown below:

| Name: Chase Davis<br>Chase has completed all his assignments to date. His current grade is a B.<br>Teacher: Mrs. Marketine<br>9/15/11 | Student: Max Capel<br>*Max turned in an excellent science project on which he received a 98%. His grade in my course to date is 94% overall.*<br>*Sincerely,*<br>*Ms. Varnette*<br>*Nov. 30, 2011* | Caley Moralez  Grade 1<br>Reading: Above average<br>Writing: Average<br>Math: Needs Improvement<br>Social Studies: Average<br>Phys. Ed.: Participating<br>Date: 9/1/11 |

In 21st-Century classrooms, many progress reports may actually be electronic. Many schools now have portals that parents can access at any time. Teachers are expected to put notes to parents on those portals as needed. Once again, the rules are the same for those portals as for all other communication with parents. The information should be factual in nature and content based.

## BASIC CONCEPTS IN CHAPTER 13

A) Grading will be a part of your job as a teacher, and it can be an enjoyable part.

B) Determining the weights assigned to various assignments is based on:
    1) the school policy (if there is one related to it)
    2) the objectives
    3) what the teacher feels demonstrates true assessment of the students in that content

C) Report cards are semi-legal documents.

D) Comments on report cards should strictly be factual.

E) In 21st-Century classrooms, many reports to parents, and possibly the report card itself, may be electronic in nature and accessed by parents through a portal.

NOTES:

# CHAPTER 14

# *Are All Those Squigglies Supposed to Mean Something?*
## Interpreting Standardized Test Score Reports

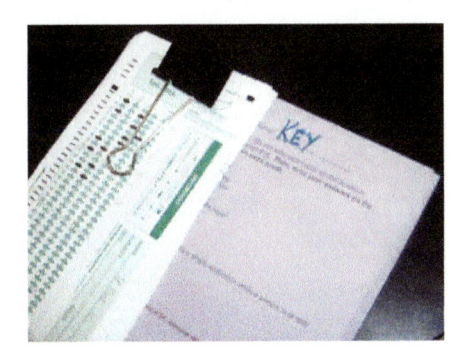

**KEY CONCEPTS:**
General Information about Standardized Tests
Percentiles
Stanines
Grade Equivalents

*It is possible to store the mind with a million facts and still be entirely uneducated.*
—Alec Bourne

Interpreting the outcomes of standardized tests for the students and their parents will be an annual event for you as a teacher. Standardized tests are typically administered near the end of the school year (in late April or early May). A test is considered to be a standardized test if it has been aligned with standards, is administered widely, using the same protocols, and interpreted using norm referencing.

A set of standardized tests are typically administered during a single week for a few hours each day. The entire set is called a *battery* of tests. The *complete battery* includes all of the subjects being administered to that particular grade level. A fifth-grade battery of tests might include the subject areas of reading, writing, math, and science. A content area that is assessed on an achievement test would be the equivalent of a subject area in school.

Standardized tests have been a mainstay of American schools since the middle of the 20th-Century. However, in the 21st-Century, the outcomes of students on these tests have become associated with the money the school receives from governmental sources, so the role these tests play in public education has increased. They are definitely "high stakes tests" now. And, that has made them controversial. Certainly, as an educator, you may actually spend some time engaging in discussions of the role that standardized tests should have in the educational process. However, for our purposes here, I'm going to stick with the "practical aspects" and simply give you information that you will need as a new teacher administering standardized tests and interpreting the score reports.

"The typical standardized test that you will be analyzing and explaining will be an *achievement test*. An achievement test is simply a test that assesses to what extent a student has *achieved* the skill set or *attained* the knowledge base expected of a student in that particular grade level" (Lovern, 2010, p. 161). In some schools, old achievement tests (ones that have been released) are administered a few times throughout the school year simply to get an internal measure on how the students are doing in their preparation for the "actual" standardized test that will take place at the end of the year. These practice tests can help point out to you as a teacher which areas that your students are already mastering as well as those you need to emphasize more.

You obviously will follow the directions provided to you by the administrators concerning the administration of either the practice (old tests) or the actual tests. Because the outcomes of the students on the standardized tests have made them into "high stakes" experiences, some teachers and administrators have chosen to be unethical in either the administration of the test or the submission of the score sheets. Do not be a part of that, no matter how tempting it may be. Your students doing poorly in your class on a standardized test is something you can overcome. You having been dishonest concerning a standardized test is not, however, easily overcome. It can be career-ending, in fact. So, follow the rules and be very careful in how you handle standardized tests and score sheets.

**FROM THE PRINCIPAL'S DESK**

The importance of testing has been recognized for years. Large-scale group achievement tests have been around about as long as school districts.

As late as the mid-1990s, there were few repercussions for teachers of students who did not perform well on these assessments. But all of that changed with the advent of *No Child Left Behind* in 2001. NCLB's required annual testing program raised the stakes for teachers by not only publishing school test scores in the local newspapers, but in many states, tying student performance to teacher evaluation. Today large-scale high-stakes standardized tests are now part of the accountability system for every state in the union. Increasingly teachers are being held accountable for their students' results on standardized tests.

Whether this is a fair and appropriate use of testing is a topic of current debate. But no matter how one feels about the present use of these standardized tests, there remains broad agreement that teachers need timely and accurate feedback on the progress of their students if they are to achieve high standards.

It is my belief that if a teacher sticks with the curriculum standards (provided by the state), teaches the students those concepts and engages them in work that allows them to interact with the concepts, the standardized tests will take care of themselves. A teacher may want to spend a couple of class periods a week or two before the test explaining the format of the standardized test and allowing students to practice some old released items. But, I don't believe preparation for the standardized tests should go beyond that.

When you receive the score reports for your class, the first thing you will want to do is look for trends among the outcomes of your students. If you were an elementary teacher, and your students were average in all areas on the science standardized test except for the "science vocabulary" section, during the next year, in your lesson plans, simply be more direct about making sure the science vocabulary is taught.

> **FROM THE PRINCIPAL'S DESK**
>
> Teachers must be able to understand basic descriptive statistics in order to compare the performance of a given student against the required standard. But that's not all. Teachers must also have some understanding of what we call inferential statistics. That is, the ability to look at a student's test score report and accurately analyze the meaning of that student's performance data. It is also necessary for teachers to be able to read a schoolwide achievement report and understand where the school is performing well, and where improvement may be indicated. When added to the skill set the teacher needs to manage the classroom assessment program (such as writing objectives, test items, etc.) great teachers possess an impressive amount of statistical knowledge.
>
> But possessing statistical knowledge is only half the job. Perhaps the more challenging parts of the teacher's duty lies in his ability to express the meaning of test data to parents in non-technical language. This will be particularly important for those parents who have limited literacy skills themselves. It has been my experience that even the least educated parents care about their child and want to know how they're doing when compared to other students of the same age.
>
> Conferencing with parents is an important part of the teacher's duty. And it is also a very good way to build trust and mutual respect between the family and the school. It is worth every teachers' time to build strong relationships within the school community, and it returns great dividends throughout the years.

On the score report, you will find *composite scores* and *sub-scores*. For instance, in the area of science, there will be overall scores (raw scores, percentiles, stanines, grade equivalents) for a particular student's achievement in that subject area. Those would be called the composite scores. Then, that subject area will typically be broken down into sub-scores. For instance in science, there might be sub-scores on chemical/physical changes, computation, and science vocabulary. Sometimes, all of the subjects on the entire battery will be combined into a final composite score. It may be referred to as the *overall composite* or the *complete battery score*.

While the various statistics provided on a standardized score report are addressed more fully in other sources (including *Statistical Measures in Real-Life Educational Settings*, Pearson, 2010), there are a few main statistics that you will have to explain to parents. They are percentiles, grade equivalents, and stanines.

## PERCENTILES

When talking with parents, you will have to explain the difference between percentages and *percentiles*. While percentiles and percentages are both out of a possible 100, they definitely mean two different things. Percentages are simply determined by dividing the number of points a student achieved by the points possible. However, percentiles are determined by putting the scores in order from lowest to highest and then dividing all the scores into 100 equal groups. Each group is then assigned a number from 0 (the lowest group) to 99 (the highest group). They can also be referred to as *percentile ranks* or *percentile rankings*.

Sometimes, a parent will come to see you because her child (who is a B student in your class) has percentiles in the 60s on her standardized score report. She will want to know what happened. You will have to explain to her that a percentage grade of 85% in your class would indeed correlate to the 68$^{th}$ percentile if approximately two-thirds of the students who took the assessment scored lower than her. Since 50 is the middle percentile (meaning average), her child having a percentile ranking of 68 would put her above average, just as she is in your class.

On a standardized score report, percentiles are used to interpret how a student did in comparison to the students in his grade that took that same assessment. They compare him to:

    A) all the students in his school or district (*local* percentile ranking)
    B) all the students in the state (*state* percentile ranking)
    C) all the students in the nation (national percentile ranking or *NPR*).

Remember: percentiles won't tell you how your students actually did on the test. It only tells you how they did in comparison to the others who took the test. Thus, if all the students who took the test scored relatively high, a student who achieved 80% of the right answers could actually have a low percentile. Likewise, if most of the test takers scored relatively low on a test, a student who achieved that same 80% might have a very high percentile. Thus, percentiles should never be used to tell the whole story. They are simply a part of the profile.

## STANINES

Stanines, named for the fact that there are *nine standard* groups, are different from percentiles because there are not an equal number of scores in each group. Instead, the stanines are based on a normal distribution, which is often called a bell curve. Stanines have the following percentage of scores in each group:

| 1 | 2 | 3 | 4 | 5 | 6 | 7 | 8 | 9 |
|---|---|---|---|---|---|---|---|---|
| 4% of the scores | 7% of the scores | 12% of the scores | 17% of the scores | 20% of the scores | 17% of the scores | 12% of the scores | 7% of the scores | 4% of the scores |
| BELOW AVERAGE ||| AVERAGE ||| ABOVE AVERAGE |||

The important thing to consider when talking with parents about stanines is to remind parents that approximately half (17 + 20 + 17 = 54) of the students are in the average area. Also, if a student scores in the 9th stanine, he is in the top 4% of his peers, while a student who scores in the 1st stanine is in the bottom 4%. It is not uncommon for a student to score in the three broad bands (*below average, average,* or *above average*) across subjects. If a student moves a little in one direction (e.g., from 4 to 3) in a single area one year, it is not a cause for concern. It may simply mean that that particular test wasn't as good a fit for the student on that particular day as the one he took another time. However, if a student moves from above average down to average, or from average down to below average, in a single year across most of the subjects, it can indicate that a student did not achieve the grade-level knowledge and skills for that year.

## GRADE EQUIVALENTS

The one statistical measure that interests most parents (as well as teachers and administrators, for that matter) is the *grade equivalent*. Grade equivalents indicate how a student's outcome on a particular part of the test relates to what would be expected of him at a particular time in his academic preparation. For instance, if a student has a grade equivalent (designated as G.E. or GE) of 7.3, it means that student is performing the same as would be expected of a student who is in the third month of seventh grade.

Most standardized tests are administered in April or May of the school year. Thus, a student who is *on grade level* would have a GE that includes her grade level as the numeral before the decimal point and an 8 or a 9 as the numeral after the decimal point.

If you were a fourth-grade social studies teacher, and on the standardized test, most of the students in your classes came out with GEs of 4.8 or 4.9 on the social studies portion of the test, it would mean that they are *on grade level*. Likewise, if several of your students came out with GEs of 4.2 and 4.3, it would mean that there are concepts in the 4th-grade social studies curriculum that were not achieved. In other words, the outcomes were indicating that they were performing the same as students in the early fall of 4th grade would be expected to perform.

There are a couple of things that it is important to remember when looking at grade equivalents:

> When considering standardized tests, it is important to remember that a particular form of standardized assessment taken by a particular student on a particular day (yes, I repeated the word on purpose) may have a different outcome than if that particular student took a different form of that standardized assessment on a different day. Thus, standardized tests should not be used in isolation.
>
> Also, any particular sub-score on a standardized test that is way below the others should not be alarming. Conversely, a sub-score that is way above should not be predictive that the student is advanced. For instance, on a vocabulary section, if a student simply isn't familiar with the vocabulary that is typical for that grade, and she doesn't read much, she may have a lower vocabulary score than her other sub-scores in the language arts. If on the other hand, a student with *on-grade-level* GEs for the language arts section of the test has very high GE on vocabulary, it may be that the passages being used on the test are ones that she has recently been reading (e.g., the *Harry Potter* books). Thus, when looking at a standardized score report, it is best to consider the *whole picture* it provides about the student, and how that picture fits in the *broad landscape* of the student's educational attainment provided by all the assessments you have on the student. (Lovern, 2011, p. 175).

Sometimes, you will have students who will come into your class who are significantly below grade level. While it will still be your goal to help them accomplish the curriculum for your grade level, when you look at their grade equivalents, a measure of success can be considered if you have increased their GEs by one full grade level.

## BASIC CONCEPTS IN CHAPTER 14

A) Standardized tests are assessments that are administered in the same manner to a wide group of students and norm-referenced.

B) The standardized tests that most teachers will administer are achievement tests.

C) Teachers should prepare students to take the standardized tests by teaching the state-mandated curriculum throughout the year.

D) Teachers will often be called upon to interpret standardized test score reports for parents.

E) The statistical measures that will be most interpretable to parents are percentiles, stanines, and grade equivalents.

NOTES:

# CHAPTER 15

## *If Only Billy Would Apply Himself...*
### Communicating With Stakeholders

**KEY CONCEPTS:**
Parent-Teacher Conferences
The NOTS of Talking with Parents
Written Communication with Parents
Communicating with Non-stakeholders

*Education is
understanding relationships.*
--George Washington Carver

## PARENT-TEACHER CONFERENCES

Parent-teacher conferences probably began the first time some parents sent their child to be under the tutelage of a more learned person. Why? Because parents care about the well-being of their children and want to know about what is taking place with their children when they are away from them. Ask any Sunday School teacher, and she will tell you that some parents will ask, after having dropped off the child just one hour earlier, "How'd he do?" So, parent-teacher conferences will be a part of your job as a teacher.

Based on research that showed that children whose parents were involved were more successful in school, formalized parent-teacher conferences became a mainstay of the American education system in the mid-20th-Century. Rather than having some parents stop in to the see the teachers at various times, schools began having specific time periods in which parents would come to the school and have interactions with the teachers. In some cases, parents were sent a 30-minute appointment and basically told to show up to discuss their child's work. Of course, that was less than successful as some parents would comply but others wouldn't. Later, other methods were employed like having

> **FROM THE PRINCIPAL'S DESK**
>
> One of the most important functions of a good teacher is to effectively communicate with parents. This is done in a variety of ways: in person, on the phone, through report cards or other written notice, and increasingly by e-mail, text messaging, classroom blogs and more. In fact, when one considers what teachers do all day it is not an exaggeration to say that teachers communicate for a living.
>
> Moreover, we know that when parents and teachers work effectively together for the benefit of the child it has a great impact on student achievement. For that reason, the best teachers I have known begin the school year by calling each of their students' parents. They introduced themselves, express optimism for their child's success during the school year, and let the parents know the best way to get in touch with them. Starting the school year with a positive phone call will help promote the parents giving the teacher "the benefit of the doubt" should she have to make a negative phone call at a later time.
>
> If you are sharing good news with parents it's probably okay to leave a message. But if you need to discuss a problem it is better to ask the parents to call you back.
>
> If you need to have a conference with the parent as the result of a disciplinary matter it is best to include the student so that communication is clearer. This also gives the teacher an opportunity to share some good examples of student work thus adding something positive to the meeting.

"Open House" where the parents were told that their child's work would be on display, refreshments would be served, etc.

So, what is the purpose of a teacher talking with parents? First, let's remember that parents want their children to succeed in life, and success in school is a stepping stone toward that. Teachers feel like they are successful at their jobs if their students succeed in the classroom (and on the standardized tests). Therefore, let's establish that both parents and teachers are interested in that particular child's success. So, what is the purpose of a parent-teacher conference? To stabilize the "team"! You, the teacher, wants the child to succeed. The parents want the child to succeed. You are on the same team. A parent-teacher conference brings the team together to work toward the same goal.

In 21$^{st}$-Century classrooms, parent-teacher conferences have given way to parent-student-teacher conferences. This is because 21$^{st}$-Century students are encouraged to take responsibility for their own learning. We used to teach the children, and then test them to see if they had met the "secret" goals that we, the teachers, set for them. However, now we tell the students what the targets are, and we ask them to constantly reflect on how close they are getting to the target. Teachers used to tell the parents, often in hushed tones, that "Billy is just not living up to his potential". Of course, Billy's mom would immediately go home and scream at Billy about not "working hard enough".

Now, the secretive nature of school is gone. We want the children to know what they are supposed to be learning, and we want them to know when they've reached that point. Grades are not arbitrary any more. Students who lose points should know what those points are, and what they can do to avoid losing those points in the future. Thus, many schools have adopted the model of having the student actually conduct the conference.

| **EXAMPLE OF A STUDENT-LED PARENT/TEACHER CONFERENCE** |
| --- |
| "Billy, please start the conference," Ms. Wallace said. |
| Billy went and got the large pizza box with his name and drawing attached to the front of it. He and his class had created the "portfolio" the day before. "Here's my drawing. . ." |
| Ms. Wallace cleared her throat. |
| "O-oh. Uh. Ms. Wallace, this is my mother, Mrs. Howell," Billy says. "And, |

Mom, this is Ms. Wallace." They exchange pleasantries. Then, Ms. Wallace makes eye contact with Billy so he knows he can start explaining his work.

"I drew this ALL ABOUT ME picture. It shows a soccer ball 'cause I like soccer. I colored the background blue 'cause I like blue. And, that's Rover," Billy says, pointing to a drawing of a dog next to his picture. He then opens the box. A large piece of construction paper on which he has written LANGUAGE ARTS covers the work. He places it face down in the top of the box.

"This is the first time I tried to write a story about Rover," he says showing a paper with edits on it. "Then, I tried again," he says, showing the next page. I fixed some of the things on the first paper, like using capital letters in the title. But, on this one, I added more details. I got some of the words spelled wrong, but the teacher liked the adjectives I used."

"What were some of those adjectives?" Ms. Wallace asked.

Billy looked at the paper. "Furry, sloppy, messy, and uh, here he licked my face with his *rough* tongue."

"He does definitely have a rough tongue," Billy's mother responded.

"And, this is my finished story," Billy says, holding three pages folded in half and turned sideways to form a booklet. He thumbed through the booklet and beamed. "We call this publishing," he added. It was obvious that he was very proud of using that big word as well as of his booklet.

The next piece of construction paper had MATH written in large letters on it. Billy turned it over and placed it face down on top of the language arts items in the top of the pizza box.

"This is my chart that shows how good I'm doing with the multiplication numbers," Billy said.

"Multiplication numbers?" Mrs. Howell asked.

Billy looked at Ms. Wallace for help. "What do we call those," she helped. "We call them the multiplication. . ."

"Tables!" Billy responded. "Yes, this shows how I'm doing with the multiplication tables. I used to only get a few right, but now I get a lot."

Ms. Wallace stepped in. "The first row shows that in late September, you were able to get 10 right in three minutes. But, now you are getting. . ."

"Thirty-five!" Billy said proudly, pointing to the bottom row of the chart. "Oh, and this is where I showed that 3 times 4 is 12 by having three baskets with

> four puppies in each. One-two-three-four-five-six-seven-eight-nine-ten-eleven-twelve," he counted as he pointed to each puppy. "Three times four equals 12!"
>
> The next construction paper divider said SOCIAL STUDIES. Billy looked hesitantly at the teacher. She turned the paper over to reveal a social studies test on which Billy had made a 67%.
>
> "I did awful," Billy said, looking down.
>
> "Oh, my," said Mrs. Howell. "What happened?"
>
> Billy didn't respond at first.
>
> "How did you prepare for the test?" Ms. Wallace asked.
>
> "I didn't read the stuff. I should have, but I don't really like it," he said. He quickly turned the test over and began showing a map he had colored and labeled. "This is a LEGEND," he said proudly.
>
> "Wait," Mrs. Howell said, turning the test back over. "What are we going to do about this test?"
>
> Billy looked down, and then sheepishly over at Ms. Wallace. At that point, Ms. Wallace asked, "Billy, you were really proud of the story you wrote about Rover. True?"
>
> "Yeah, but. . ."
>
> "Did you know that the reading in the social studies book is a bunch of stories that other people wrote. Only they are true stories. What does it mean for a story to be true?"
>
> "It means it really happened. Like part of my story about Rover was true. He does sleep under the table, and he did chew up Dad's gloves," he said. "But, other parts, like him being able to jump as high as the basketball hoop, was not true."
>
> "Good," Ms. Wallace said. "So you know what true stories are. And, they can be interesting to read about."
>
> "Like Dad getting mad about the gloves, but then laughing when we bought him new ones for Christmas and said they were from Rover."
>
> "Exactly," Ms. Wallace answered.

In the above scenario, the student is showing off his work. He is revealing what he is learning, and he's admitting areas in which he's not being successful. It's not a confrontational experience, but a conversational one. And, if we go back to the purpose of the conference, it is to stabilize the "team". To further the sports analogy, the owner of the team (the parent), the coach (the teacher), and the quarterback on the field (the student) are all discussing successful plays that have been made (learning to use adjectives to enhance writing, learning the multiplication tables) as well as ones that weren't as successful (the social studies concepts).

Whether you conduct a traditional parent/teacher conference, and whether you have the student present or not, keep in mind that the purpose of the conference is to *stabilize the team*. Your job as a teacher will be made much easier if you and the parent become partners in educating that child.

There are some "NOTS" you should keep in mind when talking with parents. These were originally published in my book, *Statistical Measures in Real-Life Educational Settings*, 2nd edition (Pearson, 2011). They can be found on the next two pages.

## The NOTS of TALKING WITH PARENTS

1) Do not characterize a student.
    NO: *Billy is a good student.*
    NO: *Wilma is lazy.*
Instead, stick with the facts and the numbers.
    YES: *Billy's assignments were above the class average in all areas except the unit test, and it was just below the class average. His grade in the class is a 92% at this time.*
If you characterize the student as an excellent student, and then he ends up with a B in your class, the parent will think it is your fault since you had characterized the child as an excellent student. If you characterize the student negatively, the parent will decide that you don't like their child and think that is why she doesn't receive good grades.

2) Do not characterize the work if it is below the upper A level. (You can definitely tell the parent that the student's work was excellent if it received a 98%.)
    NO: *Eldon's doing well in the class.*
    NO: *Farrah did poorly on her tests.*
    NO: *George's projects were well done, but his writing is unsatisfactory.*
Some parents will be offended if you characterize their child's work as "well done" and the child has an 87% (thinking you don't have high enough expectation for their child). Others would agree with you that 87% is "well done." Since you don't know how the parent will receive it, stick with the numbers and the facts. You can compare her grades on the various aspects of the course though. However, even on those, stick with the numbers.
    YES: *Darlene has an 87% on her exercises, but only a 78% on her tests. Her overall average is an 82%.*
    YES: *Milton had his highest percentage on the tests. It was a 92%. His lowest percentage was on his literature quizzes, but that is partly related to the fact that he didn't take one of them.*

3) Do not characterize the student as struggling.
    NO: *Harold had a 90% on his projects, but he struggled with the lit quizzes.*
You don't know that he struggled. He may not have even cared. Again, stick with the facts and the numbers.

4) Do not postulate as to why the student didn't do well.
    NO: *Mary didn't study hard enough for the test*
    NO: *Ira didn't put in much effort on his projects.*
In fact, don't even postulate as to why a student did well.
    NO: *It's obvious that Lisa put a lot of time in on her project*
    NO: *I can see that William really studied for that test.*
Mary may have studied really hard for the test while William may not have studied at all. Remember, parents go home and talk to their children about what you said. And, if William didn't study at all, but you said he did, he may decide that you are obviously not very smart (at least about him). On the other hand, if you talk simply about his outcome on the test, that is indisputable. If Ira's mother tells him that you said he didn't put much effort in on his projects, but he knows he did, he will probably not even try the next time.

5) Do not make promises or predictions.
    NO: *I'm sure if Paul simply puts in a little more effort, he could bring his grade up to an A.*
    NO: *Since Quint did well in all the areas except the projects, I'm sure that if she spent a little more time on them, she could do as well on them as she did on the other aspects of the course.*

> NO: *Mavis just needs to study a little harder and I'm sure she'll be able to bring her grade up.*

If you tell a parent that if the child *studies harder* (or *puts in more effort* or *spends more time on his projects*), you're sure his grade will improve, and then the child does that but his grade doesn't improve, the parents will think you didn't do your part. Again, stick with the facts and numbers.

6) Do <u>not</u> make suggestions unless the parent asks.
>    NO: *You should work with Larson in the evening on this.*
>    NO: *Getting Raquel a tutor is advised.*

It can offend parents.

7) Do <u>not</u> indicate the student's ranking in the class.
>    NO: *Nancy has the highest percentage in math in the class.*
>    NO: *Dion has the third highest ranking in the class.*

It is illegal and unethical to reveal student achievement to anyone but the student and the parent (and members of the educational team). However, by stating that Nancy has the highest percentage, you are revealing to her parent that the other students have a lower percentage. When Dion's father tells him that he has the third highest ranking in the class, he will immediately know who the two students above him are (students know how other students in the class are doing from talking with one another). You would have thereby revealed their grades. Also, don't tell parents that their child has the lowest grade in the class. Instead, use the class mean (only call it *average* when talking with parents) and discuss how the child did in comparison to it. (Charley had an 88% on the exercises which was just slightly above the class average or Olivia had a 72% on the projects which was approximately ten points below the class average.) You can use significantly above the class average, above the average, almost exactly at the class average, below the class average, or significantly below the class average when talking with parents.

8) Do <u>not</u> offend parents or try to shame them into making their child work harder in your class. You want the parents on your side. So, choose your words carefully. Also, do not baffle them with statistics.
>    NO: *Diane has raw scores of 142, 211, 41, and 167, which correlates with 64.5%, 78.7%, 88%, and 92.4%, respectively, on the various aspects of the course. Using the measures of central tendency, she is above the median on most categories, but below the mean on two of them.*

Stick with whole-number percentages when talking with the parents. Even though you will have figured the mean to the tenths, use the whole-number percentage when talking with parents. You want to show them your expertise, but not put up a wall that makes them think you don't want them to be a part of the child's education.

9) Do <u>not</u> tell parents their child is a joy to have in class unless you have actually experienced that. It's much better to discuss something you actually know about the child.
>    YES: *Gina really likes to play soccer. She often includes that in her writings.*

This will tell the parents that you know their child. Also, remember that parents talk to one another. Thus, if you said one child was a joy to have in class, but you didn't say that to another parent, that second parent may think you don't like her child. You can find something good to say about every child, and it is best if it is something that simply reveals that you recognize the child's individuality.
>    YES: *Connie wrote a really funny story about jumping on the trampoline with her sisters.*
>    YES: *Carlos is always talking about Fluffy.*
>    YES: *Carrie Ann shows me the earrings she's wearing every day.*

10) Do <u>not</u> turn a parent/teacher conference into a confrontation. You are both on the same side: that of helping the child learn. Don't play the blame game, and if a parent attempts to blame you, simply steer the conversation back to the facts and the numbers.

## WRITTEN COMMUNICATION WITH PARENTS

Most of the communication you will have with most parents will be in written form. It may involve notes to parents, e-mails, a weekly or monthly newsletter that you send home, or notes you place on an electronic site that the parents access through a portal. It is very important that you re-read anything you have written before you release it to go to the parent. You know what you meant to write, but sometimes what you actually write doesn't match what you meant to say. There are legions of stories where the word "not" was left out of an important communication.

In addition to proofreading your written communication before sending it, re-read it a second time from the perspective of the parent. Think about what it will feel like to that parent when he/she is reading it. Does it have the tone you intend? What is your intention in sending it? And, what response do you want? If you are frustrated because it's obvious to you that "Billy just isn't applying himself", telling the parents that is not likely to get the response you want. Instead, providing the parents with information that will motivate them to join you on the team in getting Billy to apply himself is what you want. Look at the two notes below and think about how you would respond to each if you were a parent.

| Dear Mr. and Mrs. Baldwin, | Dear Mr. and Mrs. Baldwin, |
|---|---|
| Billy just isn't applying himself. I think he's probably smart enough, based on that B he got on the one test we had, but I just hate to grade his classroom assignments. I know they're going to show his lack of effort. In fact, sometimes I'm actually glad that he doesn't even bother to hand them in if he's not going to even try. Could you please talk with him so he'll start living up to his potential! | Billy has not turned in three of the assignments we've had during the last two weeks. And, of the ones he has turned in, he made a 36% on one, a 57% on one, and a 64% on another. This has brought his percentage in class down to a 70% even though he made a B on the one classroom test we've had so far. I believe the last paper that required a signature was the test, so I wanted you to be aware of his current grades. |
| Thanks,<br>Mrs. Belvin | Sincerely,<br>Mrs. Belvin |

The first note is likely to make the parent mad AT YOU. Later, she may get mad at him too, but her initial thought is going to be "How dare she talk about my little boy like that!!!" In the second note, you are simply stating facts. And, while it's not good news, it definitely does not demean the child. And, it shows your concern. Sometimes, teachers think they need to state things like "I'm so concerned about Billy" or "I know he's bright enough" when talking with parents. Those kind of notes can get the response you want from *some* parents. But, the note on the right will evoke far more appropriate responses from parents. Some parents will call and ask for advice about what to do. Others will take privileges away from Billy at home and you will see his work improve at school. But, a note that shows your frustration (like the one the left) not only shows your lack of professionalism, but it also seldom will get the response you are seeking.

## COMMUNICATING WITH NON-STAKEHOLDERS

Sometimes you, as a classroom teacher, will be asked by a relative of a child (who is not the child's legal guardian), by a neighbor, or even by the media about an assessment that has taken place in your school. Remember that it is your job to teach the students assigned to you, and to communicate about *those students* only, and only to their parents (or legal guardians) and others directly responsible for their education (the school counselor, the principal). If you keep that in mind, you will not find yourself in hot water.

I once knew a high school football coach who was always asked, "Coach, are we gonna win Friday night?"

His response was always, "We will if we score more points than the other team!" It didn't put him on the record saying anything about his team or the opposing team, and it always evoked a laugh from the person asking the question.

If a "dear aunt" asks about Suzie, you simply respond that she'll need to talk with either Suzie or her parents about how she's doing in class. You can then soften the situation by adding, "If it were up to me, I'd love to talk day and night about my students, but we're simply not allowed to do that." Or, something similar. You can add, "We're studying photosynthesis right now. It's one of my favorite topics." In other words, you can say things that show that you enjoy your job, but you can't talk about students or assessments to anyone who does not fall into the two categories of:

    A) parent (or legal guardian) of the child
    B) person directly responsible for the child's education

If the media wants a response from you as a classroom teacher about the outcomes on the standardized tests that were on the front page of the newspaper the night before, once again, do not respond by giving them a comment about the assessments. The students in your class may have done well, while the overall school may not have, and you may feel like you want to defend that fact. However, remind yourself of your job. Refer them to the school authorities. Even if they press you for a response by saying, "We just want a teacher's perspective," don't be lured in.

## A FINAL WORD ABOUT ASSESSMENT

Back in the first chapter, we discussed that the purpose of assessment is to make educational decisions. That doesn't change, no matter the level of the assessment. Whether it's a simple formative assessment taking place in the classroom or a standardized test at the end of the school year, look at the outcomes, and like a doctor who uses test results to determine what to do, use those outcomes to make a plan of action!

## BASIC CONCEPTS IN CHAPTER 15

A) The purpose of a parent/teacher conference is to stabilize the team (the child, the parent, the teacher) so that the child has the best opportunity to be successful.

B) When talking with parents about a student's grades, discuss the facts and the numbers.

C) As a classroom teacher, you cannot talk to anyone about any assessments that take place in your classroom except the parents (or legal guardians) of your students and people who are a part of the child's educational team.

D) Never forget that the purpose of assessment is to make educational decisions.

NOTES:

# References

Bandura, A., Ross, D., & Ross, S.A. (1961). Transmission of aggression through imitation of aggressive models. *Journal of Abnormal and Social Psychology, 63*, 575-582.

Black, P. & William, D. (1998). Inside the black box: Raising standards through classroom assessment. *Phi Delta Kappan, 80*(2), pp. 139-149.

Bloom, B.S., Hastings, T., & Madaus, G. (1971). *Handbook of formative and summative evaluation of student learning.* New York: McGraw-Hill.

Bloom, B.S. & Krathwol, D. R. (1956). *Taxonomy of educational objectives: The classification of educational goals, by a committee of college and university examiners, handbook 1: Cognitive domain.* New York: Longmans.

Childre, D. EQ quote: HeartQuotes™: Quotes of the heart. Retrieved from http://heartquotes.net/Education.html.

Cohen, E.G. (1994). *Designing groupwork: Strategies for the heterogeneous classroom.* New York: Teachers College Press.

Costa, A. & Kallick, B. (n.d.). Habits of mind. Retrieved from http://www.habits-of-mind.net.

Csikszentmihalyi, M. (1990). *Flow: The psychology of optimal experience.* New York: Harper & Row.

Emerson, D.M., Johnson, R.N., Milner, S., & Plank, K.M. (1997). *The Penn State teacher II: Learning to teach, teaching to learn.* University Park, PA: The Pennsylvania State University.

Goleman, D. (1995). *Emotional intelligence.* New York: Bantam.

Green, S.K. & Johnson, R.L. (2010). *Assessment is essential.* New York, NY: McGraw-Hill.

Inger, M. (1993). Teacher collaboration in secondary schools: CenterFocus Number 2, December 1993. University of California at Berkeley: National Center for Research in Vocational Education. Retrieved from http://vocserve.berkeley.edu/centerfocus/CF2.html.

Johnson, D.W. & Johnson, R. T. (1989). *Cooperation and competition: Theory and research.* Edina, MN: Interaction Book Company.

Johnson, D.W. & Johnson, R.T. (1990). Social skills for successful group work. *Educational Leadership, 47*(4), pp. 29-33.

Johnson, D.W., Johnson, R.T, & Holubec, E.J. (1993). *Cooperation in the classroom (6<sup>th</sup> ed.).* Edina, MN: Interaction Book Company.

Kagan, S. (1993). The structural approach to cooperative learning. In D.D. Holt (Ed.), *Cooperative learning: A response to linguistic and cultural diversity* (pp. 9-19). McHenry, IL & Washington, D.C.: Delta Systems and Center for Applied Linguistics.

Kaufman, D.B., Felder, R.M, & Fuller, H. (1999). Peer ratings in cooperative learning teams. Proceedings of the 1999 Annual ASEE Meeting, June 1999, Session 1430. Retrieved from http://www4.ncsu.edu/unity/lockers/users/f/felder/public/Papers/kaufman-asee.PDF.

Krathwold, D.R. (2002). A revision of bloom's taxonomy: An overview. *Theory into practice, 41*(4), 212-218.

Kubiszyn, T. & Borich, G. (2010). *Educational testing and measurement: Classroom application and practice.* Hoboken, NJ: Wiley & Sons.

Linn, R.L. & Gronlund, N.E. (2000). *Measurement and assessment in teaching (8<sup>th</sup> ed.).* Upper Saddle River, NJ: Pearson.

Little, J.W. (1987). Teachers as colleagues. In V. Richardson-Koehler (Ed.), *Educators' handbook: A research perspective* (491-510). New York: Longman.

Lovern, J. J. (2011). *Statistical measures in real-life educational settings.* (2<sup>nd</sup> ed.). Boston: Pearson.

McMillan, J.H. (2008). *Assessment essentials for standards-based education,* pp. 10. Thousand Oaks, CA: Corwin Press.

Milgram, S. (1974). *Obedience to authority: An experimental view.* New York: Harper & Row.

National Commission on Excellence in Education (1983). A nation at risk: The imperative for educational reform. Retrieved from http://www2.ed.gov/pubs/NatAtRisk/risk.html.

National Council for Accreditation of Teacher Education (2007). The NCATE unit standards. Retrieved from http://www.ncate.org/documents/standards/UnitStandardsMay07.pdf.

National Research Council (2001). Classroom assessment and the national science education standards, pp.39. Accessed from http://www.senacyt.gob.pa/media/documentosDireccionAprendizaje/evaluacionEstandaresNRC.pdf.

Organisation for Economic Co-operation and Development (2008). Assessment for learning formative assessment. Accessed from http://www.oecd.org/dataoecd/19/31/40600533.pdf.

Patterson, K., Grenny, J., Maxfield, D., McMillan, R., & Switzler, A. (2008). *Influencer: The power to change anything.* New York: McGraw-Hill.

Petrulis, B. (n.d.). Grading in collaborative classrooms. Retrieved from http://www.evergreen.edu/washcenter/resources/acl/b1.html.

Roediger, III, H.L., & Karpicke, J.H. (2006). The power of testing memory: Basic research and implications for educational practice. *Perspectives on Psychological Science, 1*(3), p. 181-210.

Scriven, M. (1967). The methodology of evaluation. In R.W. Tyler, R.M. Gagne, & M.Scriven (Eds.), *Perspectives of curriculum evaluation* (pp.39-83). Chicago, IL.: Rand McNally.

Shachar, H. & Shmuelevitz, H. (1997). Implementing cooperative learning, teacher collaboration and teachers' sense of efficacy in heterogeneous junior high schools. *Contemporary Educational Psychology, 22*, pp. 53-72.

Singhal, A., & Rogers, E.M. (1999). *Entertainment Education: A communication strategy for social change.* Mahwah, NJ: Lawrence Erlbaum Associates.

Slavin, R.E. (1990). Research on cooperative learning: Consensus and controversy. *Educational Leadership, 47*(4), pp. 52-54.

Sternberg, R.J., & Lubart, T.I. (1995). *Defying the crowd: Cultivating creativity in a culture of conformity.* New York: Free Press.

Stiggins, R.J. (2001). *Student-involved classroom assessment ($3^{rd}$ ed.).* Upper Saddle River, NJ: Pearson.

Stiggins, R.J. (2008). *An introduction to student-involved assessment for learning ($5^{th}$ ed.).* Upper Saddle River, NJ: Pearson.

Stiggins, R.J., Arter, J., Chappuis, J., & Chappuis, S. (2005). *Classroom assessment for student learning: Doing it right-using it well.* Upper Saddle River, NJ: Pearson.

Stiggins, R.J., Arter, J., Chappuis, S., & Chappuis, J. (2008). *Classroom assessment for student learning: Doing it right-using it well ($2^{nd}$ ed.).* Portland: Assessment Training Institute.

Tegano, D.W. (1990). Relationship of tolerance of ambiguity and playfulness to creativity. *Psychological Reports, 66,* 1047-1056.

Thorndike, R.M. & Thorndike-Christ, T. (2010). *Measurement and evaluation in psychology and education ($8^{th}$ ed.).* Boston, MA: Merrill.

Urban, K.K. (2003). Toward a componential model of creativity. In D. Ambrose, L.M. Cohen, & A.J. Tannenbaum (Eds.). *Creativity intelligence: Toward theoretic integration.* Creskill, NJ: Hampton.

Webb, N.L. (2002). Depth-of-knowledge levels for four content areas. Retrieved from http://prcband.com/docs/curriculum/webbs%20dok.pdf.

Wiggins, G. & McTigue, J. (1998). *Understanding by design.* Alexandria, VA.: Association for Supervision and Curriculum Development.